VENus

A PERSONAL MEMOIR AND A TELLING
HISTORY OF THE LONGEST-RUNNING
REGIONAL WOMEN'S THEATRE IN THE U.S.

PALMETTO
PUBLISHING
Charleston, SC
www.PalmettoPublishing.com

Copyright © 2024 by Deborah L. Randall

All rights reserved
No portion of this book may be reproduced, stored in a retrieval system, or transmitted in any form by any means–electronic, mechanical, photocopy, recording, or other–except for brief quotations in printed reviews, without prior permission of the author.

Hardcover ISBN: 979-8-8229-4817-4
Paperback ISBN: 979-8-8229-4818-1
eBook ISBN: 979-8-8229-4819-8

VENus

A PERSONAL MEMOIR AND A TELLING
HISTORY OF THE LONGEST-RUNNING
REGIONAL WOMEN'S THEATRE IN THE U.S.

Deborah L. Randall

Contents

Prologue	i
PART ONE	1
Chapter 1: ACTION!	3
Chapter 2: CALCULATED RISKS	10
Chapter 3: LIBERATION EXISTS (AND IT'S MINE!)	17
Chapter 4: THE SUMMER OF '86	31
Chapter 5: SOMETIMES YOU HAVE TO SAVE YOURSELF	46
PART TWO	57
Chapter 6: COMPASSION AND LOVE	58
Chapter 7: UNIVERSITY - THE FIRST IN MY FAMILY	66
Chapter 8: LEGITIMATELY REAL NOW	89
PART THREE	120

Chapter 9: SETTING FLIGHT TO THE VOICES
OF WOMEN   121

Chapter 10: DAUGHTERS OF MOLLY MAGUIRE   133

Chapter 11: BAD GIRLS!   139

Chapter 12: "TAKE WHAT YOU CAN USE AND THROW
THE REST AWAY" -BUD STRINGER   196

Chapter 13: UMBRELLA ERA   205

Chapter 14: FOCUS!   221

PART FOUR   225

Chapter 15: FIRST JLT IN THE
HOUSE-THAT-LOVE-BUILT   226

Chapter 16: SECOND JLT IN THE
HOUSE-THAT-LOVE-BUILT   240

Chapter 17: THIRD JLT IN THE
HOUSE-THAT-LOVE-BUILT   289

Epilogue   409

About The Author   414

Prologue

I crave experience! Always have.

I think experiences are more important than transactions. I think transactions are how a lot of people relate to one another and the world. I have always liked not knowing. I used to drive until I was lost just to try to find my own way back.

It's easy to assume this is a direct result of trauma. But, I'm not sure. Maybe it's just my soul making itself known.

From the time I was one year old I had a best friend. The day he was born we were like siblings. When both of our mothers separated from both of our fathers, we lived together. We slept in the same room, we were bathed and fed together.

I didn't know he had leukemia. He died when he was four and I was five. Mostly I remember laughing with him. I remember his laugh. His smile. I remember the way he liked to bury trucks in the mud.

Subconsciously, I started marking time in four year increments. JLT's.

Jimmy-lifetimes.

Living like this made me crave experiencing whatever life had for me. It forced me to be inside of the given moment and to experience what that moment had to offer. Twice. Once for me and a second time for Jimmy. I've always known that time is fleeting. At least, I've known since the age of five.

And then, theatre came along and taught me that character flaws were what made life most interesting. Experiences married observations and those two things have shaped my life.

Time ticked by. Looking back I realize that environs changed with the times as much or sometimes more than I did.

This is a story about the moments I have been gifted. It's a story about living through the experiences that life brings.

It's a story of me and of Venus Theatre.

I hope it's a veneration of US.

For
Alan, Amy, Laura, Myrrh, Navie, and Maria

Part One

Chapter 1:
ACTION!

Objective: Imagine it.

The CV had finally begun. Having seen what would later be identified as an improv troupe that wore black leotards in the elementary school cafetorium, the decision to perform had been made long ago on the asbestos-tiled floor where Chief Turkey Tayac told us the indigenous tale of his people. It was the same multi-purpose room where three holocaust survivors told us their stories about sucking out puss to keep each other alive and showed us the numbers still tattooed on their arms. It was the place our PE teacher kept a larger-than-life cardboard box and did not allow us to ask what was inside (PROBABLY A BODY!!). It was the location of a local news celebrity visiting us to bake bread so they would have something to run on the evening news. That is a smell embedded in my gastronomical senses. "The Skin of Our Teeth" by Thornton Wilder would be the Senior Class Play in High School. The role of Sabina was on the radar but it was to be a student production and the student director was committed to giving jocks the lead roles. No Sabina for me but a series of small ensemble roles that were a lot of fun to play.

The drama teacher, Bud Stringer decided the Spring show would be a musical. A student-created musical.

Life jumped onto a live rail seemingly all of a sudden.

Mission: Get CAST!

My acting career began with "Little Red Riding Hood" as Red. It was 4th-grade extra credit in elementary school because Tanya Hill and I finished board work too fast. BORED-WORK!

We were sent to the multi-media room. That was a fancy early 1970's term for LIBRARY.

I was cast as the Easter Bunny in elementary school as well. I never went to any of the rehearsals so they had someone else ready to go on. But, I showed up offbook with my own costume and Easter basket ten minutes before showtime and they all breathed a sigh of relief. So, I already knew what it meant to be a *STAR*. ALSO, I invented a character called the Avon Lady for a school assembly in elementary school and performed in every talent show in Junior High School.

In High School, I took every drama class that was offered by Bud Stringer during my time there. The only reason I didn't do full plays or show up for rehearsals was because no one would drive me. It was the same with majorettes. I would just show up for the parades not knowing the routines and they'd throw me in between all of the metalled girls who already know they were supposed to tuck their socks in.

Once I got my driver's license I was allowed to stay after for rehearsals because I could drive myself. I was given a car. It was a blue Nova V8 and I liked to race other cars on occasion.

When I found out the student-written musical had only two female roles, a cafeteria worker and a Mom, and both were already cast I immediately became enraged. I stormed straight to Bud, and I confronted him. He had a shared office with the work-study teacher. That's where those of us who had no future in higher education took classes and learned how to balance a checkbook while staring at posters high up on the wall that read: "Give a man a fish and he'll eat for a day. Teach a man to fish and he'll eat for a lifetime."

This was a place where we were being taught how to stay fed, clothed, and sheltered into adulthood by way of balanced checkbooks, generic brands, and blue-collar jobs. It contrasted with the other side of the building.

The other side held rooms with glass tubes, colored liquids, and periodic table pull-downs. Maps of the world. Frogs in formaldehyde.

I told Bud that there was no role for me in the play. I explained to him that after doing every school assembly drama performance I should at least have a chance to audition for an after-school production NOW THAT I FINALLY HAD A CAR AND IT WAS POSSIBLE!

I'd kept up with my observation notebooks. I'd passed every quiz on the Greeks and Shakespeare. What was the problem here?

He promptly told me that I would have to go to the writers meetings. UGH! Even though they were mostly held in the basement bedroom of a boy named Jay who liked to make out with me at night and ignore me during the day, I WENT! I watched Jay develop his relationship with the known girl and I became the scribe for our show. Pen in hand, I sat on the floor and scribbled away, interrupting a lot.

The boys had already decided they were writing the next John Hughes film, only theirs would be better. Hindsight's a kicker on that one! Their play took place in a High School.

Imagine.

Their concept: a foreign exchange student from Russia was being chased by the KGB. The KGB infiltrator was an undercover janitor.

There were two female roles in the whole entire script, and that's the reason I had to show up, invite more women in, and write more women in. I guess they called us girls. In the end, we had over thirty female characters. I ended up getting cast as the main kind of Cinderella character. I had to play opposite Jay.

Here's what I wrote in my journal:

I can't believe it! AH! I have the lead and I've written the lyrics for almost all of the songs and I'm singing and I'm dancing and I'm CAST!!!! I've been waiting my whole entire life for this.

In every class today, I asked for a bathroom pass. I kept going down to the box office window to check to see if the cast list was up. I'm FREAKING OUT! Finally, during 4th period, there was already a group of girls gathered around the list during the class break. They broke away like it was choreographed. Like I was Alex in Flashdance and they gracefully formed a tunnel that I could walk through to see my name printed on a cast list as the lead for the first time in my life. Like they were holding invisible swords and I was being inducted into the greatest group of creatives that anyone in the Universe could have ever imagined. There was music playing in my head. Journey. But not like after the carnival.

The carnival ride boy Rudy kept giving me free rides so he could watch my miniskirt fly up. I realized that part later. Initially, I just thought it was because I was a charming and compelling character. Faithfully, it will always be OUR song. We made out in the rain. I may have been his first kiss. His Dad seemed a little charmed. Alas, the carnival had to move on and the light rain was wilting my heavily sprayed hair. I sat in the backseat with my hand against the back window as Journey sang, "Circus Life. Under a big top world. We all need the clowns to make us smile." Rudy was my rustic town-to-town one-makeout rain clown. I was his first real kiss (possibly). Forever yours. Faithfully.

Wait. Did I mention, I've been CAST! I screamed a little. The bell rang but we girls stuck together because we were all excited. I was surprised that they were excited for me. It was new and I liked being a part of a group. The excitement mounted as to whether or not Jay and I would actually kiss on stage. It's a hormone thing! The way he smokes his Marlboro outside in the designated High School smoking area on breaks. The way we thumb-wrestle during Mr. Meehan's film showings of the "Red Balloon". So much magic! Someone knew what class he was in and we went running through the hallway, no passes or anything. We were the drama-girls and we had special permissions! He was already taking notes in some advanced European History class that would make him college-prepared. He saw us at the door. I was jumping up and down waving at him while making squeaking sounds in my attempt to make no sound at all. I could almost taste his make-out Big Red gum that did nothing to hide the taste of cigarette smoke inside of my own mouth. How exciting!!

This is everything I ever want to do with my whole entire life. MY WHOLE LIFE DREAM IS COMING TRUE RIGHT EXACTLY NOW!!!

I feel blown up by the force of living. I feel like my feet will never touch the ground again.

"Shoot for the moon. If you miss you will be among the stars."

Journey plays in my head, "Anyway you want it, that's the way you need it, any way you want it!"

I feel so in love with love and art and theatre and...

I just feel so in love.

Even if he is sitting in his advanced whatever class with his one leg flung out trying not to roll his eyes and ignoring all of us. So full of himself he's HOT. He's the one who told me I should be auditioning in the first place. I'll never be leather-jacket-wearing-cool like him. I would think that he never even knew I was alive if it weren't for so many secret make-out sessions.

OH!

I'M GONNA BE ON STAGE!!!

Deborah L. Randall

[flourish: MT1]

She's there
Not really seen or heard
She's there

Her heart beats
Inside of me
I dance to the rhythms

Hair whirling
Spinning spiral
She twirls

Laughing
Heart beating
Out loud

She's only seen
On the periphery
That's her thought

The stares
Were there
She danced

On that line
Between
Danger and Love

Purity and Sex
Passion and Punishment
Indelible Ghost!

Her job was clear
Feel their pain
Take it all in

Touch the lust

And lose
The person

She was
Always meant
To become

She releases
Again
And twirls

It takes decades
To feel the digs
To heal the slights

Right now
She dances
As she laughs

Chapter 2:
CALCULATED RISKS

Objective: Become Sophisticated!

A swimming pool awaited in the backyard along with a part-time job. Several different part-time jobs. One running copier machines. Another taking orders at Shakey's Pizzeria. Also, lifeguard Red Cross certification, although that was just to protect anyone swimming in the pool at home. There was a car to maintain and take care of. The rules were still strict but clear.

Their roof + their food + their clothes = their rules.

It was impossible to become sophisticated in that place. Sophistication would require carefully calculated and explorative venturing out. Not the kind allowed whenever I had a boyfriend when I was 13. Those were fun days. Certainly, somewhere in Ohio there's a modest family still completely damaged by the strange teenager hanging out in the public bathrooms near DC's national statues striking up drunken conversations.

A decision was made to sophisticatedly venture into the fairly new metro subway system. The one my Uncle Goerge helped to build. I think he installed the seats. My Great-Grandfather Leitch helped to hang the replacement lightning rod on the Washington Monument. I was born in the city my ancestors helped to not build so much as tangentially maintain. Still, I felt very confident that the city was in my blood the same way I knew theatre was in my blood.

I signed up for The Actor's Center. Another move of sophistication. In their newsletter, I read about a place called Backstage Books. It was located in a land far far not-so-far away called DuPont Circle. These two things represented a different lifestyle. I was used to shopping Fashion Bug and playing frisbee in Fort Washington at the Forts. I also had a solid line on every lovers lane but none of this could come close to a place called DuPont Circle.

I did not endeavor to drive directly in but would be given clearance by the authoritarians to park at a metro station and take the train into the DuPont Circle stop.

It was here I would spend several weeks worth of paychecks on scripts. Not food. Not savings. Not Fashion Bug. Scripts! Classic, contemporary, and some that simply had compellingly colorful jacket covers. It was my money and that's how I was going to choose to spend it.

I would spend that summer poolside reading plays. A very sophisticated thing to do, if you ask me.

When I ran out of plays, I would endeavor on that same adventure all over again. I loved losing myself in the world of plays. It was even better than shopping for clothes. It was beyond trying on different outfits. It was about trying on different people who wore lives that I could never have even imagined on my own.

THIS IS MAGIC!

Mission: Become Different.

Public transportation. What did I ever know about that? I remember taking the bus with my Grandmother around 1970. We lived in Forestville just off of Pennsylvania Avenue. They call it Penn-Randall Drive now. Back then we ventured in on a hot day. Giants surrounded me. Perspiring giants. I don't remember stores. I remember stalls. And stuff. And rugs. And things made out of various metals. We walked and we looked and we chatted with complete strangers. For me, public transit has always been something on the Orient Express spectrum. It's intended to take me on an incomparable adventure through its portal via Backstage Books and into the kaleidoscopic floors and shelves of worlds upon worlds.

Into the unknown!

Bud taught us that we should keep observation notebooks. I watched and I made notes of the characters that surrounded me. Because that is what Bud said to do. Saturday, June 9, 1984 was a magical day. It's the day I ventured through the portal into the land of sophisticated and unending expressive ideas for the very first time in my very human life.

When I stepped off of the metro, I found an escalator awaiting me in the cool underground cavernous platform and watched as it stretched up into the sky. I was compelled to jump onto a corner of its metallic ever-moving magic carpet ride. I've never seen an escalator that long and I imagine a relative of mine probably helped to build it or at least polished the metal or something.

I felt like I belonged. It's glorious to feel like you belong.

I learned quickly that I should stand to the right because people were two-stepping all the way up into the sky. I'd never been able to master the fine art of double dutch jump rope so I had no desire to attempt such an athletic feat. Especially not on the longest-moving staircase I'd ever seen in my life. The stakes were too high. There's no way I was going to end up concussed upon arrival to Wonderland. Then again, you only live once!

The clouds came closer. I stepped to the left and slowly began my pilgrimage UP, and quickly stepped back to the right whenever I heard,

"Coming by!" or "Watch it!" or "BEHIND!". And then, back. I courageously ventured to the left and stepped up, up, up. I WAS BORN ANEW. A babe. A wee one learning to crawl up a razors-edged-constantly-moving-staircase.

Before I saw anything, I heard music. I heard whistles blowing. I heard a lot of very excited voices. The secret must have been leaked. Some secret security was breached. Wondrous characters in the wonderland were calling me up, up, up to join them in their circus life under a big top world.

This was DuPont Circle!

It's loud and it's festive. Hairy men wore leather underwear on floats and threw things from them straight at my face while they laughed and waved and hugged each other.

I stepped onto the concrete and walked towards P Street so that I could walk down 21st. At least that's what I'd scribbled sideways on a piece of old crumpled-up paper bag. The parade route was coming down 21st.

More fascinating than all of the almost naked and very happy men were the storefronts. So many different tiny businesses! I was focused on finding Backstage Books. The place that's about to change my life. Just like my Nanny, I start asking people I've never met. Some of them acknowledged me and pointed me in the proper direction.

I found IT! Backstage Books was a white house with tables on the sidewalk selling things for the parading people. I walked up the not-too-straight steps into the center floor of a house. I stood mesmerized staring at ceiling to floor scripts where walls should have been.

I had never seen anything more exciting or promising in my life. Worlds and worlds piled in stacks. Scripts are so thin, you can fit a lot of them into a small space. It must have been obvious that I didn't know where to begin because the person behind the register started making suggestions. I stood frozen with possibilities. I wanted to buy the whole store.

Behind the counter, there's stage makeup for sale and boas and props and so many costume pieces. I had no time for any of this. Who would? There are WORLDS spread out in layers all over the place.

Purchases were made. Done! Must get back to the authorities before the street lights come on. Time's a tickin…

There's no time to stop. I walked faster back to the metro station, the smells were almost overwhelming. Sweet and savory fill the air so fully I can still taste them on my lips. Falafel and fish and fries and sweet desserts and it just goes on forever. People were waving from their floats. I averted my eyes because I didn't know where I was supposed to look and I was on my vision quest. I was waiting to fill the life that had been handed to me with worlds, words, and ideas I never could have imagined on my own.

I spent hundreds of dollars from months of paychecks saved up and left holding two bags bulging with scripts. I could not believe this was possible. I could not believe this world existed, never mind all of the ones I was carrying back down the long escalative descent back to Persephone's Hades. I couldn't wait to get home so that I could start reading, and I hardly ever wanted to get home.

I seriously considered reading one on the metro ride, but I'm too sophisticated for that.

I was experiencing effective structure for the first time in my life. Structure I CHOSE.

The predictable world disappeared and I was walled in with my plan and stacks and stacks of worlds holding all of their characters to explore inside of my private journey that no domestic abuse would ever have the power to interrupt.

After each script was read I would dive into the pool and swim laps. My normal drip dry in the sun wouldn't work. I needed two towels to de-liquify so I could hold the next script in dry hands. This felt so civilized. So privileged. Entirely decadent. It felt so decadent that surely it must be forbidden.

There were so many different styles of writing. Some characters jumped right off of the page at me. Other styles of dialogue had no characters at all, just fragments of thought. Ellipses and words and rhythms that flowed between them made music like I had never experienced before.

I'd dive and swim and drip and shake and towel off to go into an entirely unknown and unexplored world again and again. Until I was exhausted and finally discovered what it was to sleep well.

I found plays that turned pain into an actual journey to the other side and I couldn't believe all of the possibilities. Sure, there are the Greeks and Shakespeare, but THIS?!?!? This is NOW! Contemporary writers. What a wild discovery. Playwrights were still alive and walking among us. They weren't the stone busts on the dusty private library shelves of the rich.

This was a whole new and immediate intimacy.

Their works played live inside of me.

This was freedom.

[flourish: MT2]

I can make this work
She said this to herself
Several times a day

When things
Were not
Working

I can make this work
The twisting and the torquing
Followed

I can make this work
Some sort of luggage
Maybe it was red

Unclenched its
Iron-jawed opening
And took it all in

Shoving it down
Compacted
And crammed

I can make this work
No one is ever going to tell me
This is not working.

Chapter 3:
LIBERATION EXISTS (AND IT'S MINE!)

Objective: Become A Director While Simultaneously Ingenuing!

The CV gained a life of its own aligned with the official age of consent. Thanks to my Aunt Deb and Uncle Bob nudging me to go to college, I decided to attend Prince George's Community College. It was a numbers game and my monster mother decided she wanted to support me all of a sudden. In a landslide vote, I was elected President of the Drama Club (long story). Working with the head of the program and advisors, we spearheaded the relaunch of The Experimental Theatre Program there. Through this program I was able to lay hands on new work by producing, designing, performing, and directing. On the Main Stage, I was cast regularly in classics and known contemporary works. These shows included a dinner theatre production as well as Reader's Theatre productions. In addition, I joined the Forensics Team and competed against sometimes highly reputable Universities throughout the upper Eastern seaboard. I was the only forensics team member to never receive a trophy. Even this "failure" inspired one teammate who had suddenly been thrown into the community college circuit and pulled from the Ivy Leagues due to a family crisis, to create a persuasive presentation about my passion, verve, and drive.

That was annoying.

Some of these credits include:
Mainstage -
"Flowers for Algernon" by Daniel Keyes and David Rogers Cast as Alice Kinean,
"Comedy of Errors" by William Shakespeare Cast as Adriana, "Gemini" by Albert Innaurato Cast as Judith Hastings, "Agnes of God" by John Pielmeier as Assistant Director, "A Christmas Carol" by Charles Dickens as Properties and Crew
Dinner Theatre -
"They're Playing Our Song" by Neil Simon Cast as Ego and Assistant Director Experimental Theatre -
"Baglady" by Jean-Claude van Itallie as DIRECTOR, "The Actor's Nightmare" by Christoper Durang as DIRECTOR, Designer, and Producer,
"This Property Is Condemned" by Tennessee Williams Cast as Willie and Producer
Readers Theatre -
"The Great American Funeral" by Janey Richards as Assistant Director and Producer

Forensics categories: Informative Speeches, Persuasive Speeches, Dramatic Interp, Extemporaneous, and Scenes from Plays

Mission: Become the Most Desired.

I signed up for Mr. Weller's English class immediately the semester after I flunked out of a 7:30 am English class in the dead cold of winter. That Ice Queen Professor was some other life form. I can't be certain. She was always wide awake in the cold darkness while things of nature with a pulse slept. She said words. I don't know what they were. I hadn't become a coffee drinker yet. I took her exams and failed.

Mr. Weller changed everything for me. I took his class and I aced it!!

I was sitting in class surrounded by people wearing football jackets with big letters on them during Mr. Weller's English class one day. The lights were out in the classroom and he had a slide show going. "These are slides of modern art." He asked the guy in the jacket who appeared to have already peaked in High School what he saw. "Brown and blue lines??". Then, Mr. Weller said to the whole class, "Watch this".

"Deborah?" I looked at him. I was a little stunned because I felt put on the spot so I think I grunted quizzically in an attempt to hold onto my persona of sophistication. Then he said, "What do you see?" I told him and the whole class that I saw emotion and movement. I went on and on about it in detail, in the way that I've always been able to keep talking. He interrupted me. He addressed the class again. "Do you know why this is?" What? He's asking them why I am. What? By now, we're all just staring at him.

With passion, he said, "SHE'S AN ARTIST! Artists see things differently. She doesn't think the way that you do".

I couldn't believe it. I honestly could not believe this entire hour happened.

At the end of the semester, he handed our graded journals back. This assignment was a little like Bud's observation notebook. Only, Mr. Weller had us write stories and he was not grading on spelling or punctuation, unlike a certain Ice Queen. You could scribble sideways and draw pictures like Emily Dickinson did if that particular spirit of expression moved you. He wanted us to make up short essays and just leave them in our journal for the three-month duration of the semester. I loved it. I wrote a piece about Vending Machine Nutrition and how it had its own kind of structured graduating system. There were 101-level snacks, all the way up to advanced that held slight nutritional value.

I wrote about being a girl running down my hallway being hunted by a monster at home from the perspective of the walls that seemed to be moving against me and shifting all around as I tried to get to my room at the end of the hall.

I was writing!

I peeked at my desk and saw that he gave me an A+. I mean, I was sure I was stupid. Just a few months prior I'd been an English flunkie. The next thing I knew, I was holding an A+ in my hands. When the bell rang I ran. I wasn't trying to run but somehow I was absolutely running. I was leaping through the hallway. I jumped up and touched the ceiling mid-gallop. People walking past me pretended not to see me screeching and jumping and leaping and, OH, MY GOD!

I'd met myself for the first time as AN ARTIST! An artist who just received an A+ in English. From a Professor who spent his summers in Europe directing Shakespeare. From a man who came to every theatrical project I was a part of on campus because he viewed me as a fellow artist. As kin. He didn't see me as a blue-collar kid who worked in a plumbing shop. He didn't see me as the abused and neglected girl who was destined to disappear. He saw ME. He told us things from the perspective of a generation much closer to us than any of the teachers I'd been used to.

He was different, just like me. As he walked down the hallway, he saw students sitting on the floor reading Shakespeare and listening to Prince on their Walkmans and he didn't see that as a bad thing. He reported back that Shakespeare would have LOVED that.

I could hardly believe it. The way lives touch. The way one person with one set of experiences can share those experiences and change a multitude of lives through conversations. This is not anything I'd been used to. Where I came from you sit down and shut up. Where I came from you work to be the most desired. That's the biggest accomplishment. How many Romeos can tink pebbles against my window? That was the question. I was an object. Always on the verge of being a burden. I was never meant to be here. I was never meant to be going up against the young women pausing Ivy League with all of the family connections and theatre credentials slumming here with us Community College people. I was supposed to be the invisible girl. The late-night make-out.

The throwaway.

Only, I WASN'T!

Because no one paid much attention to me, I tried things. I dove into text in ways I wasn't supposed to. I had a budget. I had vision. I'd always had vision. Now, my grades were made of my own voice, and my own choices. I had facility. I was the unexpected. The one no one should take seriously or fear. I took notes.

Being the ingenue on stage taught me a lot.

I read all of the books of STAN (ivslovski) when I worked on "Flowers for Algernon."

Who was Alice Kinean anyway? Why was she in this field? Did she really fall in love with Charlie? If so, what's the backstory? Where'd she get the mouse? What happened in the moments before the play began? We played basketball with kids like Charlie just to be a part of the environment and we had a lot of fun. I was playing opposite Paul on that show. He dove deep. His performance of Charlie was covered in the local papers. He was so solid. I liked being the anchor for another actor.

The hardest part of that show was having to do a stage kiss with him while his girlfriend stood behind a leg stage left with her arms crossed and foot tapping. That was weird but it didn't stop us because we were both committed to this show.

In the musical, I had to learn to blend into the chorus. I couldn't sing. I held onto a vocal tension from a childhood of abuse for decades. These days there are Vagus nerve exercises for people with that kind of blockage. A few years later I would study the Alexander Technique as well as Linklater. But, that hadn't happened yet. The director was hired from DC. She'd have B, the lead, watch me play her role one scene at a time, and then tell her to play it exactly as I just did. Because of this, I was adored and hated by my cast.

This is when I realized that one person could talk out of two sides of their face. People would gather around and tell me how talented I was. And then, they would go party while I was working on two other projects and stab me in the back. They'd come back SO HIGH. My father used to be a fireman. He told me that marijuana smelled the same as burning human flesh and that I should never touch it. I felt like my pet duck Donald in that I seem to have imprinted on my Dad the way the duck imprinted on me. Needless to say, I never touched the stuff. It wasn't a hard decision. At my grandfather's pig roast one time, I saw a man with no nose. He just stood eating pork, not wearing a shirt with two nasal holes right in the middle of his face. A drug deal had gone bad. Someone held a gun to his nose and shot it off. Like ya do. I was wearing one of my new Fashion Bug outfits. I figured, make an effort at least, you know? I just didn't want to end up without a nose consuming the smells of human flesh. That's all I'm saying.

Initially, I'd felt proud of my commitment to the work and that a director who lived in an apartment RIGHT NEXT TO ARENA STAGE trusted my acting chops. She'd asked me to be her assistant director. I drove her from her home in DC to the college and back again. I didn't realize at the time how many boundaries were being crossed.

The Tennessee Williams piece was pure magic. Shelley, a fellow student, was my director. My Nanny came to see that one. The experimental theatre shows shared the performance space with the audience. That got my brain humming about alternate staging.

We couldn't find a male actor to play the other role, I think he had about three or four lines. So B played him. She had been the female lead in the Neil Simon piece. I don't like Neil Simon, for the record. Too boysee. Too self-conscious. Too look-at-me! If he and Wendy Wasserstein ever had a child I swear it would come out wearing cable knit and aspiring to mediocrity at best.

Nanny was sitting in the audience and B tripped over the train tracks in character, just like Shelley directed. Nanny chimed in before my first line, "Hurtcha self?"

I was so embarrassed.

YEARS later I would find out that my GrandDad saw me in that show. I had no idea he was there. He sat in the proscenium audience seats and watched me from that distance. One day he told me about it. He had really big beautiful blue eyes and I'll never forget him looking right into my soul and telling me he was there, and he saw me. I asked what he thought. He said, "I think maybe you've got something there and you should keep going."

I cry just thinking about that.

When he died I gave the eulogy. At the burial, when I thought everything was over, his wife received the flag from the soldiers after a three-gun salute. I don't think we could afford the full gun salute. It was so stoic. The way they move. And so hilarious the way we all tried not to laugh.

The family thought they'd hired a man to fire the three shots, but he told them, "I jus' say FIURE!". Sure enough. Through the stoicism when the whole world seemed to spin so slow it felt like it was going to stop. When it felt like gravity was about to disappear and we were all on the verge of floating up on the ceiling like unwanted balloons with too much helium. Through this still-weighted feeling we heard it.

"FIURE!!!"

Three times.

That's the number of comedy.

After that, my Step GrandMother turned on her heels holding my Grandfathers's flag as solemnly as the soldiers and walked straight toward me. I couldn't believe it. She handed it to me.

I said the only thing I could think to say, "Why?" He had EIGHT children. I was the oldest grandchild. And, I was a girl. This was unlikely.

She told me that they had discussed it. They appreciated the time I spent with him in the hospital. I tried to read the newspaper to him every day just so he knew what was going on. She told me that if they gave it to the daughters or the boys they knew it would end up in shreds with the infighting. They knew I would take care of it and protect it.

When I was the first in my family to graduate from University, cum laude at that, my GrandDad was there. Cheering and clapping. I didn't know at the time how precious that moment was. But that's the thing about moments. They come and go, and we can't know, we can only live them honestly if we're at our best.

After reading about Shakespeare in High School and playing Hamlet's Mother for a school assembly, it was nice to be in a full Shakespearean production. In High School, Jay played Hamlet and he went up on his lines in front of the whole school, but I got him back on track as Gertrude.

In Community College, I played Adriana in the "Comedy of Errors". I don't much like many of Shakespeare's women. The men have a lot more depth. Probably because men played all of the roles and so the understanding of the female character was more of an assumption than an experience.

Playing Judith in "Gemini" was something completely different for me. I loved that I played the role that Sigourney Weaver premiered on Broadway. It made me feel something special inside. In that show, I had to say a line that went something like, "If one more person tells me how beautiful I am I'm going to stick my face in acid." I hated that. I also had to pitch a pup tent on stage during a scene. My director and teacher at the time was Cyril J. Carrol. He was old school, but he was also a badass with his own brand. One of the other characters kept going up on her lines. I had to memorize her lines as well as mine. While I was putting up a tent on stage by myself, I oftentimes had to jump out and save her from herself. We ate in that show too. Spaghetti. It was cold but we had to "eat it like it was hot". That was acting right there.

During the final dress of that show, I was in the costume shop for one thing or another. I think getting measured and seeing my wardrobe for that show. There was another student down there with us. I remember she looked at the costume director and told her she wanted to do what I was doing. She wanted to be on stage and play a lot of roles. The costume director quickly pointed to a pair of bell-bottomed jeans lying on her table. She told that girl that when she could fit into a size 3 the way I could maybe then she could start thinking about it.

I didn't like that.

I never wanted to be like my Monster so I worked out a lot. The more I worked out, the more compliments I received. So, I started eating less. After a while, I ended up living on one small french fry from Roy Rogers and a six-pack of diet Coke every day.

I don't think anorexia was a word yet. I just felt fat. All the time. One little fat spot on my body sent me into starvation mode. And when my stomach growled I was glad. I dared it to be hungry. I ended up catching colds or whatever was going around all of the time. I had these sores on my back. But I could fit into the costume so I kept getting the roles.

I grew to hate playing ingenues.

Maybe I didn't want to be the most desirable after all.

When we competed in forensics, I watched the highest-ranking competitors. The ones that went on to become news reporters. I watched a persuasive speaker on the James Madison campus and my teammates too.

I was shocked when I was not cast in "Agnes of God". I think the head of the department was sick of me. This was a two-year program after all and I was exceeding those two years. I was just doing one show after the next treating the green room like my personal apartment.

I assistant directed "Agnes of God". They couldn't do much with the woman playing the therapist. The director asked me to "fix" her. So I staged her step by step through her scenes and she still couldn't hold onto her character or remember her lines.

This is the show where I fell in love with designers and technicians. I sat in their booths with them and I watched from their side. During one of her stumbles, one of the technicians looked at me and said, "You know her lines, right?". I said, "Yeah.". He said, "Let's drop a house on her and get you out there and get this whole thing over with."

I understood at that moment that the people to care about were the designers and technicians. They ran the show. If I was good with them, nothing else really mattered. I stopped caring about what other student actors thought and found myself checking in with the tech crew.

I worked props on, "A Christmas Carol". That show had a lot of missteps and I was so glad I wasn't in it. One of the ties came loose on a flat that was hanging over Marley's head. Half of the 4x8 piece of wood dropped from the ceiling. There was one rope on the other end holding the whole thing to the baton so high above. It just dangled there. When the flat swung it hit a lighting instrument. That came crashing down and landed two or three feet away from where the actor sat on stage.

There was a pulley system on the family platform. It took 10-20 really strong people to grab ropes and pull this platform upstage as the curtain was closed across the front leaving the audience at intermission. The pullers did not pull fast enough and the curtain closer closed too fast. The actors were singing on top of this platform as it was being pulled backward. Tiny Tim was standing on the table. The curtain pulled across way too fast and knocked the crutch out of Tiny Tim's hand. Suddenly the actors were behind the curtain and the spot on the apron highlighted Tiny Tim's fallen crutch. The kid was fine. But, that was not the intended beat the audience was to be left with at intermission.

We had busloads of audiences too.

Some of the actors liked to hang out at the pub with pitchers of beer before and after shows. After a few pitchers, the Ghost of Christmas Present was singing, "I Like Life" wearing these stilts to make him 7' tall and he tripped over one of the tracks for that insane moving platform. He lay on the ground and kept singing because he was drunk and he couldn't get up.

The children in the audience seemed to enjoy it just the same.

I don't know how much I like proscenium stages.

"BagLady" was my first directing gig. It was a one-woman show. I cast a woman named Sunday Wynkoop. The playwright Jean-Claude van Italie became my FB friend decades later. Sunday was so good. The play was so good. The entire set consisted of wooden electrical spools placed all over the stage. They came by way of a retired Navy man named Charlie. He had a boat trailer and a shouty voice. I had to follow the largest spool strapped behind Charlie's truck on the highway. Charlie said if it was going to come undone, then I was going to have to be the first one to take the hit. I thought that was fair. When we arrived he needed help so he shouted at me. He said,

"I need at least five strong men and I need them in less than five minutes. GO!" I think I was wearing a miniskirt and had just done my nails. I went running to the pub and grabbed at least five buff dudes waiting in line for food. At the time it was understood that if I was wearing a miniskirt I could ask buff men to do things and they wouldn't hesitate. I saw the back of Charlie's boat trailer before the boys were back in line for their beer and pizza.

The programs were xeroxed on a single sheet of paper and stuffed in a brown paper bag. I had the ushers throw them at the audience as they entered.

I was still working in the plumbing shop. Sometimes, on lunch breaks, I'd meet Sunday in the parking lot of a park with a lake. I'd direct her right there in the hour that we had. I have always believed that theatre can and should happen anywhere and everywhere.

In final tech, Sunday and I had run through the show twice with the tech crew. It was all so close, but I knew I could take it further. I told her that I wanted to run it a third time. She simply said, "NO!".

I couldn't believe it. I thought I was all-powerful. Director. Directress. She explained that if she ran it one more time she was going to lose her voice and likely get sick. The best thing I could do was release her.

That's when I learned that actors have limits. Even when I can see in my head what needs to happen next, that has nothing to do with whether the person or people in the room with me are up for it. If they aren't up for it, might as well release them. Can't make energy appear when it's not there. Otherwise, you'll just create a tangle that you'll have to spend precious time undoing for the next week or so of rehearsals.

Let actors take care of themselves. What is a show without them? It's nothing. So, taking care of actors who know how to take care of themselves is the real critical job of the director, and by extension the stage manager.

I bumped into Sunday decades later at 1409 Playbill Cafe. She told me she used monologues from that show for years and years and landed lots of work in the city. Seeing her made me light up all over again.

"The Actor's Nightmare" was the second show I directed. I can honestly say that there's no experience like the Christopher Durang experience. The man knows comedy. Luckily, I had a cast who seemed to be deeply gifted with comedic timing. That was the show where I fell in love with comedy. There's nothing like making an audience laugh. NOTHING!

There was a lot more I did in those two and a half years. It was a time of liberation for me. I never wanted it to end. The social life was incredible. I'd ride with my fellow actors into DC and we'd dance all night long, usually at gay clubs. It was such a relief because I could just dance and let go of the pressure of being wanted.

Traxx was a favorite place, as was DuPont Circle. Traxx was in the old Meat District where the very expensive stadium is now. It had an outdoor sand pit where people would sometimes play volleyball. It had three dance floors and a billiard area. It had giant screens showing music videos of the Psychedelic Furs, Tears for Fears, and all the rest singing and making visuals. A lot of my peers shopped at thrift stores. Most of the guys wore black trench coats. Shelley always had an old man's hat and a thrifted tweed vest or something or another.

The school was maybe one mile from the Capital Center. So, we saw concert after concert. I once went to a Philosophy Class wearing a Leopard print spandex bodysuit, yellow leg warmers, and heels, with fully teased out and sprayed hair so I could get to the rock concert in time.

Those were liberating days.

[flourish: MT3]

Grabbing those sails
She flies
Canvas billows
Colors
Sky
She flies

Take no
Responsibility
For the weather
Or the clouds
That loom
Overhead

She
Floats
Drifts
Soars
Dancing
In the wind

It's a
Glorious
Day
To
Be
S O A R I N G

Water
Below
Crystal
Blue
Green
Slow

No anticipation
Of
Storms
Or
Rip tides

Deborah L. Randall

Underfoot

Up
She goes
Sailing on
Her own
Seas

Valiantly

UP!

Chapter 4:
THE SUMMER OF '86

Objective: Become A Paid Working Actor!

Bud Stringer was hired to direct the theatrical events at Wild World Theme Park in Largo, MD in the Summer of 1986.

I was cast to play the heroine for the outdoor Train Show. Our cast was encouraged to paint our own set and we spent Memorial Day doing so.

I would once again be cast against Jay and the leading men from the Community College stage too. They were beautiful young men.

We were housed in an abandoned snack shop called, "Sofari-Sogoodi". It had been the place where the elephants were kept the year before. Unlike the elephants, this cast would have no running water and no electricity.

Sofari Sogoodi and my blue Nova

There were ten males and two females total cast to play a three-person melodrama.

We tended to work in bathing suits so that water battles could launch at any time. It was hot. No a/c. Just wood chips and tackle football games in between performances and extensive water battles.

When it rained, the cast working that day would take off in a cluster, leaving the utility-free "holler" we were housed behind, splashing through the main park. We would jovially stroll past leary park-goers huddling under overhangs in their dripping wet bathing suits to avoid the rain, we would often laugh and splash them by jumping in huge puddles. Most thrilling though, was the absolute need to ride every roller coaster when the tracks were getting drenched in a downpour and were slick.

Bud also directed a Main Stage production indoors on the big stage. It was a medley of theatre musicals. And when that show wasn't running, "Talking Heads: Stop Making Sense" played.

The Train Show cast bonded in a feral way. We were the creatures of the wood. We were forbidden to eat at the employee dining hall in any number greater than two.

We joined the park's softball league. We aimed to lose every game. If we found ourselves winning we would walk off the field and leave the game. We took it upon ourselves to create a theme for each game and to costume ourselves accordingly. These themes included: the beach party, the slumber party, the formal game, and the savage game. Soon, the other teams were forfeiting before the game was to begin based on our terrible reputation.

I also created a clown character. I was proud to be paid to do it. It was so much better than playing a park costume character. Those costumes were usually years old, made of fake fur, and impossible to clean. Actors assigned to that job had to step into a suit of DNA sludge created over years of sweltering summers. Whoever wore the suits, smelled of the suits until a proper decontamination took place. This was all to help entertain the people waiting in line.

My clown name was Penny. I was waving and gesturing to children in line and this one special needs child was nonverbal and being held by her Dad, staring over his shoulder and looking backwards at me. We locked eyes and I performed for that child for the duration of her entire wait, which was almost half an hour. Just as the child was about to approach the gate, she held out her hand. In it was a shiny penny. It is one of the most powerful gifts I've ever received. I tried not to take it but she and her Dad insisted. Knowing I'd never be able to keep track of the coin, I chose Penny as my clown name.

Connection became the theme of that entire summer.

Mission: Hold True To This New Way of Existing

I WAS CAST!!! FOR THE SUMMER!!!

I was a PROFESSIONAL! That means I earned a living acting. That was going to be my plan moving forward.

Yes! Earn a living acting.

Sometimes I would wake up before the sun. I'd hop in my car and drive 30 miles south and back again just to take in the rising of the sun and expel some of my bursting energy. Then, I'd go pick up Jay and the rest of the crew. This was my paradise. I was practicing my craft and getting paid to do it.

I was a part of a cast for the entire summer. We became our own kind of bonded tribe.

Jay and I, when we were working on the same day, made a pilgrimage to the ice machine each morning. We'd fill two buckets up and we'd dump that ice into the Sofari Sogoodi soda machine ice compartment that didn't work. It was luxurious to have ice all day.

Nav and I would journey into "town" to use the locker room bathrooms that were women-only to get a break from all of that testy testosterone. Sometimes the boys just wouldn't stop!

The Facade

Here's what I wrote in my journal:

There's no way I'm dating Jay. He can forget that. He has his girlfriend back at college. It's clear he's just here to make as much money as possible to get him through the next semester and pay his tuition.

It's CLEAR!

I get it.
....
I went out on a date with a clown in the park. We ate at the employee dining hall together and no one stared at us like we were the people-of-the-wood. Daytime dining in the mess hall of the boys of summer, so forbidden and fancy. After that, he tried to impress me with his juggling skills. He threw a bean bag to me, but I missed and it landed in a little stream behind me. All of the individual beans inside began to expand and explode so we called it a day.

The clown escorted me back to Sofari-Sogoodi. I tried to introduce him to the crew but they were having none of it. Jay had taken Shaka- a metal rod the boys used to smash things when they would play out their scenes from "Thunderdome" on our little back patio- and he'd smashed a chest of drawers that Bud dropped off for us. I mean he turned it into splinters. I don't know what his problem is!

Jay and I take turns driving our crew to work. Sometimes, we sneak people in through my trunk. Gordo has taken a liking to riding in the trunk. Phil Collins's "In the Air Tonight" played on one of my mix tapes and I think that drum solo may have blown Gordo's mind. I heard a little landshark voice coming from back there saying, "Can you rewind and play that again?"

NO, GORDO!

We tried to explain to him that Phil Collins wasn't a real rocker but he wasn't buying it.

Jay drives the "monster-machine". It's an ugly green Toyota pick-up truck.

We're always listening to "Purple Rain" at full volume. And sometimes, if it's raining on the way to work or the way home, I pull my car over, insist that everyone leave the doors open, and get out and dance on the side of the road in the rain.

Nav had to stop driving her parents' car because I sat in it all day one time so I could experience the air conditioning and we killed the battery or broke something. Her sisters told her we smell like livestock.

I've learned to just be hot. Sweat. Live with it. I had to put away my pumps with babydoll socks and I got myself a pair of white jellies from the Fashion Bug.

Charles kept getting high and he tried to convince Nav that he could fix the dead battery in her parent's car with some sticks, a rock, and some mud.

Nav screamed and started storming around in a random pattern until she disappeared behind Sofari Sogoodi. I found her lying face down on the little back driveway behind the Sofari Sogoodi patio area just mumbling incomprehensibly and giggling while laying flat on her stomach.

We sometimes have these psychotic break moments. We seem to take turns.

I heard the train whistle which is our cue to put on a show. I knew she wouldn't be able to do that one so I took off running with two of the guys. As soon as we heard the train whistle we had to run out of Sofari Sogoodi, through the paved compound with wood chips in the middle and then up the steps to the platform. After that, we jumped off of the platform, ran up the hill that was covered in poison sumac, and ducked backstage before anyone on the train could see us. Our costumes were hanging back there and we jumped into them and started the show as soon as the train conductor stopped talking through his CB radio.

We usually do about four shows an hour. Every 15 minutes or so. It depends on how crowded the park is. It stays crowded.

I love everything about life now!!

....

We metroed in to see SPRUCE at RFK. He was on his "Born In the USA" tour. We stomped the stadium so hard singing along, we cracked its foundation.

It's so wild to feel this happy and to be this free. I love it.

I was tired and still had to drive everyone back from the metro. We were riding backwards on the metro sitting in the orange seats that my Uncle George probably installed. I was trying to keep it together, to engage in conversation with the rest of the group but I was really tired. Jay touched my leg and said, "Rest". I felt like Buttercup in the "Princess Bride", even though the boys already nicknamed me "Boop". The whole ride back he had his arm around me and the only expectation was that I shut my eyes and rest. Honestly, no one has ever asked me to rest before. Also, he tells me to "relax" a lot. Which I mostly can never do. So, I do hang out with him a little.

I trust him. But, not.

I trust him with my thoughts and ideas, but not with my body. I like knowing he wants me though and I push that out to every limit. It makes me feel like I won something.

....

On the fourth of July, Jay, Nav, David and I snuck onto the backstage area of our facade after hours and watched the fireworks after dark. They exploded far away in the park after the sun went down. We watched from the second deck. Jay's fingers brushed mine and suddenly we were holding hands. We made sure no one saw that. He says he broke up with his college girlfriend. But, I think we should just stay really good friends.

....

Well...

I resisted him for a long time. He swooped in for a kiss right at the beginning but I was not going to let this happen. We're around each other a lot. And we laugh, A LOT. And there's just some pull between us. Chemistry. Maybe it's love. If he says it I'll say it.

We mostly meet at the waterfront in Tantallon after work. It's around the corner from the marina. You have to walk through the woods to get there. It's very hidden. I swear, the other night he must have seen three different falling stars.

Every time we took a break from kissing he would look up and see a falling star.

These other kids sometimes walk up with beer and watch us make out like they're at the drive-in or something and we're the show.

The embarrassing thing happened.

SO EMBARRASSING!!

We heard people coming through the woods, so I jumped up from lying down on top of him and I lost my balance. And, I fell sideways into the water with a little splash. It was muddy. Only it wasn't mud because we were right around the corner from where all of the boats were docked at the marina.

I was 3-5 feet below the top of our makeout wall and he was still up on top of it. The three people with their beers just kept watching us like it was still some kind of show they'd already paid for and they weren't about to give up their tickets. I couldn't get out of the water.

Jay started laughing his ass off. He thinks this is funny. Which makes me more frustrated and stuck. Now, he's laughing so hard he can't even help me get out at all! Eventually, the guy watching us stands up and grabs my other hand. They both pulled me out. Just then it started raining.

I was covered in yacht excrement when the rain fell. It was so gross.

I went back to my car and assumed he was going back to his truck which wasn't parked too far away. But he followed me and even though I was covered in all of that yuck he gave me a sweet kiss on the lips, in between his continued chuckles.

So, I guess you can say that our relationship is full of stars and also full of shit.

I don't think anyone knows about our hookups. It's private anyway.

……..

I play the girl who needs to be rescued because she can't pay her rent. Sometimes, I prefer to play the villainous landlord.

The other day, Paul was playing the villain. I was laying on the old sawmill that we'd built. I was spinning the wooden blade over my head repeating, "Turn it off, turn it off" over and over. Paul was milking the train packed with people. So, I just kept spinning and repeating. He asked if they thought he should let me live. This three-year-old girl screams at the top of her lungs, "KILLLLL HERRRR!!".

I stopped spinning the wooden blade, sat up and gave the whole train a deadpan look. The more still and disgusted I seemed the more the whole train laughed. I didn't break character at all. I was incensed and waited until they stopped laughing. Well, my CHARACTER WAS. I love that. Holding for laughter might be one of my favorite things in the world.

We were supposed to have three different shows in rep. The Melodrama, a clown show with ladders, and some excerpts of the "Music Man". The "Music Man" is Bud's most favorite musical of all time, I think. We had to learn the songs, "you can talk you can talk you can bicker you can talk, you can talk talk talk talk, bicker bicker bicker bicker, you can talk all ya wanna but it's different than it was…"

We only ever performed the melodrama. It's for the best. Diving through windows on the facade with ladders everywhere would have landed at least half of us in the emergency room. I don't think anyone could ever play a bigger Music Man than Bud himself. Sometimes we're strolling characters.

Bud bought two different dresses for Nav and me. Hers looks more comfortable. And the boys dressed up. We strolled as char-

acters from an earlier time period. I'm not sure which time period. I think we were supposed to bring some kind of dignity to the park.

Jay told me I should primp like that everyday. He said that was how I was supposed to be. He gave me those eyes. To be honest, I love getting sweaty and jumping around without care almost as much as I love clothes and makeup.
……
I've been writing poetry on the inside walls of Sofari Sogoodi. I started writing on paper and taping it up. But, when the pump heels and baby doll socks went away somehow I just took to writing straight on the walls. They are covered ceiling to floor and now the summer is over.
………
Jay brought his things in to work this morning. His brother came to pick him up at the gate and drive him straight back to college.

We cried when we said goodbye. I'm still crying. He came to work one more shift so we would be his last Maryland experience before heading back. That was nice. He got in my car and I drove him to the front gate and we waited for his brother to pick him up with all of his stuff for college. We sat there holding hands staring at each other and kissing a little. Mostly, we were quiet. Neither one of us could talk much without getting upset. He had a tear or two on his face.

We're both determined to keep this thing we have going. Deep down though, I think we both know this is our last moment. It's beautiful. It's really sad too.

This was the greatest summer of my life.
……
Jay dedicated a lot of songs to me over the summer. I still have the list.

Some were off of the Don Henley, "Boys of Summer" Album. One was, "Land of the Living". "I wanna stay in the land of the living with you. I want to stay here with you."

I miss him. I miss his quirky habits. He says we'll make this long-distance relationship work, but it's not going to. I write to him every week.

I couldn't go back to work without him there. Time to get ready for the semester anyway.

I miss how he used to take a paper wax-coated Coca-Cola cup and turn it upside down. Then, he'd rip the bottom up to make a wick and he'd light it. It was a very unique meditation candle. I miss our Hibachi. I ended up buying it and burgers every week so we could cook for ourselves all summer to avoid the main park. We became so self-contained. I miss our talks. Even though they seemed like they were about nothing a lot of the time, the absence of them has left a hole in my heart.

My heart aches. I'd gotten used to all of that touch. I feel shut down without it.

…..

I miss my poetry wall. Each of us cast members had our thing. The poetry wall was mine. Better than tackle football in the wood chip yard. Or ninja darts ripping up every wall in the place.

Once, Jay and Joe stole my car. Jay found the mix tape section of my glove box and then he just kept playing "Hot Blooded" over and over while he drove in the circle that went around the wood chip yard. Joe jumped in with him and they sped off with my car. I tried to chase them. They took off leaving puffs of dust behind them like a cartoon. I ran as fast as I could until I had to stop. Nav started laughing at me screaming and crying and just then, I was stung by a bee. I screamed primally, NOOOO!! She laughed harder.

We each had our moments of psychotic breaks.

Nav and I had to retreat to the girl's locker room after that and we stayed there for a couple of hours that day. We started to feel guilty about getting paid to make the boys work, but they had it coming.

Anyway, it was a lot to process.

Jay was the person who sat next to me in the High School Auditorium and told me I should be auditioning. We traded journals that summer. Mine was from Mr. Weller's class. It had all of those spontaneous essays in it. He gave me his journal from College too. We each took a week or so and read through them.

When we returned our journals to one another he told me that my writing was "refreshing". Refreshing. I liked that. I suddenly liked very much being known and seen as a creative person.

I liked the words he used with me. I miss THAT!

He became my best friend. I'd never laughed that hard with someone and had so much lusty fun with them at the same time.
. . . .
I miss him too much. We each send a letter to the other every week. He sent me the lyrics to "Wish You Were Here" by Pink Floyd. He wrote them backwards so I had to read them in a mirror.

The times I visited he took me out to dinner. But when we were driving back, he ducked when he saw someone walking on the sidewalk.

I have a solid way of ignoring what's staring me right in the face. But, I want to hold onto this just a little bit longer. I don't want it to be over.
. . . .

I couldn't take it. I needed to feel his touch. I needed his kiss. After work on Friday, I drove down to Richmond and onto his campus at VCU. I knocked on his door but no one answered.

I needed him. I needed to touch him.

All other touch is violence but not with him.

I imagined where he might be.

A strip club.

I walked around and stepped into one. It was mostly empty. Topless college students walked across the stage without much dancing. Like they were taking their turn in a three-dimensional catalog of wares.

Hardly anyone was there except for a priest and a couple of friends. The priest seemed most engaged.

I left immediately.

I was walking around Richmond after dark until I ended up leaning on my car and staring at his door. I know. After having stalkers I was becoming one.

In the final moment, I saw him. He was walking down the sidewalk. He was surprised to see me. Thrown off but also happy.

He invited me inside.

We talked for a bit but I needed him to touch me. Just hold my hand. Kiss me. It felt like I was drowning and I'd come for his oxygen.

After some chit-chat, we decided to take a shower. This was a thing we did whenever we had the opportunity.

It was always beautiful and sensual.

I needed to feel the water and I needed to be kissing him and feeling him skin to skin. It seemed to be the only way I knew I was still alive.

We would kiss. His hand would drop low caressing me. I would grab his hands and lift both of our arms over our heads and we'd never stop kissing.

He took a break from our kissing just to look at me, and I would drink him in with my eyes too. He looked me over and then his words came at me again. The way he chose them and the timing of his delivery. It was too much. He said, "You look like the Venus DiMilo". We kissed more and we lifted our arms in a time-stretching pace.

Over time, he'd slowly slide his hands down over my wrists. He'd keep going until the same pattern repeated. We would kiss for an hour in that water until it ran cold.

That night we slept in a loft. I had to leave and I remember him scanning the place for anything that I might leave behind. At first, I thought he was so tidy and I was such a slob. Looking back, I think that he was removing all evidence of me.

This was a deeply familiar feeling. So familiar I may have mistaken it for normal.

That was our last interlude as young lovers.

Summoning the gods of wind and rain from the rooftop of Sofari Sogoodi

[flourish: MT4]

Something about that
That heat
That fire
That steam

Something about it

Something about that
That touch
That freedom
That dream

Something about it

Something about those
Sensual nights
Adventurous days
Endless energy

Something about it

Something about those
Private Moments
Untouched emotions
Music and dreams

Something about

That Summer

Echoes
In
Me

Chapter 5:
SOMETIMES YOU HAVE TO SAVE YOURSELF

Objective: HONOR

I had to break away from my dream.

It was heaven living the life that I saw out in front of me. It was amazing to make it all appear. But, I couldn't control the toxic dynamics around me.

My Mother was a monster who wouldn't stop raging no matter how many ways I tried to get her to calm down. I could see that her rage was in me. I could not allow myself to become her.

My Father had disappeared entirely. The last time I was with both of my parents was my High School graduation. June 4, 1984.

He would not answer my calls. His wife slammed the door in my face. As best as I can tell I was a bad debt that had been paid in full by my 19th birthday. I did not exist to them after their debt was paid. They were free and clear and GONE.

I was always an object one way or another. That never stops leveling me.

I had become a pronoun by that time. That's why I prefer proper names instead. They never used mine. I was a she/her. I was a credit card my Mother could never pay off. I was money owed and had to be careful not to create more debt for either of them. I understood everything I did came with a price tag. I tried to not eat much, I bought my own clothes. Ultimately, I needed my own place.

There became nothing more important than getting out of that house. It had me trapped even when I was only really sleeping there during the best summer of my life.

The summer was gone.

It was brutal.

....
The theatre CV takes a pause here.

Mission: Hold My Soul As I Crack This Cycle

The truth was there was no more Wild World to escape to anymore. I'd lost my tribe. Suddenly we were all supposed to be adults who knew what to do. I'd exhausted my two-year college programming.

This is what I wrote in my journal…

Truth is truth. I live with a Monster, a hybrid monster-parrot. I mean not both, one or the other. She's either a red-faced-spitting monster chasing me down the hall and tackling me, pinching me, hitting me in the face with her many-ringed fingers, or she's a parrot. I thought she was an interesting woman before I realized she was a parrot. It's taken a while to realize that the brilliance I thought was her was always someone she was parroting. So, in that way, I think I was raised by a lot of different women, all channeled through the one.

I don't know what to do with her rage. I carry it. She has pounded into me that I will not be like the failures in my family. She has violently pounded into me that I will do better, I will be better.

I remember when my Monsters' oldest half-sister was babysitting me right after Jimmy died. I was five. We were in that room that GrandDad was building. It was missing a wall. There was just a big piece of plastic dividing the room from the outside. Sometimes it would blow in the wind. The Evil-Half-Sister had done one or two modeling gigs for the Sears catalog so she thought she was the shit. She kept tapping this flyswatter on her thigh. She was in a chair leaning back with her legs crossed tapping her top thigh with that fly swatter as the plastic wall rustled in the wind where brick and mortar should have been. She seemed to love leering at me. Daring me. I'd been crying and I got in trouble for crying. So, that's why we were in the position we were in, the one where she brought me into this room with a saran wrap wall and two chairs facing 6 and 9 o'clock. She was terrifying with her 20 pairs of socks scrunched down above her Chuck Taylors to show the world she was a real redneck.

I started to sob and to tell her that I missed Jimmy, but before I could finish, she dropped the leg that had been up and crossed down and went into a quick squat, slapped the fly swatter on her thigh, and screamed right in my face, "Stop feeling sorry for yourself!".

My GrandDad's house had a lot of detritus lying all over the mud yard. I say mud because there wasn't any grass. Just mud and stuff. Lots and lots of stuff of all kinds next to the big hill where we once tried all day to dig our way to China.

My GrandDad had a racist dog. I don't think the dog was born that way, but he was taught to hate. He matched the redneck socks and Chuck Taylors and cigarettes smoked by five-year-olds and noseless drug dealers at pig roasts.

I thought it was a rug or a blanket or something just lying around in the yard like everything else. I stepped on it thinking I'd get in one dry mud-free step.

Teeth!

Snarling teeth arose from the mud and were headed straight toward my face. All of the girls were there. They were screaming my name. I should say they were screaming the name they called me. They were saying, "RUN DEBBA-LOU, RUNNNN!!!"

I was little. I ran.

This is something they all witnessed but I only experienced from the inside.

I became a bluebird.

I flew to the top of the swing set. I mean, I was straddling the very top above where the swings were mounted. That dog was not giving up. He was leaping and growling and trying to grab my foot to pull me down. He was a German Shepard and he wasn't playing around with his hatred toward me.

The point is, they all saw me fly.

I think that's maybe why I never really fit in.
....
Something happened!

Something bad. Like worst-nightmare-bad.

My half-sister is 13 years younger than me. She's five and still sometimes wears a diaper. So spoiled. We were in the basement and she screamed and said I was hurting her when I was on the other side of the room. It's a strange temptation, this rage I've inherited from my Monster. My sister makes me SO angry because she's always lying like that even though she's so young. How is that even possible? It's striking to see someone so young behave with so much manipulation. I don't like her. My Monster always spoke to us as if we were the same age. "Girls!".

Here's the problem, my monster has Cinderella'd this dynamic. I had to wait until I could drive myself to school in 12th grade to stay after to do plays or anything else because I wasn't allowed to take the bus and no one had time to drive me. My Monster *is building a school for my sister after she just attended child ed at my High School and had a graduation at the age of 4. Something she and the entire family seem to view as equivalent to a High School diploma. I just cannot catch a break. My Monster will add a new class level to a school she decided to run as my sister grows up. My sister will be driven to and fro and never have to worry about anything. I had to get a quarter or two and eat whatever they were serving. But, my sister *doesn't like SANDWICHES*. So, she will get a charcuterie packed cooler on the days they don't order in for pizza or whatever. Everything I had to work very hard to earn, was handed to my sister. So, I simply feel a lot of resentment toward her. Like, all-the-time-resentment. I have had to feed her and change her diapers and be the "built-in-babysitter". But, I'm not allowed to correct her. In fact, she corrects me in these ridiculous ways. I just cannot take it anymore.*

In the basement, my Monster's old rule just started playing out with me. It was the old, "I'll give you something to cry about!" adage. I lifted her left arm into the air by the wrist. Her feet came off of the floor and with my right hand, I whacked her diapered butt.

Thing is, it was NOTHING compared to what I was used to enduring. Not even close. Still, it was way too much. She started screaming. I told her to stop being a brat. But when I went to change her diaper, my handprint was still on her little butt.

That's it!!!

Change of plans.

I HAVE to go.

I took on more lovers and fell into sensual dynamics with men and I just let everything else go with one promise.

No kids. No kids for me. I NEVER want to have kids.

I moved out. I rented the smallest room in an apartment in the cheapest town I could find in 1987. I committed to paying $175 a month plus utilities. I was informed by my Monster that there was no coming home. So, once I left, I would never be welcomed back to live.

One of my exes showed up with a pickup truck. I was still friends with his sister. I was able to bring the twin bed that I'd used as a toddler and a three-drawer dresser. No sheets. No towels. I'd purchased all of my clothes, so I still had an extensive wardrobe.

On that first night, my nose started bleeding. My new roommate taught me about frozen peas on the back of my neck. She told me to tip my head back. And she sat with me for about ½ an hour. This was different.

Usually, when I had a nosebleed, I just had to tuck away and hide until I could get it to stop. The bleeding happened more and more.

The nosebleeds started when I came home from a visit with my Father one weekend. I was so sad, I couldn't stop sobbing. My Monster informed me that if she ever heard me crying again after a weekend with my Father she would never let me see him again.

I taught myself to hold my cry inside. I would smash my face into a pillow to cover up the breathing sounds and I would force myself not to make any vocal sounds.

This was around the same time that I did my mirror transformation. Whenever she would terrorize me down into a sobbing mess, I would run downstairs into the bathroom. I would watch myself cry in the mirror and observe the shapes and the different muscles. After that observation, I would begin to change the shapes in my face as tears rolled down. I would not leave that tiny bathroom until I was laughing my ass off.

If I'd accepted just being a pronoun, and never being a proper noun, I don't think I would have made it. Allowing people to generalize me down into a pronoun would have meant accepting all of the labels they chose to slap onto me and none of the identity I was discovering for myself. All of those she and hers felt like darts in my back. They sent the clear message that my name meant nothing. I was just another nameless disposable. Holding onto my individuality, my sensuality, and my overall desire to do whatever "they" said was impossible were the things that kept me alive and present.

The PennySaver had a lot of jobs listed. I applied for most of them and held down four jobs at once sometimes. I was very excited to be hired to work at Petrucci's Dinner Theatre on Main Street. This meant I got to watch shows all of the time. My dream was not dead yet.

This is from my journal:

Well, I didn't get cast in "Fiddler on the Roof". I auditioned with a monologue I'd written myself. It was about an orgasm capsule that women could take during boring board meetings. Everyone seemed engaged. It was no match for "Fiddler", though! I guess that particular tradition does not include female orgasms. Go figure. The director is a man name John Palmer Claridge. I saw him in the theatre. He said he thought there was something to my writing worth exploring. He said that if I wanted, I could drop monologues in his mailbox at the theatre and he'd be happy to give me feedback. He encouraged me to keep writing.

The THRILL OF IT!! This is the first time EVER that I auditioned with a monologue I'd written myself. I felt like I was soaring. I had to be back there for my shift that night. But, I was soaring so high I had to jump inside of my bitchin blue Camaro and drive. I followed the water and somehow ended up at the Kennedy Center. They were having an open house. I parked and I walked and it felt like I'd finally found home.

Working at The Paper Moon in DC is a demanding thing. We do fine dining until midnight. And then we transform the whole restaurant into a dance club until around 3 in the morning. I've gotten good at table service. The first time I opened a bottle of champagne I let out a little shrill sound though. The guy who trained me there has long blonde hair cut in a harsh straight line. He's constantly flipping it around because he's a true asshole. He seems to think he's a beautiful mermaid and he will live his mermaid life even if a table has been waiting ten minutes for water. He tried to tell me that I should make people wait ten to fifteen minutes before greeting them. That's not my style at all. He loves himself and he loves it when the whole room notices him.

One of the busboys grabbed my boob and I slapped him in the face. He got angry with me and told me I should not have hit him. I told him that if he didn't grab my body I wouldn't hit his face. Seems like a fair deal. But, sometimes I need him to froth the milk for the cappuccino, I'm no good at that. I hate being dependent on people. Especially grabby ones.

I have to show up early to set the place up. I like to roll my sweatpants down to get more air on my midriff because it's summer and DC is a reformed swamp. He told me I was too sexy. I wasn't trying to tempt him. Then we argued over whether I was sexy or not, which is something I didn't have any kind of time for. Anyway, it's all weird.

Lily Tomlin came in and I think she was staring at my butt, but I'm not sure. My table offered to buy her a bottle of wine. She said she'd already been given three and asked if my table might like to buy her a cup of coffee instead. So, I served her coffee. She was so much nicer than Oprah. I made the mistake of saying something to Oprah when she was at a two-top at Philip's Flagship. She told me she was working and that I shouldn't be interrupting her. She was right. I've learned to play it cool around celebrities now.

No biggie.

I think I don't want to be intimate with anyone without my clothes on because of AIDS. Have you seen what it does?

It's turned DuPont Circle into a zombie land. There are these men wearing sweaters that are three sizes too big with reddish-brown almost pulsing sores all over their faces. They are so low energy and weak I can hardly believe they are out and about. One waiter at Bay 'n Surf where I work convinced everyone on our shift to give him our tips so he could buy one experimental treatment. But then, he went and bought street drugs with our money instead.

Then he died. So, I guess I can't be too mad at him. I work hard for my money and giving it to him was an act of generosity. People are gonna peep!

There are a lot of people dropping dead from this thing.

I'm so glad Planned Parenthood is inside the mall. I go there to get my exams and my birth control pills. And IF I want to have intercourse with a guy, he has to go and get tested for AIDS. It takes a week or two for the results to arrive. So, the spontaneity of traditional sex is gone for good it seems.

I don't want to die.

I work at the box office at Petrucci's. I run lights and I run sound. I manage the Broadway Club. That's the balcony. Only once did a person not show up on their designated night to sit at their designated table. I called to inquire and found out she had died.

That's the only no-show I've ever experienced here. People in Laurel are dedicated.

My manager throws temper tantrums. I mean he throws erasures and his face turns red and he screams and we all jump around him to get done whatever he needs us to get done. His other gig is impersonating Edgar Allen Poe. I think he wants to be a celebrity and he doesn't like watching other people doing the acting work.

Tammy Tappin came out dancing with us at Mac's Place behind the Giant. We danced to a lot of Prince songs. She has a singing voice that shakes souls. She was in "Annie" and when she sang, "NYC" my soul melted down into my feet. She's touring with Andrew Lloyd Weber now.

I love being surrounded by all of this talent.

ven*us*

[flourish: MT5]

Freed
She
No
Longer
Longed
Wondered
Grieved

Freed
She
Fled
Danger
Into
Stranger
Sensual
Things

Freed
She
Felt
The
Buried
Pain
As
It
Appeared

Freed
She
Broke
Out
In
Hidden
Hives
Doctor
Makes
Clear

Freed
She
Is
Told
What
Is
Without
Is
Also
Within

In
Terms
Of

STRESS

Nosebleeds

Hives
On
The
Skin
Living
Within
the
Body

Still
She
Felt

Freed

Part Two

Chapter 6:
COMPASSION AND LOVE

Objective: Evolution Is for the Adaptable

Lots of jobs still.

Mission: Let Go of NEEDING and Embrace BEING

This is what I wrote in my journal:

This is the night that changed everything for the rest of my life.

As hard as I work, I like to dance even more. Jen and I waited tables together and one day she asked me if I wanted to join her to go clubbing. We sort of made a pact. We worked a lot but when we weren't working we decided we would go out dancing. We'd meet up and choose a club. If there weren't many people there we'd move on.

Being young, white, attractive women comes with benefits. We know this. We know we can get into any club for free just by showing up. They pull us to the front of the line and wave us through. We know we can drink all night without spending a dime.

We're sort of bait for men who have money to spend. We understand this and we don't care. We're tired of working, working, working. We want to play as much as we work. Besides, we can't make what men make even when we're working the same job so this is a kind of leveling as far as we see it.

It's the evening of May 4th, 1989. All over the city, we see posters for "Batman". Looks like it's going to be good.

What if I'm a free agent?

Jen and I are FREE. We go out, we dance, we move on. We cannot be trapped like those butterflies behind little glass frames.

I am wearing my black and white polka-dotted mini dress, black and white striped leggings, and black leather boots.

I love this outfit because it's comfortable and fashionable at the same time. Also, it keeps me connected to the Wild World summer which seems to be drifting further and further away from me.

I'm not even the same person anymore.

I still have my baseball glove with "Boop" written on the pinky side. This is my Boop-outfit.

I've been dancing for a few hours. One guy has dreadlocks and is from Hawaii. He's nice. We dance a song and then we leave in separate directions and then we dance another. It's like this code. An unspoken language that understands we could use each other or we could just step away and see what else is going on.

This is an underground club, meaning you have to go down steps because it's under the street, no windows and I'm sweaty with all of the dancing. By now I've learned that while free champagne may sound like a good idea, it doesn't mix with constant dancing. Too many bubbles.

The scene in the women's bathroom was something to behold that night! It was like someone dropped a whole row of Mentos into Coke bottles stall by stall.

Tonight, I'm not drinking. I'm just dancing. I've stepped away from my aloha-guy and I'm leaning against the bar. It's the ideal location because the air conditioner vent is in the ceiling and it's perfectly drying my hair and cooling me off.

My hair is short now because one of the guys I was seeing said I looked like a greyhound and he wanted to see me sleek. Turns out he was a gay man in denial who would sneak to DuPont Circle late at night. He'd pretend he couldn't remember where he parked his car and when a man helped him he would give him an oral service as a thank you. Another heroine saved by the hero.

I'd say that relationship was sexually dysfunctional. It kind of worked for me because I didn't want to die of AIDS and he was only really attracted to men so he couldn't do the deed with me and we never kissed. Which was a relief.

He also liked to snort cocaine. I've watched a lot of people do a lot of drugs. Cocaine scares me the most. I can see their eyes dilate and it's easy to tell their heart is racing. It always seems like people on cocaine are a half a step away from having their heart explode inside of their chest. Creeps me out. Especially because they seem to feel so liberated and energetic while all of this is going on.

Once I found him completely naked laying fetal on the floor in my apartment after I came home from a wait shift. He did organize all of my albums alphabetically first, which was a kind of consideration.

He was fixated on Amway.

Pyramid schemes! He stayed up for three days and nights listening to Amway motivational cassette tapes. It made him completely delusional. By the time he got to the Amway convention in Richmond, he grabbed the mic from the speaker's hands in front of thousands of people.

He couldn't stop talking and became so disconnected and excited that he stripped all of his clothes off in front of everyone. So they arrested him.

That was a final flag for me. Time to move on.

Tonight, I'm doing what no single woman is ever supposed to do in a club. I'm leaning on the bar alone without a drink in my hand. Pretty soon I can feel eyes on me.

I stare directly back at the eyes staring at me.

These two guys across the way are at it and mumbling. I read the lips of one as he speaks to the other saying, "Check her out". Next thing I know, a man I've never seen before pulls his broad shoulders back and is striding toward me in an exaggerated and pretty comical way.

We were equally satirical.

I pulled a real "boop" and batted my eyes in a cartoonish way. He pulled his shoulders back further and strode ridiculously.

This was definitely satire.

We started talking satirically. With distance.

We kept talking.

Songs rolled by.

We danced. I waved to my aloha-guy.

We talked.

We danced.

We talked.

Jen began to walk by me saying things in my ear and tapping her watch.

Like I was on the clock.

"45 minutes." (tap tap tap)

"THREE HOURS!" (tap tap tap)

I'm not a prostitute.

I wasn't working at all. I was off the clock. This was the longest conversation I'd had with anyone in years.

I was telling him, this guy Alan, about playing Penny and about being a paid performer at Wild World and about the shows I'd done in Community College. He told me that he was a musician and he told me about the bands he was in and the shows he was playing and he told me the names of his guitars.

This was completely different, outside of my experience. He wasn't trying to catch a glimpse of whatever of my body parts. He was TALKING to me. He was HEARING me and SEEING me.

I wasn't this young woman who had to prove herself anymore. For the first time, with him, I felt already established. He wanted to hear more about what I'd done and what I wanted to be doing next.

I'd dated musicians. Famous-ish ones. It was great to be backstage and to watch them do their thing. But, they never really wanted to know much about me. They just wanted to be seen with me.

Alan was listening.

He gave me his phone number and I tucked it into my boot. But, I lost it. So, I set my answering machine to say, "Thanks for calling, I'm not in right now. And, if this is Alan, I lost your number so please leave a message".

He looked me up in the phone book and called.

I made it into the city to watch him play a house party.

He has the most beautiful singing voice I've ever heard.

He has a fuchsia guitar named Giles and a bright green one too. He sang a Terrence Trent D'arby cover, "Sign Your Name Across My Heart".

He's so talented.

....
Alan lives with me now.

Sometimes he writes songs that he says are about me. One is called, "Beautiful Like This".

<u>*Beautiful Like This*</u>

She bathes in blue and yellow like a red star
Moving to the light she bends everyone
She reigns like all the love you ever buried deep down
Move into the light
So long black star

Beautiful Like This
Beautiful Like This
I feel like I'm falling into the sun

Beautiful Like This
Beautiful Like This
Is this how it feels to fall in love
With an everyday angel from above
The beautiful life has just begun

She rides on blood red clouds melodies pouring out
Moving to a sound only she can hear
She sings a melody underneath my skin
I can almost hear the words
Beneath the scars

Beautiful Like This
Beautiful Like This
I feel like I'm falling into the sun

Beautiful Like This
Beautiful Like This
Is this how it feels to fall in love
With an everyday angel from above
The beautiful life has just begun
-Alan Scott

Back when I did "Gemini" there was an actor from Brown University who played a character named Bunny in the show. She told me that all I, or anyone, really needed to succeed in theatre was ONE person. One person who believed in me. One person who would always show up. She'd done the role all over the country and she had one friend that was always there. She told me it was all I needed. But, I never thought I'd find one person who could see the artistry in me first, before anything else.

I never knew anything like this was even possible!

Miracle.

[flourish: MT6]

Remember when you thought you knew
Remember that?

That time when you had it all planned out
Remember?

That's not how it works
Nope.

The only reason to make a plan is to take the next step
Simple.

See it
Let it go

Love is not what anyone told you it was
Love

It's something else
Something you've never seen before
And as soon as you're sure that you know
You're lost

Trust

Trust this path

It's finally found you.

Chapter 7:
UNIVERSITY - THE FIRST IN MY FAMILY

Objective: Home base. What happens from here?

The Theatre CV is underway yet again. During my time at the University of Maryland, Baltimore County, I received scholarships and grants.

Some acting credits include:
Shakespeare On Wheels - "The Merry Wives of Windsor" by William Shakespeare
Maryland Stage Company -"The Persecution and Assassination of Jean-Paul Marat as Performed by the Inmates of the Asylum of Charenton Under the Direction of the Marquis de Sade " by Peter Weiss Mainstage -
"The Tudor" by Jacob Lenz adapted by Bertolt Brecht Second Stage -
"Cinders" by Janusz Glowacki "Don Juan Comes Home From the War" by Odon von Horvath.

I participated in protests to save the theatre department, with guidance from the University President, Freeman Hrabowski.

I participated in improvisational student productions both acting and dancing.

Dance credit:
Kimberly Mackin Dance Project "Pictures At An Exhibition" by Mussorksy, the Baltimore Museum of Art.

I not only was the first in my family to graduate from University but I graduated cum laude.

I continued to wait tables at the Silver Diner.

I briefly trained to teach ballroom dancing for a living.

Mission: Remember YOU ARE A Proper Noun PERSON!

I was singing along with Tracy Chapman in the scene shop, "Don't cha know they're talkin' bout a revolution…". My theatre practicum teacher Drew took exception. The riots aren't only happening in LA. We've got some action here in Baltimore too. Drew was trying to take his wife and his baby across town. At a stop light, rioters started shaking their car with the baby inside and everything. Drew told me we didn't need to be singing or encouraging revolutions.

Drew's Theatre Practicum class is no joke. It's the first theatre class I've enrolled in at University.

I heard the man before I ever set eyes on him. We all did.

The scene shop smelled like my paternal grandfather's barn behind my Nanny's house when I was very little.

I love the smell of wood.

Drew bellows. He doesn't even yell. He bellows. It's as if the wind fills his entire being. Like his body becomes one big giant hot pocket of air. That air creates a breeze and that breeze full of tonal demand enters the room five paces before his physical body does.

He's very clear. He calls us idiots and says he doesn't want to see digits flying all over his shop. He points to a chalkboard with "Drew's Rules" written out in chalk.

1. Measure twice, cut once.
2. Assign the laziest person the hardest job and they'll find the easiest way to do it.
3. Drew's Laws of Demographics: Out of 100% of the people you'll meet in the industry, 80% won't be worth knowing. 15% will be kind of okay. 5% will be worth truly getting to know.
4. Early is on time, on time is late, late is a failing grade
5. No two objects can occupy the same space at the same time. (including saw blades and digits).

He REALLY doesn't want our digits flying around his shop.

After we were clear on all of that he showed us every piece of equipment in the shop and told us how to use each thing. Specifically showing us the precise location on the blades where our digits would likely be severed and go flying.

It was weird because before I always had other people doing that kind of stuff. I was the visionary ingenue thinking of new ways to run programming. Suddenly I had to sweep floors, hang lights, and sign in on the sheet five minutes early or face extreme consequences.

I once witnessed a car accident on 95 on the way into a show call. I kept driving because of the consequences and repercussions! I told Drew about it and he SCOLDED me. His voice pitched up and bellowed my name, "RANDALL! If you see an accident, stop and report the accident. Jesus!"

Sometimes it's confusing.

First rule of theatre: SHOW UP.

The professors are characters in their own right. Each one is so full of passion and each one has a unique kind of stamina.

I'm finally seeing theatre as a possible lifestyle and occupation again.

It's all so far beyond my wildest dreams. I have to keep stepping into it to see where it leads.

Here's what I wrote in my journal…

Wendy is amazing! She's my advisor and she is training to be an Alexander Technique practitioner. She invites us all to sign up for one-on-one adjustments with her. She's so excited about what she's learning you can feel it.

She teaches me to stop doing. She encourages me to BE. She says I have to get out of the way of myself. I'm still figuring out what that means. I've got a lot of tension spots in my body. Her warm ups make it possible for me to embody characters in new ways. Her vocal teachings are freeing up my whole vocal mechanism. The tone of my voice is changing. Again, I can play around with my voice to create different characters and it's SO MUCH FUN!

Sam is my Euro/Mod Professor. He is one of the founders of the Lyric Theatre in Ireland. He says that when we read a script we should be able to tell which ones still have life to breathe into the world and which ones are a matter of record. He says young artists don't know how to dress anymore. He eats the whole apple. I mean, the WHOLE thing, the stem and the seeds and every single molecule in that bag of apples while he's giving us notes.

He told me I should play Virginia Woolf. He called me one of the Bronte sisters. He didn't specify which one. There's nothing like hearing Sam's laughter during a performance. It's fuel!

Alice is the oldest of the group. She teaches Theatre History and Speech. Alice has a system. She doesn't know that referencing blackamoors is an offensive thing to do. She loves to show her slides from Greece and the surrounding region that she took on a trip a while ago with her now-deceased husband. She loves Michelangelo's David. She lingers on that slide for quite a long time just taking in his "beauty".

Then, there's X. He's a mostly bald chain-smoking director. He likes to rub his forehead a lot with his cigarette wedged between his fingers. Sometimes this is a good thing and sometimes this is a bad thing. It's good if he repetitively says, "wunnerful wunnerful

wunnerful" while quickly rubbing his forehead with the padding of his cigarette-holding hand. It's bad if there is no sound. If there is no sound but he's rubbing his forehead slowly, he's likely about to tell an acting student their work is mud. Or that they are wooden like a tree. Or that their performance was entirely unbelievable and they'd have to go back to the beginning of the scene. When this happens, other scenes get bumped to later in the week. So, a person can be sitting there ready to perform and then the scene in front of them may take the entire three hours of class. Watching X dissect scenes is new for me and I'm learning a lot from watching the way that he works. It seems like if the actors are not in the zone going in with all pistons firing it can quickly become a tedious dissection of trying to make sense of the pieces that aren't working for students who generally don't get it from the beginning. X will get them there by spending hours on a single moment. He comes at it from more angles than anyone ever thought was possible.

Last semester I chose a scene and read it for X to approve for my upcoming scene study class. I was really into it. I was hoping for something positive from him. Like he would say, you're really onto something here. Let's go with this one!

But all he said was, "You just did it."

I was confused.

Then he went on to say that there was nothing to work on because I'd just found what needed to be found in that scene. I needed to find something I could work on for three months.

X doesn't really teach a branded method or a style. It just has to work. He either believes the character or he doesn't. X says there's no such thing as a transition. Meaning, every moment on stage is a live moment. There's never permission to drop out of being present. He believes in rehearsing a show for three months to be performed for one or two weekends.

X says we can only ever play one moment at a time. Trying to play many things at once creates "mud". The reason he wants us to experience a three-month process is that he believes it takes at least that long to understand a work.

It's like he thinks we have to make every possible mistake to find out what works.

It's exhausting.

Some Xisms:
-Impulse is golden.
-Hesitation is death.
-You must compress singularly true moments together tightly and then trust yourself to play them in quick succession without thinking or controlling.
-Expect nothing from your audience. "You take your guts and you put them on a plate for your audience and if you're lucky, they will slurp them up. That's the compliment. Maybe they'll belch in your face. That's it. Expect nothing else."

We watch one another's work as we sit in chairs in a single line against the wall.

X cast me in "Marat/Sade"! WHAT!?! I get to sing!!!

His cousin is Z. A famous conductor.

X tells me I have "good intonation"! WHAT!?!? I'm in a state of complete disbelief. This is not just a Main Stage production, it's a professional Maryland Stage Company Production.

I'm getting paid to act again! (in class credits).

Holy.

X casts at the end of a semester and then we rehearse for three months and perform the show for two weekends.

For "Marat/Sade" he has us working in the rehearsal room with all lights off wearing straight jacket-robes.

I've volunteered to be the pyromaniac. I'm excited to push myself! I love pushing myself. A fellow student volunteered to shave her head but then she never did. He told us not to shave anything. There's some idiot in the cast who keeps trying to catch his sleeve on fire. The last scene is a riot. X staged a riot and Drew is doing the fight choreography and special effects. They've soaked something in chocolate sauce and staged it to look like a castration with the castrated testicles being force-fed to one of the characters. It's so disturbing that some audience get up and leave. X tells us that's a good thing because we've had a real effect on them. I always thought we were supposed to keep audiences in their seats. But, he's a genius and as artists, it's our job to collectively transport people to imagined places they would otherwise never know.

So…

At the very end, before the lights go out, my character holds a bucket of fire. I stare into it. And it's the last thing that goes out on stage when I cover it with a hidden lid. but this idiot actor is throwing his 8' sleeve directly at my bucket of fire. Drew has made it very clear to everyone that it's my job to prevent anyone from catching on fire. Or, if they do, it's my job to put them out immediately. I can still hear him bellowing, "STOP, DROP, and ROLL!". We all know where the two water sources are on stage. I decide I can stay in character and give the show a dramatic last fire beat while at the same time preventing a man from setting himself aflame in my bucket. So, I have to stay in character and gently move the bucket around in a seemingly catatonic state. Backstage, I tell him to stop trying to set himself on fire. I told the stage manager. But, no one cares because he's another diva-dude who thinks everything revolves around him. He doesn't care what happens if the theatre goes up in flames. He tells me he's just trying to catch on fire "a little bit".

JeeeeSus!!!

The only people who will listen to me are the costumers and I think that's because they don't want the costumes destroyed.

Muslin costumes.

Going up in FLAMES! I can see the impending inferno and Drew's screaming face in my head every day.

Not setting the theatre on fire while staying in character becomes my singular focus.

It's very different from the lighting for "The Best of Burlesque" at Petrucci's Dinner Theatre.

The thing a few of us learn most in doing "Marat/Sade" is that we work very hard to get into character. X brought in campus experts and we studied the French Revolution, insane asylums, and the RSC production in FULL detail. But, no one ever showed us how to get OUT of character.

To prepare for "Marat/Sade", I met with Drew before Algebra every day to practice my fire breathing. Drew had me breathe grain alcohol over a match. But, I ran out of wind. I think I burned all of the cilia out of my lungs. So, I ended up squeezing powder out of a bottle over a flaming match instead.

Suddenly, algebra became entertaining and interesting. It took me a couple of weeks to realize why. Even though I wasn't swallowing any of the alcohol it was being absorbed in through the membrane in my mouth. I was walking around campus drunk. Drunk in Algebra. And, I got an A in the class. Third try. I had always failed before.

Stress.

Geez!

Sam wants me to play Mistress Quickly in, "The Merry Wives of Windsor". Shakespeare on Wheels is a program he and Bill Brown put together. It's a tractor-trailer that unfolds into a set and then folds back up again and drives off. It tours the eastern seaboard.

I can't.

I tell them I can't. I feel like I can understand Jay from Wild World more now. I have to make money all summer so that I can afford to go to school during the semesters ahead. I have a mortgage and a car payment.

I have very adult responsibilities while I'm in school. They call me an unconventional student. It applies.

I have to work. I have to work for every single thing I have.

To be honest I'm disgusted by students who have their parents paying for everything. Like they're doing them a favor by coming to college. I have to upsell milkshakes to pay for every credit hour.

And, let me tell you. When you've closed down all of the stations and the rodeo or square dancing party or whoever those taffeta taffy colored short skirt wearing people are with their cowboy hats appear at the doors in droves to take up half of the restaurant, it wears on the psyche. Especially when a station wagon-driving lazy busboy ducks out and leaves you to stay until the sun comes up re-cleaning. I screamed so hard at him as I ran down the gigantic booth seat and slammed a full buspan against the window. I called him a bastard and watched him smile and wave as he drove his slow boat of a car. Cindy, was the other waitress and she was laughing so hard at my fury she peed herself. And then she went over to the soda station, the one where I had to make all of the upsold milkshakes and she just laughed maniacally and sprayed the whole station with whipped cream.

I couldn't be mad at her though. Her husband is abusive and she has two kids. He pays for rent and utilities and she has to pay for groceries. So every weekend she works a double shift and whatever money she makes that night is the budget for her to feed her kids all week. She goes straight to the all-night Giant after work and by the time her kids wake up the next day, the cupboards are stocked as well as she can stock them.

So, when a design teacher tries to end his class two hours early, having spent the first hour talking about how he used to live next to Bob Marley, I become furious. I confront him just as students are excitedly packing up to leave early. They are giving me evil side eyes.

I am telling him that essentially, I am paying him to teach me and he's not doing that.

He says, "This is the easiest A you'll ever get."

I say, "I don't WANT an easy A. I WANT TO LEARN."

So now, a lot of people hate me.

Somehow I agree to tour as Quickley with Shakespeare on Wheels. I worked it out with the Diner. I will pick up as many shifts as possible in between.

I'm stressed out and grumbling. Kind of complaining to a fellow student that they've essentially begged me to do this so I have to say yes to stay in good standing with the department. She eloquently tells me to shut the hell up. She explains that she and many others will do anything to take any role to tour all summer. She says she's sick and tired of hearing me complaining about something any one of them would kill to have.

I feel like an asshole.

I am an asshole.

I'm the asshole now.

I'm the one taking things for granted.

Having performed outside for an entire summer with no running water or electricity, I know I can handle this. We have two vans, a stage manager car, plus a tractor-trailer. We have a big cast, a production manager, a touring manager. The works.

Still.

We have one dude who is not stable. He is always going too far on stage, and off. This one night he was driving the van somewhere near the Finger Lakes. He was blasting metal music and it was late. The people in the van told him to turn the music down and he lost it. He pulled the van over and threw everyone out. He left them on the side of the road in the pitch-black night in the middle of nowhere.

Somehow the Stage Manager found out and got in her car to go and find them and bring them back to the motel. She was successful. Some had to ride back in the trunk. Les was an older actor who wore hearing aids. He dealt with this tour by mostly turning his hearing aids off and closing his eyes. But, this night, he was tossed out on the shoulder of an unknown road. At least he didn't have to ride in the trunk like some of the other actors did. So, that's good. The wild guy stayed on the tour and started dating the Stage Manager.

A few of us went skinny dipping when we were in St. Mary's. We broke into the graveyard and made our way to the water. It was a full moon. I would find out very soon after that there were jellyfish in the water. Not ideal.

We got out of the water. We laid back to stare at the stars. As we lay between the tombstones in that colonized graveyard, one of the actors used a burial marker as a pillow. It was one of those moments on tour where I felt at one with the Universe. There was another. We were in someone's house near the ocean and there was a pool in the backyard. I was floating and staring up at the Milky Way. Weightless with no real direction, only sensation. No artificial light. Just me and the whole Universe.

Profound.

All of it.

We're lying around the cemetery in St Mary's and I guess because we were thinking there were probably ghosts we started singing, "Unchained Melody" from the film "Ghosts".

We're singing, "...and time...goes by...so slowly...and time... can do..so much..."

Right about then the metal crazy dude and the Stage Manager walk up on us. He decided to start singing. Only he's out of key and loud. He has no sense of atmosphere or, as Wendy would say, "he seems to have no kinesthetic awareness."

By now, we are having a hard time pretending he's normal.

Because he's an absolute whackamole.

He decided to "take center stage" and he wails..." are you...still mine...I i I i I NeEeEeEd..."

By now Jason who was using the tomb as his pillow blurts out an explosive sneeze laugh. That breaks the seal of self-imposed restraint. We all burst and find ourselves rolling around laughing at this guy.

He's asking what's so funny?

That makes us laugh harder.

Oblivious, the stage manager takes him back to her car.

And, we howl for a solid half hour. Once we all stop, one of us will let out the slightest sound and we will all be rolling around in laughter again.

Whew!

I needed that.

The production manager found a dead squirrel and put a note on it to tell us this is what was going to happen to actors who didn't behave. I think she must have thought it was funny. But dead squirrels lack humor.

I finally confronted the wailer at Strathmore Hall after he went ballistic on one of the actors there. He didn't like that. No one backed me up. Once again, I found myself in a standoff with someone who was not in their right mind. It shook me up. I left to go cry alone under the bushes because we only had about ten minutes until places and that wasn't enough time to find the van or an indoor space. I felt arms circle around me from behind and hold me tight. It was the Stage Manager. She was apologizing while squeezing me and saying that she should have been the one to manage him and thanking me.

Ugh.

I think about money and management structures in theatre. Shakespeare had already killed Fallstaff in "Henry IV". But Queen Elizabeth loved the character so much that she requested he appear again.

A quandary.

Queen Elizabeth was Shakespeare's benefactor. So, he had to meet her requests or not write plays. Shakespeare wrote "The Merry Wives of Windsor" as a prequel to "Henry IV", and as a comedy. What kind of wizardry is that? Playwrights can bend space and time. They are the Gods and GodDesSes of their worlds. They determine every single detail on the page.

I often wonder what Shakespeare wanted to write about.

Of course, some people think Queen Elizabeth was Shakespeare.

So many theories.

It's amazing. Unfortunately, I am a bit young to be playing Quickly, and Sam, for purposes of run time, has cut many of my scenes from the show. I do get to play Queen of the Fairies. Love that.

One of my castmates keeps getting injured. She has a mild concussion so there were a few shows where I had to put myself in the scene just to keep her from falling over last week.

The other week the entire crew had heat stroke. We showed up to our site somewhere in Virginia and there was no crew. They were all in the hospital. So, we actors had to put the stage together before performing. I'm so glad it held.

We were at this train museum on a farm in Pennsylvania or someplace. I could not show it to you on a map if I tried.

We're set up in front of a cornfield. Storm clouds are overhead. And the truck is all metal.

So, we started the show THREE different times. All three times a storm drops down on us just as we're getting started. When this happens everyone jumps off the truck from wherever their location is. From the audience's perspective, they just see actors in capes leaping off of the sides of the truck. All three times this happened after my entrance.

I'm feeling really good. I enter. I deliver the first couple of lines of my monologue. The only other person on stage with me is the ASL interpreter. We've worked her in the show as a character. So, I'm talking to her during my monologue.

Suddenly, the Stage Manager screams from the middle of the crowd, "GET OFF OF THE TRUCK!!!"

Three times.

I loved entering and watching all of the faces in the audience light up at my entrance. For a split second there, I felt that I was their favorite character.

It was then that I heard a thunderclap the likes of which entire Universes are formed. As it turns out, it wasn't that the audience had chosen me as their favorite character at all. The look of awe and wonder on their collective faces was not about my brilliant performance.

They thought they were about to witness nature murder me. They saw a lightning bolt strike directly behind me. I jumped off within milliseconds of being electrocuted by a lightning strike on the truck. Although to be fair, lighting never actually struck the truck that night. But, it was close. It was a close call.

Another time we were performing beside the famous Wye Oak. It was a nice day. Children were everywhere. I was just about to enter. Jason comes backstage and bursts into a combination of terror and laughter. My cue is coming up. I'm trying to ignore him and stay focused. But, what if he's not okay?

He suddenly blurts, "I think I kicked a child up into the Wye Oak!" "Whaaaat???" "And he never came down!" By now, he's laughing but he also has tears pouring down the white makeup on his face and I have to enter.

This tour taught me that a cue is a cue.

In Havre De Grace, we had bats flying at us. At UMBC we had to compete with three different firework displays. In Ocean City, there was a plague of frogs on the field where the audience should have been seated. One actor grabbed one and took it to the top of the truck where it lept to its death. There was an issue of performing in masks in the summer and eye infections. In Fort Washington, one audience member under the influence of we'll-never-know-what stood up in the middle of a performance and declared, "I AM SHAYAM!!!" and then bum-rushed the stage. In Gaithersburg, the train plowed by blowing its steam horn so all I could do was hold onto a door frame on the set and pretend to not be sucked away because there's no such thing as a transition.

Everyone should tour.

ONCE.

When they're young.

I like always working on plays. I like working on two or three at a time. It's hard to believe how they can resonate with one another.

I finally found a physics teacher I can learn from! They say he's specifically geared to teach the artistic types.

Did you KNOW that there's a formula for impulse!?!

It's mind-blowing. I walk out of Xs' acting class where he says over and over, "Impulse is golden. Why do you think we can have so many different Hamlets? Impulse is golden." And then, I'm taught this formula: $J = F * \Delta t$ in the next hour. Impulse is the product of the average net force acting on an object for a certain duration.

The actor is the object. The net force is the culmination of audience and script and preparedness and sometimes bats and frogs and trains and lightning strikes.

It's so hard to quantify and this is helping me a lot. You have to put your soul, your specific energy, into the work for it to convey to other souls, and people. This is the sacred bond between the performer and the audience. And you have to let go of any idea that you have control over the net force. You just have your piece of it. One variable among many, mostly unpredictable, variables.

Bringing plays to life is science.

I'm taking it so seriously with everything I do. The next director tells me I can play any of the roles in the show after my audition for him but other students can't. So, he gives me the less likable character with fewer lines. I'm loving it. I LOVE not being the ingenue. I get to smoke and terrorize people. I get to spit on the ground and make another character clean it up with her hair! My character rapes other young women with coke bottles. Not really. There are no rapes on stage, but that's her rep.

I understand now that theatre is the original simulator. Before machines were invented, people were trying on other lives by experiencing different people living lives other than the ones they knew, or in a different way. Just to see what it felt like to be a completely different person having a completely different experience.

Wendy has me working on some John Guare scenes. I'm playing a terrible person. So, I told her in front of the whole class that it was hard to play a terrible person. And then, she told me, as an actor you have to love your character. Even if you're playing a serial killer, you have to love that person. Good acting means not holding judgment over your character. It means accepting them exactly for who they are. That's the journey of discovery. The whole process of building a character is respecting who they are as a whole human being. It helps to understand why they are that way too. Compassion for the character is really important.

So, now when I build a character I stand in awe of them. Because they exist. I know it's my job to stay true to who they are.

I'm thinking, or maybe hoping, that one day this will be the way I view all of the people in my life who set out to do me harm. Maybe one day I will be able to stand in awe of them for existing at all. It's a working meditation. A good practice.

Theatre is like trying on outfits with your soul.

X says we have to hand over what we have created as a kind of an offering. It's not up to us to try to make the audience feel. It's up to us to be honest in our performance and accept that the audiences will experience the journey in their specific way. And, that is none of our business.

What's great about theatre is that plays need conflict. That's what makes them interesting. That means the more extreme the characters are one from the other, the more interesting the work can be. Also, playing characters very much alike can be interesting. The whole thing is an experimental journey.

We can stage a riot and look at it detached and decide how we feel about that. This is much better than being trapped in an actual riot. Theatre gives our brains ways to experience things without ever leaving our seats together as one established community of audience on any given night.

The audience is the fuel. Trying to perform without an audience is simply rehearsal. There's an energy exchange that is never the same each night.

X says to never try to play the show that happened the night before. It's a different audience on this night. Same formula, but different matter making up the variable of the equation. The audience will have a different way of interfacing with the work. Keep it open for them to experience that. Don't put limits around it by trying to do what you know worked yesterday, that's death on stage.

As Sam says, theatre is a living breathing thing. It's no good trying to trap it. We're here to feed it and to let it grow.

We have to remain open to experiencing each moment as it arrives.

I'm thinking, if I can really commit to doing this onstage, maybe I'll get better at doing it in my own life.

I find it's a lot like a rollercoaster. We spent three months laying tracks and inspecting the engine. It's a lot of work on a lot of dif-

ferent levels. When it's time to perform, our only power is to get inside of the thing, throw our hands in the air, and take the ride.

Skipping the process that puts the thing together is a travesty. A perfect way to set any actor up to fail.

X directed a Beckett series and I got to see all of my Professors performing. This was different from being on stage with them.

X insists the room must be completely black. Not even a pinpoint of light can leak in. I know he must be driving Drew crazy. I'm laughing about it inside but my respect for X grows. The precision that man captures in his direction is stunning.

Stunning.

Every single millisecond each of his actors is on that stage is overflowing with unspoken intention.

That's my goal. To be that kind of performer and maybe I'll direct that way too someday. Completely uninhibited and absorbed in the world the playwright has penned.

That's how we touch the truth together.

That's the dream.

I'm a dance minor too! There's a dance improvisation class almost every semester. Each time it features a guest instructor. I sign up every single chance I can get.

This feels like Bud's improvisation classes every semester all over again. I just can't get enough of this.

Talk about impulse!

One man sent us out into the hallway, then he opened the double doors to the studio. He used the door frame to box in and define his movement and we watched him dance for over an hour.

It was completely riveting and it set the gears churning in my brain in terms of space and framing.

Final projects are a lot of pressure. I've got a Shakespearean scene, and a contemporary scene, and Alice is going to test us on the phonetic alphabet, all before lunch.

The other week, the KKK came to campus to protest. I was terrified. A lot of the time I eat lunch with X and my friend Anne. I was almost crying telling X we needed to get them off of the campus.

He stopped me. He told me, no. He said this was the best place they could be. He told me that people who wear hoods and hide in dark places will quickly lose their power when they are exposed to the light.

I hadn't thought about it like that.

The President of the college is Freeman Hrabowski. When he was a teenager he convinced his parents to let him march with the freedom riders led by Dr. King and John Lewis. They didn't want to but he convinced them that he had to live everything he was being taught in church and school.

A notorious racist spit on him and he ended up in jail when he was only 12 years old.

When we were protesting to keep the theatre program, after they threatened to cut it I was so mad at him. I went into his office and I started yelling.

He stopped me. He told me to take a seat.

Then, he told me that I needed to learn how to use my voice in a way that people would hear. He said he understood my rage and that it was justified but if I wanted to affect any kind of change I would need an audience willing to hear me.

Tricky.

It's taken a lot for me to stay on campus.

I didn't think I'd make it to my degree. I'm the first in my family.

I had to quit waiting tables at the diner. It was becoming pretty impossible to complete my dance minor because I kept jamming down on my hip when I was taking orders and then I was limping. Working two double shifts back to back and trying to keep up with dance classes after a tour has become impossible for me.

But, I know I shouldn't complain because I'm so lucky to be having these opportunities.

I was picking up breakfast shifts for a while. Jane is a career waitress and she always works that shift on the same days every week. Her nails are always spectacular and there's never a hair out of place. At the diner, we have to wear these dresses with buttons down the front and a blue gingham crown. Eventually, we were allowed to wear socks which are good for shock absorption..

I told Jane that one day I was going to run my own theatre company. I started to go on about how I was going to do it. But, she interrupted me. She said, "Yeah. I used to have dreams like that too."

I had to go.

I'm working on my final project for my dance class. Carol Hess has us work with the videography class. I danced in one of the underground tunnels on campus. There are many. Maybe from the bomb shelter days or maybe from the days when the University used to be a mental institution. I'm not sure if Zelda Scott Fitzgerald was burned to death in a fire on campus or a couple of miles away. The history is creepy nonetheless.

I included some of the underground tunnel footage with live choreography in my final dance project. I also read aloud the Maya Angelou poem, "I Know Why The Caged Bird Sings". And I did a sock puppet show too. It was a lot. But, I was in Baltimore. So, funky artistry was par for the course.

The money ran out at one point. That's why I didn't think I was going to make it.

I lost it.

I just started walking around campus sobbing.

Another theatre student saw me and jumped from behind the desk where he was working and held me. I was sobbing. I felt stupid so I ripped my way out of his arms and went up to the theatre administration office to talk to Bill, the head of the theatre department.

I couldn't stop crying.

He said he didn't have any way to help financially. Then he grinned. Then he told me to, "accentuate the positive, eliminate the negative, and don't mess with Mr. In Between". This did not help me pay my tuition. Just outside of his office, I stood sobbing and pathetic.

That's when Alice appeared out of her office. She was wearing her Thursday outfit. A light blue and white polyester business suit. Her hair was perfectly pinned and her make-up was in place. She had a sandwich bag filled with a few select apple slices. She smiled at me and said, hello.

I couldn't hide my tears from her, I looked at her and she was taken aback when she saw my face. I just said, "I can't do it. I'm going to have to quit. There's no way I can fund the rest of my education."

I saw a side of her I'd never seen before. One I'd never see again.

She stood a little taller. Her voice was a little deeper. She'd already offered me an apple slice and she pinched the whole sandwich bag with unexpected fingers as her pointer stabbed right toward me.

"Don't you quit! Don't you DARE quit!"

Something changed. I went back down to the financing office and I applied for a Pell Grant. I got it and that's why I'm graduating.

The scenes went well. I could hear Sam rolling with laughter.

Grades look good.

I'm graduating cum laude.

I'm graduating.

Cum laude.

A first.

I have officially accomplished the impossible.

About a year after I graduated college, I went back to dance in a student project. It was there that my character was required to sob as part of the choreography. All of my training had been about playing against the outburst. It had been about internal conflict adding to the drive of the show. This was different.

I felt all of the sadness that should have caused tears and went through the movements of sobbing but no tears would come. During one final dress rehearsal my nose started gushing blood again. At first I thought I was crying when I felt liquid on my hands. But when I looked down it was scarlet red blood.

A message in a bottle from the girl I used to be to the woman I had found a way to become. Rehearsal came to a halt. I cleaned myself up. From that moment forward, I could cry again.

Message received.

Healing accomplished.

Deborah L. Randall

[flourish: MT7]

Really
This time
This time is the real time
Really

Trust it
Know it
Live it
You got this

Really
This time
This time is the real time
Unlike

The old times
The fake times
The attack times
The control tims

Really
This time
This time is the real time
Now

I'm a real woman now
I can talk
I can wear clothes
Watch me dance!

Really
This time
This time is the real time
Watch

See
Hear
Me
I'm right here

This time.

Chapter 8:
LEGITIMATELY REAL NOW

Objective: Become REAL in the Real World, Officially.

Straight out of College I discovered the League of Washington Theatres. Their primary purpose was executing the cattle call auditions for every casting director in town and some outside of town too. These cattle call auditions were held at Arena Stage each year. Each actor was given 2 minutes to present their audition at the center stage of Arena Stage.

Back in the days of PGCC, Cyril J. Carrol had us go see plays as part of our classwork assignments. We had to write reviews about them for a grade. No shows were in-house back then. There were ALWAYS student tickets and group rates available in the box office at every professional theatre, no matter the size.

At Arena I was able to see in exactly this order: "The Tempest", "'Night Mother", and "The Cocoanuts".

"The Tempest" was done in the round. Never had I ever seen anything like it. Mid stride, the actors caught batons that flew up through the smallest holes in the floor. Not a gliding step was missed or delayed. Prospero seemed to fly into the rafters from two small one-foot-wide tiles in the floor. A cape placed matter of factly on the floor summoned him. Up he flew from under the floor, putting on the cape as he flew past it, into the air and landed above us.

I really didn't like the actual script but I LOVED the staging! I had no idea traps could be used in such brilliant ways. In community college Micheal had to fall backwards into one after he'd been shot during a rock opera. There was a crew with a mattress down there shuffling around holding the mattress above their heads. From what I understood they were always trying to move it into the right spot so that it would catch him. Usually he ended up at least partially on the floor. I guess they didn't know that theatre is a science.

This use of the trap door system at Arena expanded my brain.

"'Night Mother" ended with a gunshot that prevented me from leaving my seat for a solid twenty-minutes.

"Cocoanuts" was a favorite of my Community College fellow. Violet was brilliant. She told me she'd studied at Arena Stage. The truth was, she was a homeless teen who signed up for a program to expose kids like her to the arts. Technically, she HAD studied at Arena Stage and she never felt the need to explain anything beyond that. It took over a year for me to realize she was living out of her car. Suddenly her clothes seemed very wrinkled and her trunk was full of them. They didn't look entirely clean.

She's the reason I was President of the Drama Club. Everyone wanted her to do it but she didn't want to, she wanted me to do it. So she walked all over campus getting proxies. She was a presence. A character. Her cackle laugh traveled between buildings. Her hair was vibrant red and she could not be missed. I'd later find out that she was a professional dominatrix and that she worked the phones for an escort service.

We'd drive in her old car that had vintage oil. She could only add oil to it, she could never get it changed because it would kill the engine. The oil had become a part of the mechanics of the car somehow. She called it vintage and compared it to a good wine. I didn't even know what a proxy was. At the drama club meeting she showed up with a stack of over a hundred signed proxy slips from students around campus. I think there were about 12 people at the meeting. She nominated me and voted me in before any of us could blink.

Each year we'd have a wild Halloween Party that usually ended up with someone calling the police and shutting us down.

She was high most of the time and she respected that I never touched the stuff. She told me she did it because it made her a part of a community. In that community everyone loved and accepted the other without judgment, she said. One night we drove around DC with a boombox in the middle of her front bench seat playing The Rolling Stones and I watched her smoke hashish from a pipe while she drove.

She tried to tell me that being a dom was the same thing as being an actor. I disagreed.

For Violet, "Cocoanuts" was the penultimate show. The designs were flawless. The choreography was seamless. The costuming was stunning. That's why she loved it. Plus, she was fangirling over Halo Wines. Watching that show was a lot like watching a film. It just flowed so close to perfection it almost didn't seem real.

Suddenly Violet had money and an apartment. Her new car was falling apart. It was a small beige thing, black smoke came out of the tailpipe. We were dressed to the nines. The car was manual. We stepped out in heels to make curtain at Arena and fed the meter. Some people stared at us. Violet was really terrible at parallel parking and I think part of her shawl was hanging outside of her car when we arrived.

She also took me to see "Hayfever" at the Kennedy Center. We sat in a box seat, if memory recalls. We were really dressed up and she tried to set me up with a man at a piano bar after but he was old and weird. She tried to explain to me how much money he had.

So?

And, ew.

That night we left the cars and hailed cabs. I guess it was fancier. She had a hand fan and also a perfumed kerchief. One cab driver smelled like vintage pit odor. She giggled and her eyes watered and she kept holding her kerchief up to her nose.

She'd previously belonged to a biker in a biker gang. I think they broke up and that's when she started living in her car.

She liked feeling protected by big biker men. I could relate. At Wild World there were all of these young men that would form a human wall with their bodies if anyone tried to approach me in the wrong way.

It's a powerful feeling to know that this time you will not be beaten or raped. It changed everything for me. I was able to understand that I was a valuable person.

I think that's what led me to Alan, coming to understand my own value.

The first time I auditioned for The League of Washington Theatre's I landed callbacks. I did NOT expect to do this. There were about a thousand of us. The casting director that called me back the most was the casting director for Arena Stage, Jerry Manning. Jerry had passion. He read volumes and volumes of books when he wasn't attending shows. He'd come to Baltimore to see the shows I'd done in school there. He'd read about our production of "Marat/Sade" in American Theatre Magazine. He called me back five different times. I ran out of material. He kept telling me I must be equity. I kept telling him that I wasn't.

He said I would be perfect to understudy the entire Arena Season.

Jerry Manning cast me in a show of his at The Studio Theatre Secondstage.

I picked up shows everywhere I possibly could.
University of the District of Columbia
The Theatre Conspiracy, "Size Matters"; and Mary in "Why We Have a Body".
I was excited to find the SHE Company.

After University, I also began to do solo work, explore performance art, and create programming for late night viewing.
I became a satirical performer with Gross National Product.
I created my own company called "Venus Envy".

Under this title I produced works in DC and NYC;
"An Arco Accolade"
"The Voice Inside the Vessel".
 "All She Cares About Is the Yankees" by John Ford Noonan.
Venus Envy lead "Take Back the Night Marches"
collaborated with "Break the Chain", "CodePink", "The House of Ruth", and other organizations.

I also did some television and film work.

All of this happened while I held down a job in a cubicle in an insurance office.

Mission: Fry It Up In A Pan

The first thing I had to do was land a job that would allow me to pay for all of the bills and for my newly acquired student loans.

I was hired to be an administrative assistant for a very successful professional woman.

> *Here's what I wrote in my journal:*
>
> *I know I can learn a lot from her but this is a different world.*
>
> *I'm getting weird headaches. Sometimes I see in triplicate. One day I was trying to say the word "cat" but I said "table" instead.*
>
> *Alan is playing out with his band all the time and I'm going to every one of his shows that I can.*

We meet for lunch at my day job all the time. Sometimes that's the most I see him inside of any given week.

I have to be at my desk at 7:30 am sharp, no matter the traffic or weather. She calls to see if I'm there picking up the phone at 7:31. Once she knows I'm there she does her private yoga study and meditation at home and then comes in a couple of hours later. She also has a lot of brown bag lunch meetings. At these, she meets with other professional women and they share war stories.

The other day I heard her fire a client.

I thought the customer was always right.

No.

I overheard her on the phone with the woman. She'd been coached by her brown bag group. She tells the woman on the other end of the phone that she sounds unhappy. She tells her that she can't fix this and that it would be best if she found a different representative. She tells her she thinks they will both be happier.

I'm riveted.

Fascinated.

She teaches me about cold, warm, and hot contacts. She says a hot contact is a much better investment of time than a cold contact. A hot contact is someone she has a real connection with. Through that connection, she can get people to invest money.

She goes over investment portfolios with me and has me upgrade charts and make presentations for her.

She sends out sports schedules for the year instead of holiday cards because she doesn't want to get lost in the piles.

I have to stay after for many days on end to get them all printed properly, labeled, and mailed on time. I'm on a salary. No overtime. Just working for the team.

I'm on the phone when I'm not updating files.

She has spirit advisors. I think they are Sikh, but I'm not sure.

She tells them that I am like her sister and they can share whatever they like with me.

They come into her office about once a month.

I step in to give her an update on a client and one of them addresses me. He says, "you carry too much shame. You wear the wrong underwear. You should wear cotton underwear and release your shame."

I never asked.

Mrs. Belle is one of the longstanding administrative assistants. I'd say she began as a secretary back when that was a thing. She's approximately eighty-five years old and about four feet--one. I think her apartment is in the same building and that she just takes the elevator down to work. Whenever I go over to her cubicle, which is intentional because she's all the way on the edge, I sometimes find her cold asleep with her head on her typewriter. No doubt a typewriter she's been using for a long time. She always seems to be in the midst of typing the same envelope.

Every day she takes a lunchtime pilgrimage to the break room, down the long hallway. She wears flip flopish shoes that click when she walks and more often than not she lets out little farts at every step.

It's a soundtrack.

I had a conversation with her in the break room the other day. The microwave always has a line of us waiting so it's a good place to chat.

Mrs. Belle said that when it comes to criminals there's one effective and proven way to take care of them. She mentions Australia. Then she says, you give them a bag of seed, a shovel, and a bottle of water, drop them off on an isolated island and wish them well.

Survival of the fittest.

Derrick works half days. He comes in through the Arc, an organization that finds jobs for those with disabilities. He's always sticking labels on things and eating lunch at the table in the break room at the same time everyday. He's quiet as people wait in line for the microwave. He has a fried chicken drumstick and a piece of white bread that is always wrapped in aluminum foil. It's easy to forget he's there. He's shown me his music. Hand written sheets of compositions that look like they should belong to Mozart. I can tell he's got music playing in his head at all times.

These two people are gossiping while waiting for the food to heat up. Derrick is eating his standard lunch. Finally they leave and I'm about to put my food in the microwave. All of the sudden out of nowhere, Derrick blurts, "What they do!".

I start singing Backstabbers. He's a brilliant person.

Another female agent tells me she can see my underwear through my dress. And a woman working in the processing office tells me my skirt is too short. I'm mostly not really sure what's going on.

A lot of sexism is definitely going on.

One man after the other tries to bully me around and I'm not having it.

One new assistant used to wait tables in a strip bar down the street. One of the male agents "saved" her and brought her in to work for him. She's confused most of the time. The other day, she took off on Friday and just drove to Florida because she wanted to see the manatees. She floated in the Gulf of Mexico with them for a few hours and then she drove all the way back so that she could be back at work.

I asked her if she used to be a stripper. She said, no. She was a waitress in a strip club. But then, she admitted that she always wore very short skirts and when she wanted a good tip from a table of men she would pretend she'd dropped something and bend over and flash her butt toward them.

Cash tips.

I understand.

Another woman is so fashion forward. She wears dark dark lipstick, almost black. Her hair is red and slicked back and her clothing is designer. She looks like a fashion model. She takes no shit at all. She corrects men all the time. She doesn't last long but man does she leave an impression.

The woman I work for is now paying for my parking, which is a HUGE relief. The parking garage is on the third floor. So, I don't even have to walk outside in the rain anymore. Which is great.

One of the office manager women is so hated by a higher up assistant she gets scissors thrown at her back that barely miss her.

And, that was just another day in the insurance office.

I was in the middle of a project in my little cubicle when all of the alarms started going off. There's a bomb threat and we are asked to evacuate the building. I grab my purse.

My boss is being advised by her guides. I scream over the alarm system and say, "there's a bomb-threat!".

They continue to sit and stare at one another.

Nothing.

"I'm going to evacuate the building!"

They wave me into her office. I get close to them as instructed per hand gestures. All the while I'm wondering if it's such a good idea to have my car parked on the third floor because if the bomb is in a car, that's probably parked on the third floor too. And we're way up above that so I really should get downstairs and outside before the whole building blows with my car, insurance agents, and spirit guides inside.

I try to focus on what they are saying. But these thoughts are rolling loudly inside of my brain.

One of the men shakes his head slowly. He looks at me as if our ears are not about to start bleeding. He says, "This is not your day to die." I only know he said that because I read his lips, he was speaking way too quietly to be heard over the shrieking bomb alarm bells.

I thanked him for that. In a mimey way.

Still.

I will be evacuating the building.

"Thanks!"

I get out of there as fast as I can. It's a building faced entirely with glass. As I walk out the front door there's about a hundred people standing in front of it staring up at it as the alarms continue to blare.

I visualize the explosion that must be less than a minute away now. In my mind, I can see glass shards impaling all of the parts of them facing the glass building. I smile at them and wish them a good day and get the hell ALLLL the way across the street and inside of a grocery store at the opposite end of the block.

Alan visits me for lunch longer and longer. Sometimes I take three hour lunch breaks. We spend most of my paycheck on lunch and gas to get to the job. And, medical bills because the stress is costing me my health.

It feels like I can't breathe in there.

My boss comes to see all of the shows I'm in, which is really so kind. Sometimes she brings other people along.

Jay thinks I might be having mini strokes. We're friends and in touch by phone now. I go into the brain man. He runs an eeg and an mri and he tells me my brain is perfectly fine.

I ask if I can get that in writing.

He says I'm too young to be under this much stress. He says biofeedback work is really good for young women.

I just want to be able to pay my bills and live my dream life. I know that women can do it all because I saw it on a commercial in between one of the four blue collar jobs I was working years ago.

I stopped working for the one top agent lady and went to work for the entire company as the assistant manager in their marketing department. My direct manager said things like, "vanilla envelopes" in meetings.

A big conservative very rich agent is talking about Steven Covey and the "Seven Habits of Highly Effective People". He's talking down to me. He's speaking to me like I'm an idiot.

This is a regular occurrence. People assume I'm stupid or invisible. I'm just taking notes and letting them think whatever they'd like to think.

*I got the Covey book and read it. I analyze it the way X taught us to analyze scripts. I write in the margins and dog ear pages. I take it all in. The next time this man tries to belittle me I tell him that according the Steven Covey he seems to be investing in a Win/Lose *paradigm* and that's not the most effective form of management.*

He stopped talking to me.

One of his younger assistants came to see Alan play at the Bayou. She's dating a really gross man who is at least twice her age, half her intelligence level, and constantly disheveled. He never stops looking at her ass. He buys her all of Alan's CD's. He buys her a very sporty car. She quits the job, marries him, and has his babies.

I have a feeling this will not end well.

I offered to create Venus Envy through the SHE COMPANY to do outreach for at-risk women being sheltered at the House of Ruth. God's work, right?

I'll never forget that night for as long as I live.

I load in my conga drums.

I come back down the very long narrow staircase with the almost nuclear yellow throbbing glow. I can feel it in my fillings.

I have a bucket (a big container of props) that I grab and when I approach the door to come up the steps again I spot a Grandfather with his Grandson.

They are not allowed in.

Visiting hours are over.

The little boy is maybe seven years old and he's holding a toy guitar with no strings. It's plastic. I can tell he wants to show it to his Mom. The grandfather asks me to please have them send his daughter down or, at the very least, let her know they're here.

I try to be respectful but the bucket is big and I squeeze past them. I'm not allowed to let them come up to where I am going.

I'm shaken.

On the next trip out to the car those two are nowhere to be found.

As I walk up the dreaded stairway to smoking lounge purgatory, my mind starts racing.

My performers are arriving one by one. They are stepping up to me so excited. The only thing I can focus on is the residents. One by one they zombie-march in and take a seat at one of the many tables for four. Some of them have their heads down like in elementary school. As if they haven't slept in years and now, when they finally get a safe bed to sleep in, here comes the weird artsy women just leaking into their precious time.

They were broken.

Some had broken teeth, or no teeth. Their hair was frayed and snapped off. Their clothes were mostly not their own. These women had fled from terror. Maybe the terror of near matricide, maybe the straight up terror of poverty. It was clear that these women had fled and then had landed here in the yellow glowing room. The light was so bizarre and surreal you could hear it humming.

Harsh.

Everything was harsh.

As Venus Envy, we'd rehearsed a lot of improv games to share with these women. All of the performers showed up with their hearts completely in it. Each one of them experienced a stone stunned expression as they processed the room we were performing in. It came over each of them individually, one by one, but always the same expression.

It was a mix of disbelief, terror, and denial.

We were in a food desert. There was a liquor store and ATM on every single block but no grocery store. Not even a vegetable stand. Fastfood about every five blocks.

This is the Universe we'd stepped into.

Suddenly, nothing we'd planned seemed to make any sense.

I just started playing the congas. The performers started singing, of all things, "The Banana Boat Song". I have no idea why.

The energy in the room changed entirely.

DAY-O!!!

Women who had been bent over and broken popped up. Broken teeth and dead eyes became smiles and laughter. Within two minutes no one was seated anywhere anymore. Every single person was up on their feet dancing in a conga line. One of the residents perfectly balanced her purse on her head. Her arms went out flying akimbo. Hips were swaying. Everyone was singing at full volume when their smiles weren't breaking out into laughter. Bent over bottled up joy that had been so pushed down and so repressed it came flying up like a geyser washing away the stale nicotine stains on the walls and ceiling.

It overtook everything. This energy just produced a driving force. I cannot tell you what else happened because it almost feels like we were collectively abducted. I don't know what improv games or exercises came after that.

I know that when I left I had about half of the props in the bucket as when I arrived and I didn't care.

I wanted those women to feel like they were a part of something bright. We accomplished that.

As I loaded out, I couldn't help but stare at that spot by the door where the man and his grandson stood. I couldn't help but wonder where they were now. Which woman was their daughter, their mother, their beloved. There was no way for me to know. No permission to convey the message the grandfather asked me to give to his daughter. I tried. I was told it was after visiting hours, they would have to come back tomorrow, I was sworn to anonymity.

I agreed to all of it.

Still, I couldn't help but wonder if that little boy or his grandfather got any sleep that night.

The only power I have is to pull up the impulse of life in people.

That's it.

After that, it's completely out of my hands. It's their journey, not mine.

I don't know why.

I want to bring Venus Envy back to the House of Ruth on a regular basis.

None of the women working with me agree to come back. Each one tells me it was one of the most profound experiences of their lives. Not one of them is in a position to repeat it.

I have to respect that.

It's their journey, not mine.

I can only be so deeply grateful to each one of them for giving their time, talent, and energy.

Venus Envy continues to collaborate with the SHE Company. Through this collaboration, I'm learning SO MUCH.

Practical things.

Like, we rehearse in the stacks section of public libraries. It's free. Like, how to communicate with a cast of people volunteering, how to put that structure down on paper.

The House of Ruth has opened The Women's Empowerment Center now.

It's about five blocks down from the residence.

It's a church!

It has a red door just like the church I was baptized in.

Right now, I'm working with the Theatre Conspiracy. I'm playing Mary in, "Why We Have a Body" by Claire Chaffee. Only it's not the latest revision. It's an earlier draft. I am in love with my character because it's my job as an actor to find a way to fall in love with my characters.

I don't want to diagnose her, I only want to find her point of play and give it to her as often as possible. There are definitely moments she veers into a dark ditch. I'm not focusing on those. I'm focusing on her heart. Her spirit. It's lovely. She loves life and I love her for the way she loves life.

My producer is Tricia McCauley. We read, "Size Matters" together for the Theatre Conspiracy when it was run by gay men. But right now, it's mostly run by women. Tricia has just gotten back from the O'Neill workshop intensive on playwriting. While there, she met H. H has been chosen to direct.

H lives out of state.

Two rounds of auditions were held before H even arrived. H was there for the callbacks and cast me as Mary. I'm still in complete shock that I was cast in this role. Every single young woman actor in DC wanted that role. H said that I understood the character in a way that was unique and unmatched throughout the audition process. I trusted that.

It was a great process. We mostly rehearsed in different lounge areas at American University where most of the Conspirators had gone to college.

The freedom I had in developing Mary with that ensemble cast was everything I could have ever hoped for.

Mary likes to have fun. One of her favorite things to do is to rob 7-11's at gunpoint and then lose the police in gourmet jelly bean stores while they chased her on foot.

Playwright Claire Chaffee has a real gift. Her pen resonates a truth that up until now has seemed impossible to capture. She's funny and she's real. Mary believes she is the reincarnation of Joan of Arc. The show opens with her holding the audience up at gunpoint during a 7-11 robbery. "It's not your fault you don't listen to your unconscious mind, that's why it's there."

Joseph has designed a BRILLIANT set for a tiny corner of a blackbox space. I'm in love with everything all over again.

This play has been described as a memory talking to a memory. Mary has been described as a character with schizophrenia. In the play Mary has her sister Lili meet her at the airport.

In the scene Lili finds herself looking around and asking which flight Mary came in on. Mary tells her, no no, she took the bus. When questioned why, she tells her sister the airport bar is her favorite bar. She says, "The mix of terror and boredom. It's what drinking's all about…"

Every night I can hear Tricia howling at that line and some others too.

The freedom I feel each night playing that character is definitely a form of euphoria. I'm free. I'm creating in this flying freedom machine. It's glorious.

The space is not ideal. I warm up in the back alley pointing my plastic gun at all of the rat leather on the pavement. Alan runs down the back alley at night trying not to scream, while the rats climb the fencing like some kind of parkour competition. He's a city-boy. Vermin are the enemy. I'm hybrid city/country. So, I can appreciate their familial connections and existence. He's having NONE OF IT!

The other night, I became so engrossed in my sister's character, Lili, at the airport I choked myself. The stage manager keeps buying honey covered peanuts and Mary chews them like a small mammal. Nibble nibble nibble on the front teeth. The other night I kept doing this, listening to my character's sister and I forgot to swallow. My cheeks puffed out like a squirrel's. When it was time for my line I inhaled so that I could speak.

When I inhaled, shards of jagged honey covered nuts embedded themselves into my vocal folds. I suspended my breath as if I was underwater swimming. I was waiting for that moment of terror to pass. My eyes began to water and I had to find a way to choke out my last lines. Somehow we got to the end of the scene.

I ran backstage and started clearing my throat which sounded like vomiting. The trashcan was backstage, so close to the stage right entrance, the sound was onstage! Our Mother was onstage doing her monologue about bulimia, and I'm trying not to sound like I'm forcing myself to throw up backstage. Only, I kind of am.

I stopped myself from choking soon enough to get ready for my next entrance. I had to light a cigarette and smoke it as I walked in. Just then, the stage manager decided to turn on the air conditioning. I could not get out of the path of the blowers so I had to really really suck on that cigarette to get it lit.

I don't know.

It seemed like my next scene went by pretty fast.

And then, I couldn't stop babbling under my breath backstage over and over, "nicotine is a drug, nicotine is a drug…".

Rough day/rough night.

Yesterday, I went to the Women's Empowerment Center to teach my empowerment workshop.

One woman had written about her alcoholic mother hoarding dogs and naming them after alcohol. She yells out for Michelob and Heineken, Bacardi!, Jim Beam!, Johnny Walker Red!, Johnny Walker Black!, Stoly!...it went on and on. And I started laughing out loud because it was so funny.

But, some people aren't in a place to laugh at their life. I need to write that down.

Laughing was bad.

She looked at me with pain in her eyes. This was her real experience and it was landing on that meridian in my brain where tragedy touches comedy and I found it to be hilarious. So, I had to shut myself up and rethink things.

Yesterday, I was early.

I knew I was early. Maybe a little too early so I drove around the block several times.

It was three minutes til one. I'm supposed to start at 1. I parked and pulled out just one of my Conga drums. It was weird that the writing workshop wasn't happening inside of the church, The Women's Empowerment Center.

I figured maybe someone was in there and the door was maybe unlocked. But, when I got to the top of the steps and grabbed the door handle, I found myself to be very very wrong.

I leaned against the railing with my drum and my thrift store purse. It's white with beads glued on. It's like the ones they used to sell in Myrtle Beach that one time I went with my Dad and my First Stepmother. She wore a Budweiser bikini and we rode rides and shopped and had fun.

A teenaged boy is riding down the street on a bike that looks to belong to a younger sibling. It's small for him. He stops and lays it down at the bottom of the steps. So, I figure he's coming to see someone. Probably the Priest?

He walks up the steps and before he makes it to the top landing I tell him, "the door's locked".

He mumbled something but I couldn't understand what he was saying. He was wearing designer clothes. His hair was very tidy and he smelled good, like he had just bathed and then walked through a commercial ad for musk fog or something. He was wearing nice jewelry too.

I just looked at him because I didn't really hear what he had said and I didn't want to be rude.

He got closer to me and said, "Give me your purse before I stab you."

Huh?

This did not register with me. I looked down. In his right hand he was holding a philip's head screwdriver threatening to puncture a lung by plunging it between my ribs.

This seemed so unlikely to me.

I explained that I had no money. I told him I had some medicine that I needed in there.

He said, you don't have any money?

I told him, no.

He said, give me your purse.

Reluctantly, I did.

Mostly I gave him my purse because I had to perform Mary in "Why We Have A Body" that night and I knew I couldn't do that with a punctured lung. It would be impossible.

But, a part of me wanted to throw my conga on him and knock him down the steps. Then again, that would have damaged my drum.

I watched him ride his tiny bike down the center of the road, his knees were almost hitting the handlebars, and my little Myrtle Beach white beaded purse dangled from his right hand while he steered with his left.

Once he was out of sight, I ran into the street and started screaming for help.

No one in the neighborhood seemed to be home. Which was weird, because their cars were out front.

A taxi came down the street with fare but HE stopped. He actually had a phone in the console of his car. He called the police for me. I thanked him so much and knew he had to move on with his fare.

After that a lot of my students started to appear from behind corners. They said they saw the whole thing. I was so relieved. Witnesses.

I told the woman running the programming who showed up eventually. She told me two things. First, she said I should have known better. She told me I was a white woman in a black neighborhood and what did I expect? She said I was a walking target and I should have known better than to have anything valuable with me. Secondly, she told me that nothing any of these women said mattered because they were all drunk.

I had no idea.

I stayed there for hours and hours. It took over two hours for a police car to show up. Even then, the officer never turned down the volume on his jazz station or pulled to the side of the street. He just sat there in the middle of the road. By this time, I started to really freak out. I was sobbing asking him if I did the right thing. Wondering if I should have thrown my drum at the guy. Wondering what I had done wrong.

The officer just looked over his left shoulder at me and said, "Yes, Maaaaam you did the right thing." in one long droning exhale. He clearly thought I was being ridiculous.

Now it's all hitting me. I have no identification. I have no checkbook. The checkbook for Alan's Guitar business was in there too. I have no keys. No ID. He knows where I live! He has the keys to my car! I called the police over and over and they said there was no sign of the kid riding down the middle of the road on his tiny bicycle. I asked if they'd checked the closest ATM's. They said, no.

Frazzled.

Alan was home. He held me.

I called Tricia. I was crying and I was shaking.

She answered.

I told her what happened and I admitted I wasn't sure if I could do the show that night because I had to open holding the audience up at gunpoint.

I felt kind of stupid.

It's not like he held me up at gunpoint. I mean he was just holding a screwdriver. It wasn't even like it was a commercial screwdriver. It was a cheap screwdriver. It probably would not have broken my skin. I don't know. Maybe it would have punctured my lung. I don't know. It wasn't a gun.

It's like the time I was raped in a car behind a church.

We'd been drinking and I knew this guy really liked me. I was into heavy petting, but I told him no. He decided otherwise. It's not like I fought him. His member was diminutive. I could barely feel it. I just flopped dead like a fish and waited until it was over. It's not like he physically hurt me. I could have put up a fight but I didn't want to be a nuisance.

I could have thrown my drum but I didn't want to cause a scene.

I was on hallowed ground. The door of the sanctuary was very much in reach. How bad could any of this really be? I'm fine. I'm fine. No big deal.

Maybe I did deserve these things. Maybe I have too much. It's not as bad as being terrorized by my Monster. The rape and the robbery were far kinder than she had ever been.

So, not so bad.

Not a gun. Not a fight.

We're cool.

Tricia tells me she understands. She, too, has been mugged in the city.

Like it's some kind of rite of passage for women. To be mugged or raped. To be robbed just comes with being a woman. Even according to the women running the shelters to provide safe haven for women.

My mind won't stop spinning.

Tricia gives me three distinct instructions.

She tells me to SCREAM!

She tells me to kick the wall three times.

And then, she tells me to come into work.

Okay.

My car is still in the city anyway. My spare key is at home so I can pick up my car after the show. At night. In what I can only now label a very scary neighborhood.

Who cares? Who cares if it's night, I was mugged in the afternoon.

Who cares?

Alan drives me into Adam's Morgan.

I'm shaking.

We park near the Paragon and walk through to the front of DCAC.

We saw David Bowie at the Paragon on $20 general admission when he played with the Tin Machine. Which was interesting because we'd both seen the Glass Spider tour at the Capital Center but we hadn't met yet. I can stay focused on these facts. These are lovely little facts.

My mind continues to wander.

So many people were at the theatre it was weird. Usually there's hardly anyone there at my call time. People looked very worried. We had another sold out house. My understudy was pacing the stage with a script in her hand and someone running lines was walking beside.

I think I said, "I'm here".

Everyone crowded me and hugged me.

Tricia promised to stay right by the door so if I needed to run out for any reason I could and my understudy would jump on stage. She'd be sitting right in the front row ready to jump up and take over if that was needed.

Yikes.

My understudies skin was turning purple with terror which defied the expression of calm on her face.

I got this.

We get on with the show. I dropped a line or two during the initial hold up scene but then it feels like home. Alan takes me to get my car and he follows me all the way home. I go the way I like to go. One of the many wonderful attributes of Alan is that he gives me room to be me and somehow he's still right there.

I get home and I fall asleep and now I feel like I'm in shock.

The cast is going to buy me dinner at Millie and Al's before the show. Everyone is so kind. One actor's husband is a detective. He says that in that particular section of town the police are not good for much. They, in fact, are kind of notorious for corruption. Yikes.

I made it through the whole weekend of shows.

Just got off the phone!

I called the police and spoke to a detective. He lectured me.

He said I should feel lucky and happy that I am still alive. He said that if I was a really caring person I would adopt the boy who mugged me because he clearly needs guidance.

What?!?!

He mugged me. What is with this mommy-blame? Why am I expected to heal someone who meant harm to me? I feel like I disappeared. Like there was no crime. Like the fault was mine because I didn't know my place and now I should fix it.

He says that a woman and her daughter were shot dead point blank three blocks away in their car while they were getting money out of an ATM. And then he tells me a man on a bike three blocks in the other direction was turned around on his route so he stopped at a payphone to call someone and he was stabbed to death there.

He explained to me how lucky I am over and over.

Lucky.

I think the women in charge at the House also knew they shouldn't have said what they said. They came to see the show. Afterwards, they told me I blew them away and they expected to see me get a Helen Hayes Award.

I don't like them anymore.

I don't like this.

I can't drive that car.

I can't do this anymore. I'm willing to invest a lot, but I'm not willing to give up my life.

My Monster buys me a new red car. She says it's not for me, it's for her. So she doesn't have to worry about me in the city.

That guy has the keys to my car and my house and he has my address.

This woman left a message on my answering machine. She said her name was Mary and she found my purse in an alley.

I've been trying and trying to call her back.

Finally, I reached her. She tells me she's a minister. She says that she SAW my purse in an alley. I keep asking her when I can come and pick up my things. I tell her I want my checkbooks back.

She tells me that she only tore the top one off to get my information. She says she left the rest there and when she went back to look everything was gone.

None of this makes any sense.

I spent my summers in Jersey. My StepGrandFather was the Mayor. My Gram had the poorest house in the richest neighborhood. My Monster would drop me on an Eastern Airliner with my dolls Miss Beasley and Chuckie (this was before the horror film!) and we would be given little metal wings and served peanuts and walked by a tidy small airline stewardess to meet my Gram at the gate.

My Monster gave me my own $20 spending money. She always kept at least $100 in her leather cigarette case. Usually there was another tucked in her car. You always have to have your own money.

Walking through the airport I saw these socks with a small family of mice on them. My Gram and Aunt told me no, I couldn't have them. I was wearing shorts with clogs.

When I bought myself the nylon knee socks with the whole scene of a tiny mouse village to wear with my clogs, my Gram and my Aunt made me walk five feet ahead of them in the airport.

They were afraid of risk-taking socks.

We toured a show I wrote called, "The Voice Inside of the Vessel" to the lower east side of New York City. The whole thing was an adventure. Gregg built set piece scrims and my friend Deb painted them. I had to rent a 17' truck. Laura held the sideview mirror on the passenger side because it flopped. Adrian rode in between us in an old lawn chair. I may have sideswiped a car on 5th Avenue, but I hope not.

The shows went well even though collaborators lived in the space. They did their unbalanced laundry during our performance. One climbed through our performance space up into the booth to get some cables while we were performing. So there was a lot of banging and clonking that was not a part of our sound design.

People!

We had to wait it out a day in New York City before we could get a truck to bring everything home. So, I walked around the city.

I won the lottery for "Rent"! I paid $20 to sit in the third row.

I landed student tickets for "Nijinski's Last Dance", offbroadway.

OH.

MY.

GodDesSsss!

The Source Theatre had summer festivals every year. A man named Keith ran the thing. There were a lot of Keiths running things and he was one of them. He could never stand up straight because the stress of his job had him bent over in pain throughout the process.

In that festival I directed, wrote, and performed. I was coming in after the establishing generation and it was a hodge-podge of everything.

The smaller cattle calls were effective. Because they were smaller we would talk to each other in between groups of ten.

There was a singular door that led to nowhere. You could open it and there was only a small platform there. As the month rolled on it would become more and more covered in used condoms. A rainbow of used condoms that no one seemed to ever care about. I guess it was the secret place that no one thought anyone could see.

We had to enter that theatre through the back alley which could be sketchy.

To get upstairs we had to walk up these tuck away steps. Much like the Studio, the top of the steps heralded multi-use spaces. Half office organized. Half meeting space with found couches. Usually there was an area where you could tell people had been living. The Source had this gigantic sink that was covered in paint and coffee equally. Paint brushes shared space in the drainage area with coffee cups. Nothing matched. It was terribly artistic.

Between the couches we would find piles and piles of scripts that Keith had organized and left stacked on the floor. Aspiring directors from all over the area would sit on the floor or on the couches reading the singular submission copies. We'd eventually pay attention to what the other was looking for and start referring scripts to one another on the spot.

As a performer in the festival I won the Metro Arts Theatre Award for Best Actor. I'd taken one character out of my solo show and done one of her scenes. Patti. The one Tricia said I should take out of the show. So, HA!

I really appreciate the roles I've been hired to play. I appreciate writing and staging my own work. It's just not enough. It's not filling my soul. The world is such an upsetting place.

I don't want OJ to be on my TV. I don't want Clarence Thomas to be on the bench, I don't want Bill Clinton to say, "It depends on what the meaning of the word 'is' is. WHAT!?!?! I don't want Dick Chaney to be Vice President as he cashes in on war contracts. I don't want George Bush to be making such stupid decisions declaring things are over when they are not. Where is the leadership? I want them all to be held to account for abuse of power in the real world.

I want to fill my worlds with colorful characters and big dreams and not be forced to live in their worlds because in their worlds I don't really exist. I have to play so small. It hurts.

I STILL have to write in the roles I want to be playing!

It's infuriating.

I'm here to dive into the collective imaginings of colorful minds. I'm not here to appease matrocidal rape culture.

It's frustrating.

Sometimes it's hard to find my actual stage because the world is pretending to be that. The world is pretending to be an experiment in presentational lifestyles instead of a place where the journey happens for real.

Worst!

Script!

Ever!

Deborah L. Randall

[flourish: MT8]

I grew up in a house on the highway
The sound of the cars
My lullaby

The backyard
Was an offramp
That led to an unfamiliar place

For most
The stillness of the car beside them brought comfort
For me
So many colors blurred into art, yet I had no place to play

Like something I'd see
Hanging on the walls of the Hirshhorn
If I had anyway of knowing what that was

For me

The sound and the colors
Were the canvas of my knowing

For most

Just another day of work
Or obligation punctuated by fast food bags flying

My stillness
Was their smudge

Nothing

Their hurry
Was my canvas

My grandmother always used to say
That city people

venus

And country people walked differently

City people were always in a rush
Country people were in no hurry at all
And had time to take in the sights

So I always wondered about
That blur of rushing cars
And whether I was city or country

Which one of us was in a rush?
It was so hard to leave
My home on the highway

There was no subtle approach to be found
The only thing to do was buckle up
And floor it!

Which made it seem
Like I was the one
In the rush

And then I felt
The stillness that comes with speed
I could see my neighbor next to me

A first
And that little house
On the Highway

Was less than a speck of nothingness
Not even a blur
Barely a memory

I never had time
To say goodbye
Or, thank you

Part Three

Chapter 9:
SETTING FLIGHT TO THE VOICES OF WOMEN

Objective: BE THE FUTURE!

After "Til It Hurts" closed, I attended a forum of female directors in Washington, DC. It was held in the auditorium at the National Museum of Women in the Arts. It changed my life. After the feedback session that followed, I put the paperwork together. I put a board of directors together. I found a pro-bono legal team.

Venus Theatre Company would officially exist and it would be a nonprofit!

Tricia and I both began working for the Helen Hayes Legacy Project. This was a fully funded audience-development/outreach project. The program consisted of four visits, three composed of theatre workshops in various DC Public Schools with one trip to the theatre.

T had done my natal chart by now. We were bonded for life. You could tell if Tricia loved you because she would do your natal chart and keep it on file at her house. She informed me that Venus was my ruling planet.

I began working at Gymboree as a side hustle. It was nice to pay bills while working on mats and wearing socks.

9/11 brought about profound change in the world. On September 12, I observed a moment of silence with the babies at Gymboree. It was something President George W. requested from the nation. The nonverbals were wailing in emotional pain even as their parents tried to remain quiet.

That moment haunts me still.

Mission: Remember Specificity Breeds Universality!

"Til It Hurts" closed in the back of 1409 Playbill Cafe on my birthday. It began on my Fathers birthday. This was not planned, it's just how it worked out.

At my first performance of "Til It Hurts" in DC, Tricia showed up and sat on the floor upstairs at the feminist bookstore as I performed my solo show on a stool with one very harsh light mounted on the floor and making me sweat. Tricia wore a deep burgundy top with matching lipstick. She'd seen this in development from the red couch in the living room of her group house a million times. She was always right there in the front row, believing in me, cheering me on.

Gregg was a fellow UMBC alum and a technical director. He hooked me up! He sent people my way and props and whatever I needed. Through Gregg I would meet my permanent design team over time. For now Laura and Amy had my back. Kris was giving me one lighting instrument. Another alum named Tony was also around. They all ran the boards and kept me going.

> Here's what I wrote in my journal:
>
> "Til It Hurts" is a two act solo show. I play eight different characters. One of them is called Patti Androginio. Tricia says she

doesn't belong in the line up. But, that just makes me fall in love with Patti deeper and write her more.

My set is a five-wrung A-frame ladder and a bar stool. I wear a gray hoodie eight different ways for each character and I play guitar as Patti. It's sarcastic guitar. It's not real guitar. Alan has written music for my poetry and showed me how to strum it on a ¾ sized guitar.

I spend days in the library researching. Patti has a cable access show for children that goes on at four in the morning when children are decidedly not watching. Patti is mostly stoned and definitely exhausted all of the time. She fancies herself a performance artist but her parents insisted she take the safe path. She has a secondary degree in psychology.

Patti plays songs about psychological disorders for children. This is why I've spent so much time at the public library making the librarian my new best friend.

The songs are about: The Peter Pan Complex, The Wendy Dilemma, The Cinderella Complex. Odes to Chicken Little and The Gingerbread man. Stuff like that.

There's a bird.

I play a parrot. Because I was raised by people who parrot all the time and never seemed to have any ideas or real voices of their own. Also, because my Grandmother had a pet parrot named Sam. I loved that bird. So, I became him. I sit way up high straddling the ladder, wearing the hoodie backwards and say things like, "hello", "gonna get cher tail", and then laugh maniacally

> *like a bird*
>   *from my perch*
>   *atop my ladder.*

It's fun.

I also play Jimmy. My best friend who died of leukemia when he was four and I was five. I became him. The lines I've written for this are seemingly nonsensical but they are a kind of music just like him.

Believe it or not, John Palmer Claridge is running the Gunston Arts Center in Arlington, VA! He has invited me to bring, "Til It Hurts" ' into his Innovators Series.

AH!

Okay okay okay.

Laura and Amy and Tony run tech for me at Gunston. I, for some reason, agreed to set up all of the bleachers which was a lot of work for them. I feel like a jerk.

The booth is soundproof and has no windows.

This is terribly problematic.

Tony stands outside of the booth, Laura is in the booth. Tony gives Laura hand signals as to when to change the lights from the back of the house. She keeps the door open so she can see him.

Yikes.

My Gram showed up from Jersey and watched from the back. After the show she walked up to me and gave me a hug and I couldn't believe she was there.

I received a fan letter. A man said he really believed I was a four year old boy. He said he lost his son and he felt like he was seeing him again when I played Jimmy on stage.

Then, there's this woman who wouldn't shut up. At Gunston, I had to agree to "talk-backs". I hate talkbacks and I'll tell you why. It's never helpful to the artist. It's for the audience to feel like they have some kind of power over the performer.

The power the audience has over the performer is the energy they bring into the room and share during the performance.

It should be the job of the audience to experience the offering given in the performance and then take what they take from it. Love it. Hate it. Whatever. But, TALK-BACKS mean the audience has been taking notes during the performance instead of simply EXPERIENCING it.

THIS LADY!!

She just keeps saying, "What's the bird? Why's it there? I don't understand the bird?" She goes on to tell me she's seen "Annie" on Broadway more than 27 times, like that's some kind of qualifier. Like I give a shit.

I WANT to say: Look lady, that bird is clearly not there for you to understand. It has about 10 lines in a two hour piece. Psychologically speaking I can see you have issues around unexpected things and a denial system around all that you cannot control.

But, I just say the part about the 10 lines out loud.

I've performed this show in so many places it's a big blur.

Finishing out at 1409 Playbill Cafe was its own special thing. Venus collaborated with Phoenix Theatre. We've had a one month run in the back of that bar every Friday and Saturday night from the second week in September until my birthday on October 10, 1999.

Jeffrey and Said, the owners, even pop a bottle of champagne for me on my closing show. Jeffrey is the Queen of the bar and is always on the same barstool. Said runs the kitchen and he gets mad a lot. So, every night I'm there I aggressively scream, "SAID!!". And then he says, "WHAT?!?!?" And then I scream, "DO YOU NEED A HUG?!?!!?". He always aggressively screams, "YES!!!". So I run into wherever he is in the kitchen and hold him for a solid minute or so.

The bartender is mad at me.

One of the regulars named Peter came to see my show on a Friday early in the run. When I came in the next weekend to perform, the bartender asked me what I did to Peter. He is not happy with me at all.

No idea.

The bartender tells me Peter is usually in every night of the week. This past week Peter has not come in once, he explains. He won't even get off of his couch. He demands he know what I did to him.

Great.

Next thing I know, Peter is sitting in the front row!

I perform the entire two hours. I'm so grateful no one has mistaken my stage for a bathroom tonight. I can hear the 10pm drunk lady. I named her SANDY. I don't know if it's the same lady or if there is a different one each night or some combination thereof. But, I can set my clock to 10pm right when the alcohol makes her voice pitch up to that awful place and become a part of my sound texture.

It's guaranteed that every night at 10pm when I'm performing my most intimate scene weighing in whether it's worth it to keep living or best to inject the needle in my arm, every single time just at that scene, SANDY always puts on her drunk stadium voice and it becomes a part of my show.

There's no wing or offstage area at all. It's very awkward when a drunk person ready to pee finds themself standing center stage. The stupid is on them. I just hold and watch to see what they do. They usually realize it isn't the bathroom within 3-5 seconds and hustle out of there apparently thinking if they do it fast enough they will have erased the memory of everyone watching.

The backdrop of my stage is a gigantic window. It's usually the view of a lovely empty back court. But, on some occasions the audience watches things behind me. Things such as a rando tenant taking out their trash, talking on a brick of a cell phone, "walking" their dog, and picking up its poop. It's hard to compete with these things.

I don't compete. I focus.

I give up my guts as I was trained to do.

I am determined to stick to the objective of whatever character I am playing at the time.

The best I can hope for is ten audience members. A higher up of the Studio Theatre next to 1409 Playbill had a birthday dinner for her mother in my performance space so I had to hold a long time before I could set up and begin performing. You'd think she'd understand. But, no.

Why is Peter back if he couldn't get off of his couch for a week? I'm performing but the question hangs in the air with the dusty lingering of the stage lights.

A fellow Gymboree instructor watched my graveside monologue and couldn't get out of her seat at a rehearsal. She sat there crying. I had to hold her. It took the better part of 20 minutes for her to stand up. I feel like that's what X trained me to do. Touch the exposed nerve of truth.

I'm at intermission and Peter is sometimes holding his head down staring at the floor in the front row as I perform.

This is more difficult than the critic who sat in my light with the script watching every word printed on her lap as I performed right in front of her. Why couldn't she have taken a seat further back? Why'd she write that Patti wore Birkenstocks in her review? I was wearing vintage Italian leather aviator boots. Details. Ugh. Right in front of her face and yet, she cannot see. Audience should be experiencing the show. Ugh.

When I get to the end of this show I'm not even going to duck backstage. It's a public bathroom anyway. Unless I divert into the kitchen and give Said a hug. Said always needs a hug.

Okay. Show is over, here I go back IN!

…

…

…

Wow.

Wow.

Okay.

He's still sitting there with his head hung low like he's on an airplane and about to get sick. I touch both of his knees and squat down. I try to make eye contact.

"Seasons in the Sun" is playing. It's my Jimmy-song.

He looks up at me.

"Peter, what is happening?"

He says, "You know that scene by the grave where you forgive your father?"

"Yes", I say. It's the same scene that kept my Gymbo friend nailed to her seat for 20 minutes. I don't know why that scene is such a big deal for people.

Ultimately, my character gets herself to forgive her father for the abandonment and (I'd later find out) the sexual assaults while she slept.

It's what I needed to do if I wanted to grow as an artist. I needed a place to put my father-stuff so it would stop weighing me down. I understand from doing that monologue over and over that forgiveness has nothing at all to do with the person you're forgiving. It's a gift you decide to give yourself so that you can move forward into your own joy and light.

It's hard to forgive. For me, it took a lot of repetition through character.

Peter tells me, "I've been thinking about that monologue all week."

He confesses to me with a kind of guilt and shame combined, he says, "When I came out of the closet as a gay man, my entire family disowned me. My daughter was 2, at the time. I've been thinking a lot about your monologue. I've been thinking that if you can forgive your father, that maybe she can forgive me."

I was confused at first. He was not a pedophile. He was the victim of homophobia. He lost everything to step into who he really was. Somehow my story resonated with his story even though they were two different journeys.

Specificity breeds universality.

This is the power of art. It's the power of theatre.

I hope he finds peace.

Peter goes on to say, "She's 23 years old now. All I know is that she's someplace on the West Coast. I'm thinking about looking her up."

Wow!

All I can say is, "Yeah, I think you should definitely do that! I think she would LOVE to know you."

I'm just gonna sit here for a minute.

I have to load out. I have to get home.

*It's so strange that I started this journey on my fathers birthday and that I ended it on my own, unplanned. But plays, they call up energies in all kinds of unexpected ways. They nudge us and remind us how powerful we really are when we show up.
…*

I went to an open forum at the Women's Museum of Art in DC. It featured five female DC directors. I listened to what they had to say.

It's a strange time.

It's the end of the 1900's!

On December 31, we will enter the new millennia. We're supposed to prepare for all of the banks to collapse and for all of the clocks to stop working. They say that once the year goes to "00" everything will stop working.

I was able to get a cell phone. It's expensive so I only use it for emergencies. I'm glad to have it. It's shaped like a brick but it has a durable clip on the back. I like to wear skirts and dresses with boots and clip my phone on the outside of my right boot. It feels both fashionable and efficient.

At the forum of female directors I am told that theatres are not made of bricks and mortar, but of people. That's interesting. It's a good mantra.

I've rehearsed actors in parking lots, in stairwells, and near the carousel on the Washington Monument grounds.

I'm not sure if the woman who said that has ever had to perform with a dog shitting through the window behind her, but it is good advice.

At the end they ask if we have any questions. I stand and tell them about the shows I've been doing. I tell them how I've been touring around. I tell them that they have inspired me to expand into a more professional structure. I ask if they think I should start a company that empowers women in the theatre. They give me sage advice. Circles of women keep bending me into my own light and truth. I reach down to gather my things at the end of all of this and when I go to stand up I am surrounded by 15 different women shoving their business cards in my face from all sides, wanting to talk to me about my idea. It's overwhelming. I collect a lot of business cards.

I get the hell out of there.

One of the attendees and I shared the elevator going down.

She asks me if I've ever heard of the "Molly Maguires".

I say, no.

She says there's a lot written about the men but not much written about the women.

Huh.

I offer to give her a ride home so she doesn't have to deal with the metro late at night and we talk a lot more, mostly because I had no idea where I was going and it took three times longer to get her home than the metro would have.

It's December and I feel like I need to give Said a hug. It's been way too long.

I hop on down to 1409 Playbill Cafe. The TV's behind the bar are blasting George Bush on the debate stage. The world remains terrifying. Neither Jeffrey nor Said are around tonight.

Odd.

I ask about Peter. "How's he doing?".

The bartender seems to have gotten over his animosity toward me. He tells me very nonchalantly as he's polishing the water drop stains off of a highball glass that Peter is in Hawaii at the moment.

He's vacationing with his daughter.

[flourish: MT9]

Looping back to the back
Her vertigo was cured
It'd all gone horizontal

Looping back to the back
Was a rhythm
More primal than sweat

More familiar than fear
More habituated
Than the sex-on-the beach
Shots
From way back
When that sounded romantic
Good ideas
She'd found
Were relative
To the day
And time
And experience
Of the given participant

Looping to the back
While others moved ahead
Her job made clear

Cheer

Chapter 10:
DAUGHTERS OF MOLLY MAGUIRE

Objective: *If It Doesn't Exist, Create It.*

Just as there wasn't a word for anorexia when I was younger, there wasn't a word for the male-gaze during this period of my life. I could feel it though. It assumed me. It was either revolted by me or it wanted to consume me, but it never ever SAW me.

The problem was bigger than my own family. Bigger than finding out how to be proud of my gender heritage. The problem was so big and all encompassing I would have to figure out how to function inside of the walls of it.

There's so much I didn't know yet. Thank God. If I'd known, I would have cut ties and run. I was entering the Nurturant phase of my life. The Mother-phase. I was exploring Celtic Goddess archetypes and the Dead Sea Scrolls. I was learning to hold a rosary and ceremoniously burn things in effigy.

I wrote a three act play with music.

Alan composed a complete soundtrack that was both texture and song.

My research was extensive. First dramaturgical, then genealogical, then historical, and finally, a college class I could have taught in any given semester.

The venue for, "Daughters of Molly Maguire" was The Warehouse Theatre on 7th Street, NW. It cost $1,500 a week. Which was A LOT of money. But, we were now a non-profit so the pressure was supposed to lift according to my projected business plan.

What I didn't know yet was that the world hates women. Strides I would make that would be seen as accomplishments if I were a man, were reasons for multitudes of people to be jealous of me and to do all they could to cut my progress off at the pass. I also didn't yet know how dark my relationship with my Father was. I was clear about my Monster and still trying to figure out how to make it work. But, I didn't know yet that my father was a pedophile, that he did things to me that come back in memory flashes and cause me a whole lot of trauma. I don't want to focus on these things. I just want to make a note that I was climbing uphill at all times.

The design team was led by Gregg. He and Laura finally started dating during this production. Amy was in the show. She was having stomach cramps and the all female cast kept telling her she had the flu. She had a baby in her belly. It was conceived during our rehearsals.

There's something fertile and sensual about Venus!

It's a cast of 12 women. Stage management was by Alli. Costumes were by Dana. Alan made a big purchase of a double CD deck so we could run sound from the booth. We had that thing forever and only used it on that show.

Mission: Remember, Inspiration Lives Everywhere!

The Molly Magiures.

The Molly Maguires began as a group of men calling themselves the Sons of Molly Maguire. But, who was SHE? A feeble old lady who needed to be saved? I don't think so. Was she merely legend? Who were her daughters? I decided somehow that the stories of Molly's Daughters were the same as my story. At least for the sake of exploring this project.

Who were these women? They were here. They landed on American soil and some of them made their way into mining towns. Many of these women had no voting rights, no legal way to earn a living once their male counterpart was gone. Often they were left with so many mouths to feed. How did they DO IT? I became obsessed.

The "Daughters of Molly Maguire" became "Molly Daughter". In the end there were four different versions of the play. The last solo version is published by Pennsylvania University Press and distributed by Chicago University press in an anthology entitled, "Anthracite!" The editor of the Anthology, Professor Philip Mosley would write a paper about my process on the Molly Project and present it to a panel of his fellow Professors in Austria.

I staged a candle lighting ceremony for each of the ten men killed on June 21.

One night during a performance, a fierce storm blew in. Lots of thunder and lightning and hard rain falling on the flat roof of the Warehouse Theatre.

Every single thunder strike punctuated a line in the show. It took our breath away.

Audience members asked us who designed the sound. That night we could only say the spirits of the Molly Maguires.

A direct descendant of Yellow Jack was in town from California. People began whispering to me after the show. They were asking if I'd spoken to a certain person. Or if I'd read a certain book.

It became very clear that when this show closed, there was still so much more work to be done.

I thought I would solve my woman-identity problem. Instead I fell into an adventure.

It goes on to this day. We've taken to visiting the town of Jim Thorpe every June 21st to mark the Day of the Rope.

The first year I had an overwhelming urge to get myself there. Amy and I stayed at a VRBO directly across the street from the jail. We plugged in and played our "Molly" songs that morning. Later that day, we were told that it was the first year the AOH did not lay a wreath or play bagpipes.

After a few years of doing this, we were told the Alexander Campbell branch of the Ancient Order of Hibernians had been dissolved. But our commitment to telling their story has not.

In prior years, a man tried not to pay us for a tour. Serendipitously he ended up with the words of a death coffin notice on his desk. It was a document he requested without knowing what it was.

On one tour we performed with an art installation called, "The Faces of Coal" mounted all over the room. Alexander Campbell's nephew was in attendance. He stayed after and gave me praise for the piece. I'll never forget him looking at me and calling me clever. When an Irishmen calls you clever it's an incredible feeling.

On another tour I was heckled by a woman in her 90's. By the end of the show we'd become friends and I walked her to her car. It was cold and icy that day. I'd performed in an old schoolhouse somewhere in the mountains of Pennsylvania.

Professor Philip Mosley invited me to perform at Penn State a couple of times. During my last visit there I noticed the students on their cell phones. I asked them why. They told me they were texting their friends to come over and see the performance.

I will always feel the Molly's with me, I think. Amy and I have a band called the "sheshes" and we keep playing and writing new songs for and about them.

[flourish: MT10]

I had it
I thought I had it
It was right there
I stayed up so many nights
Laying it all down
It pushed through my soul
Birthing a rosary through vocal stigmata
Counting my blessings
Lucky stars
Everything became miraculous

Driving
Writing
Speaking

I can do all of these things
They could not
So, I should
I will
Keep going with this
I can
I will
Keep pushing through

With all of these
Impossible things
Waiting
At my fingertips
For me to notice
For me to speak
To move
To tell

Their story
Is
My story
Is

Deborah L. Randall

Their story
Is
My story
Is

We are

IT IS

Chapter 11:
BAD GIRLS!

Objective: Produce As Many Women As POSSIBLE!

Summer festivals and readings and productions of new works by women in rented and free public spaces.

CV:
Bad Girls Summer Festival 2002-a selection of 5-8 shorts with an ensemble cast (DCAC)
Bad Girls Summer Festival 2003-a selection of 5-8 shorts with an ensemble cast
(DCAC)
Bad Girls Summer Festival 2004 (The Redemption)-a selection of 5-8 shorts with an ensemble cast
(The Warehouse Next Door, BlackBox on 7th Street, NW DC)

Selected public readings on a monthly basis in various physical spaces including:
Art Galleries in DC
The Warehouse Theatre and Cafe.
Lafayette Park in front of the White House (in conjunction with Code Pink protesting the impending war in Iraq)

2003 - "The Anastasia Trials in the Court of Women" written by Carolyn Gage, directed by Karri Rambow
(DCAC)
2004 - "Ugly Ducklings" written by Carolyn Gage, directed by Deborah Randall
(The Warehouse Next Door)
2005 - "Cigarettes and Moby Dick" written by Migdalia Cruz, directed by Deborah Randall
(The Warehouse Attic)
2005 - "A Little Rebellion Now" written by Lisa Voss, directed by Deborah Randall
(The Warehouse Main Stage)

"How She Played the Game" by Cindy Cooper, performed and directed by Deborah Randall
(performed in collaboration with the Helen Hayes Legacy Project for DCPS throughout the city)

"The Ballad of Step-Off Girl" (A 10-minute monster truck musical) written by Kim Moore was performed at the Sewall-Belmont House after a reception and book signing for, "Inez. The Life and Times of Inez Mulholland" by Linda J. Lumesden.

Venus Theatre was invited to be a part of the Page-to-Stage Festival at the Kennedy Center from the year of the festival's inception until it no longer existed.

Venus Theatre held a successful fundraiser at the Warehouse Theatre and both second and third wave feminists gathered together.

The Sewall-Belmont House was discovered and on the radar of Venus.

Mission: Don't Stop Unless You Can No Longer Stand

Eight Jimmy-Lifetimes have passed by now. Thirty-two years. I'm 36. I love remembering his grandfather's lap now. A bony knee held each of us with every single holiday Peanuts special flickering on the box near the wall. Not really knowing what we were laughing at. Just celebrating the sights of Snoopy and Charlie Brown and Lucy. Of Great Pumpkins and ice skating dogs. It was funny. It was a joy. Jimmy's grandfather's knees must have ached.

Brushing teeth, at least the ones we had, thoroughly each night and taking bubble baths. Nothing was wanted for. Everything was already there. I guess that's why Nanny used to always say, "I got plenny". I understand that. Always going to bed at the same time. Before the adults. Always played out, laughed out, so tired. Falling asleep was a no-brainer.

To be able to sleep like that again!

Losing a tooth in a cob of corn. Seated in his kitchen around a long table. Red something smeared on the corn. His Mom noticed and found the tooth. She put it under the pillow for the tooth fairy.

These were magical times.

Being scared of blood or dangerous things was immediately met with spontaneous outbursts of the Popeye the Sailor Man song and followed up with a question about whether or not enough spinach had been consumed for the moment at hand.

Once he was gone I didn't make sense to people anymore.

It was his world. His set, props, costumes, appointments. I was just the counterpoint. Without him, I made no sense to anyone.

I made no sense to myself. I was a feral ghost.

Looking back I realize the scene I made at the funeral home. My Dad was carrying me on his hip. I saw Jimmy wearing a brown suit and laying on his back in a brown box at the front of the room. A bunch of people were just sitting in chairs staring at him. That really pissed me off.

I started yelling for that asshole to stand up. I was screaming at him. Everyone else in the room started shaking with sobs. My Dad took me outside and we sat in the car together. I was only five years old but I could tell he had no idea what to say. We sat there.

I needed to know.

"Why won't he GET UP?!?!"

"He can't."

"That's stupid."

"He's not really there."

"Well, where the hell is he?"

"He's in the sky with God."

"Floating in a cloud?"

"No, he has a home there now. Up in the sky with God."

Just then, the theme song for the Jefferson's started playing in my head. So, I figured he'd moved on up to the Easter Side.

"Can I see him?"

"No."

"Why? What'd I do?"

-silence-

My father had the good sense to drop me off at Nannies house or at Aunt Virginia's house after the divorce. My Mother and I moved into her Grandmother's house and then three or four more places in a span of three years.

There were ghosts everywhere.

My Aunt Virginia would throw me in her bathtub and scrub the crust off of me before her stories started and after she got a good cake baking in the oven. She took me to Toys R Us and let me pick out my swing set.

I played with my Uncle outback. We ran around a tree and I started singing, "ring around the collar" from one of the commercials that came on between the stories. Whatever I did I did with gusto and he just burst out laughing at me. He couldn't even play anymore because he was laughing so hard.

Jimmy and I cussed like sailors. We were allowed to. Looking back, it's because they all knew he was dying and they wanted him to have as much fun as possible. I was one of the props in his world. I was his best wing-man.

Outside of his world I didn't fit.

Aunt Virginia told me that if she heard another bad word come out of my mouth, she would wash my mouth out with soap! I laughed. I cussed. It was my hilarious vibe. Until, I was held over the bathtub and received a brand new bar of soap right in my mouth.

Disbelief.

Betrayal.

No one ever wants to experience that twice!

One thing was clear, the rules had changed.

From that point on I think I went looking for different worlds that might have some role waiting for me to play.

When I met with Wendy all of those years after college, she gave me a lot of advice. I was glad to be landing roles, but I was unsatisfied with the characters.

Wendy would tell me, "if it doesn't exist, create it". She also told me that instead of being angry or upset about sexism, I could simply view that as permission. Permission to create whatever I wanted to create with each new offense. It was all just more and more permission for me.

That was freeing.

New rule. Offensive work is my permission slip to create (and no reason to lock up).

There are always moments in the rehearsal room where I can feel the laughter and joy of Jimmy. I know I have to live moments in life twice, once for each of us.

At the plumbing shop, my boss Skip used to always talk about how he liked being blue collar and not too big. He'd say, when you get to be too big you become a bureaucracy. When you stay blue collar, you get to keep playing.

It's a simple formula. High quality of performance matched with low overhead.

I can do that.

I've drafted my contracts with actors in a certain way. I have a three month window in which to pay everyone. I know that if the show crashes, I can pick up a waitron gig and get everyone paid on time this way.

I find free or affordable spaces to rehearse and perform. This way, I can pay actors, playwrights, directors, and sometimes myself instead of spending money on rent.

I remember carport performances with my friend Joan Breummer in the neighborhood where I grew up. The ping pong table in the basement would be overflowing with costumes and we'd sing along to records and do skits. We'd also use our cassette deck to record soap operas and make up satirical jingles. "The Old and the Decrepid" has been brought to you by "Crust In Your Underwear!".

The albums we listened to all summer were incredible. The compilation album, "A Night at Studio 54" kept us dancing all summer long. Donna Summer singing "Bad Girls" was as bad as it got. And by bad, I mean cool as hell.

At some point Joan's dad took us to an underaged, non-alcoholic dance club in Virginia called, "Little Feet".

I was wearing my Gass brown suede lace up shoes and jeans. The women there, and I will call them WOMEN, were wearing polyester wrap skirts, flawless makeup, and character shoe heels. I think they'd already taken a roll with John Travolta by the looks of things. They could spin and twirl. I was still doing the toddler squat dance but my button up fuschia shirt was full of sparkling metallic threads.

I decided it would be so much fun to do Bad Girl Festivals at Venus Theatre. I would hire an ensemble group of actors and select a group of short plays and we would make an evening's performance out of it. This was a nod to my childhood, even if no one else knew it.

There were so many actors to choose from. Initially, we rehearsed in the stacks section of the Cleveland Park library. The librarians would come up and dance with us, toot tooting and beep beeping past their lockers and through the one hallway.

We performed at DCAC.

I was able to work with and meet so many amazing artists that shared similar passions with me. My soul was lighting up.

I complained a lot to Tricia though, much like I was complaining to Wendy. No matter how much I was accomplishing it was always being viewed as nothing. It's hard to slam into brick walls successively. It's important to vent and laugh with a friend. A trusted friend.

Tricia started talking to me about Suffrage Plays. In one of her classes at American University, Professor Jennings taught her all about them. Tricia gave me her xeroxed copies of the out-of-print Methuen files of Suffrage Plays. They were Edwardian comedies.

I staged almost all of those xeroxed scripts. Decades later I would download some for my cast and I'll never forget how funny it was to see them complain about the print outs after what we'd done with Tricia's xeroxed copies years before zip drives existed.

Smart! Funny! Tight scripts! They were written to keep women entertained on the picket lines as they protested inequities and fought for the right to vote. Of course, being flawed humans, many of these women would go on to contradict themselves with their own actions.

Suffrage was a one hundred year movement. The big argument was that it wasn't necessary because women would simply vote as their husbands voted.

Pamphlets are why dresses don't have pockets much, even today. The suffrage women would whip out a pamphlet and recruit on the spot anywhere any time. So, clothing for women was no longer designed with pockets. A typical short-sighted "solve" for a problem.

These women would also go on hunger strikes. They would be force fed with a tube and a funnel. "Iron-Jawed Angels".

I learned that every movement of protest that successfully changes the shape of our culture results from a process of organization. I learned that from Heather Booth when we read, "Jane: Abortion and the Underground" by Paula Kamen at George Washington University.

I love Bad Girls so much. There are so many women with so much to say. Playwrights are magical little gods of their own worlds. I'm obsessed. This festival allows me to combine lots of different types of women on one stage. It also has allowed me to explore casting men to play submissive characters.

Hoo! They generally don't like that very much. It's not familiar or comfortable. I mean they are generous and land it brilliantly. But, it's clear to see how much men are simply used to being at the front of the line. If you tell them their job is to be at the back they seem fine with it cerebrally. But, there's no familiarity for them in doing that so it can be this kind of blindfolded-grasping-through-the-darkness vulnerable experience.

The ten minute plays I used to do at the Source Summer Festival were not related to one another. It was a big hodgepodge of everybody doing everything. I'm so glad I was a part of those festivals and that I even won an award or two. The perk for Bad Girls is how much we can experiment. With all of this experimentation comes connection. There's real magic in that.

I see the benefit in having a production manager to be sure. I'm trying to be all things to all people and it's stretching me.

This is because of my desperation. I'm truly desperate to produce as much work as possible. Moreso to create as many jobs for women in the field as I possibly can. It feels like my calling. It feels like the only thing I'm here on the planet to accomplish. If I can wake up and do the work, that's all I want to be doing. There's no retirement plan in the theatre. There's only the moment at hand.

This may prove to be detrimental down the road. But, for now, I'm living inside of my WILDEST dream! I'm stepping through worlds upon worlds.

Carol is the co-director and designer for the first Bad Girls Festival. We both sip on iced chai lattes. This is the luscious taste of this summer. It cuts right through all of the sweat and anxiety and makes us feel elevated and quenched.

I expect people to be cheering us on. Every single production we land is another miracle. We're not supposed to be here. We're not supposed to be staging works by women. And yet, here we are.

Everytime I make it to the front of the line, I'm sent to the back again.

Ouroboros. I keep moving hoping I'm not actually consuming myself somehow.

Over and over.

It's maddening.

I feel trapped but I'm going to keep going anyway.

These actors are SO talented and these scripts are so much fun! Playwrights bring themselves in to see the festival from all over the place.

One night an actor comes running in to tell us she was carpooling with a castmate and they got a flat. We go running through Adam's Morgan together.

We kept running until we arrived at the car on the sidewalk in front of an apartment building on 18th Street.

Two of us changed the tire and the third woman jacked up the car. A crowd gathered. They made their call on time.

As a manager I know I have one primary task. It's vital to give every person on my team access to their own win. It's also vital, in the event that they are not able to rise up to their win, to give them avenues out. Offramps of dignity. I've learned this.

Otherwise, it's just another kill-the-messenger situation. I tire of being the messenger. My focus is landing the show.

Building the right team is how we get to paradise. When the right pieces are in place, there's not much to manage. When the right people are in the right roles, it's smooth sailing.

Post coverage is the ONLY way people come to see plays. If you aren't covered there, expect no audience. They basically tell their readers what companies exist. By omission they project which companies to avoid as well.

It was 15 minutes before go-time, and there was no one on the books. The entire cast went into Adam's Morgan on foot. They wandered around in their blacks and found people paying their checks inside of restaurants and this ensemble pulled them into the theatre. They grabbed some people walking down the street as well.

> *This is what I wrote in my journal…*
> *…..*
>
> *I've lost my 13 year old dog, Mr. Gable. I have to sit through the League of Washington Theatre cattle call auditions.*
>
> *Days have gone by now of me walking at our normal walk and times without him. Days of writing a note in his voice to tell the whole neighborhood goodbye. Days of bequeathing all of his neckerchieves, toys, and treats. Days and days of weeping at the loss of my companion who saw me through college, and late night wait shifts. My best friend was gone and I wished I could have him around just a little bit longer.*
>
> *Someone did a monologue about a dead dog at the League cattle calls, and I vowed to hate them forever.*

Another AD has what I like to call the "jaws of death" in her hands here. She sits beside me in the house at Arena Stage. It's a hard core industrial metal stapler she holds in her hands. She staples the feedback sheet to the headshot when she's done watching the actor. Sometimes, that's five seconds into their monologue. KER-CHUNK! Done for!!

I can hear it. The actor can hear it. I think they can probably hear it in the lobby.

I feel so bad for the actors. I'm proud to be one of them. I know what it's like to stand up there for two minutes. Tricia brings a sweater and represents the Stage Guild, the a/c is cranking but it's so hot outside. Sweaters are counterintuitive. I have vowed to sit through all five days, 40 hours of over 1,000 auditions, two minutes at a time.
.....
That was a mistake.

It's the third day and I'm way too punchy now.

One actor says, "so…God…SAID…"

Pausing for ungodly amounts of time with no intonation or character in a single syllable. "Pregnant pause with no conception".

With the timing of a very accomplished comedian the timer who clearly had their arm in the air for the full ten second warning right on cue said, "TIME!"

"so…God…SAID… … … TIME!"

It was comedic gold.

I laugh-sneezed right out loud because it was incredibly well-timed and hilarious. The actor looked at me from the stage with dosey doe eyes of watering betrayal and slowly made her way off.

I've become one of the terrible people.

Maybe I have now become THE MAN.

…..

Structure will insinuate itself in the worst places if it is not established from the start.

So, it's best to make friends with it, describe it, put the parameters of it in a contract. Have someone sign on in agreement so that it's clear these parameters are agreed upon. Check it off the list and get into the PLAY!

At some point, the characters have to dwell in the same world. Hopefully, BEFORE the show opens to an audience. When Zelda Fischlander said that the artistic director should have the final word, I bought it hook, line, and sinker.

To regularly just decide to show up whenever you feel like is definitely not something I can work with. It's a clean fact. I fired someone else. Inside of the CVS. Where she was shopping ten minutes after rehearsal start time. Sometimes I hate people.

………………

Oh, geez! I'm on thin ice with the janitor of the library! My whole business plan right now turns on free rehearsal space. Cleveland Park Library is ideal. I've used other libraries in the city and once was locked inside with my entire cast. I like the Cleveland Park library. They have a terrarium with turtles. So, they must be animal friendly. Right?

I adopted Davey Crockett. It's only been a month since Mr. Gable passed. I tried to sneak Crockett into the back of the library. I didn't want to leave him home alone. Alan was out of town touring his music and I was determined to make the first 72 hours with Davey Crockett a bonding time.

I did ask the shelter if I could pick him up in a month. But a beanie baby addict who looked like a beanie baby herself was seated in a cubicle at the kill shelter. Contrasts! She quickly explained to me that if he wasn't available there would be another dog of equal value. She told me this while staring at her computer screen and talking out of only one side of her mouth. I flipped out.

I busted him off of death row immediately.

HAD TO!

I took him with me to the production meeting on the Starbucks sidewalk. I don't think he's ever been leashed before. He's chasing pigeons into the street near the movie theatre and this is pulling me out of my chair. But, I stay focused even as I spill out face down on the sidewalk in Chevy Chase. I'm on a schedule. I'm not gonna let them kill this dog.

Everything makes sense. Trust me.

Nanny always said there was a difference between city people and country people and apparently this reads with dogs too. Because Davey Crockett is clearly an old country dog attempting to sit on a city sidewalk as he resists the urge to make the pigeons FLY into traffic.

I let people stare.

Whatever!

The janitor now has it out for me for the rest of my existence because he caught me sneaking Davey up into small stacks through the back door. I've violated his trust and he has choice words for me. I explained that I thought it was an animal-friendly environment and I'd only be bringing him up the back steps and into the stacks room.

No go.

Thin ice.

Davey naps in my car in the back parking lot and I check on him every hour-fifteen. We work it out.

A month after rescuing Davey, I rescued Jasmine from the neighborhood. She's a Shiba that's getting kicked in the head by the neighborhood boys. Each time Alan goes out on a tour he comes back to a new furbaby. After Jasmine, he asks me to please stop. So, I do. These two will see me through.

> My biggest objective always, is to create a playground for actors so they can jump around and laugh their asses off.
>
> My intern drives an old pickup truck and we haul things around in it.
>
> She lives in a very nice part of town with her parents and we rehearse in her room because the location is ideal.
>
> The best part of this second summer festival is the last show. It's a rock-opera trailer-park musical written by Kim Moore. "The Ballad of Step-Off Girl". I've staged a slo-mo fight between GitIt Girl And Step Off Girl with a cheap strobe light and the sound of Lenny Kravitz singing, "American Woman". It's everything I've ever lived for.
>
> We have more of an audience somehow this time.

I decided to produce Bad Girls III at the Warehouse Theatre Next Door. I bring in three other directors and a new intern.

I want to create as many opportunities as I possibly can. It's in my bones. I just feel like this is what I'm supposed to be doing.

> I'm advised that my life will be made so much easier if I lighten my load. But now, I'm having to manage so many more people. Nothing feels lighter. In fact, almost everything feels heavier. I still have to pay for rehearsal time by the minute. One of these directors doesn't seem to understand that. She uses her rehearsal time to talk about guys and who she wants to date. I'm flummoxed!
>
> I'm trying to give them off ramps and avenues and at times pogo sticks and moon shoes. The thing I love about it is the interpretations of the scripts. With four different directors it feels much more luscious. It's got a lovely depth and texture. It's working on so many levels.
>
> I'm working on an ulcer.
>
> Too many cooks in the kitchen vs. creating as many jobs as possible for women in the theatre. It's a balancing act.

I think the biggest issue in Bad Girls III is that no one involved experienced Bad Girls I or II. The audiences had. So continuity was an issue. It's a tough spot when the audience is more familiar with a project than the actors. The trade off is how refreshing it is to have new blood.

My theory earlier about it growing organically is not quite working out as much as I thought it would.

That's a really important aspect of the business model. So many women writers have been ignored. I need to embrace as many diverse styles and people as I possibly can. That's the point of the Bad Girls festival. It can never be the same thing twice.

But marketing trends are starting to pull in the other direction. These trends dictate that the audience has to know what they are going to see before they go to see it.

This defies my concept and it's really bad news for female playwrights. I want to surprise my audience with all that we've discovered in the process. I want them to experience it as it's unfolding in front of them. It would create a fourth job for me if I had to EXPLAIN the play before the audience showed up to see the play. Tease it, yes. Cliff note it, YUCK! NO!

My training taught me that this was the job of the critic. Bud taught all of us to NEVER underestimate our audience. I cannot even count how many times he told us that. I wrote it down in my notes a lot.

How will I even know what's working if the audience isn't actually experiencing it? I need to stick to my vision. New works, largely unknown women. Double (okay, triple) uphill battle, but the only way I'm doing this is by breaking in new works and holding open auditions to stay open to new talent.

So many jobs.

I went to see "A Winter's Tale" at the Shakespeare Theatre. A treat for myself. I don't know why so many characters are holding umbrellas. Is it raining? Why are they so colorful? I'm thoroughly confused.

There is a man seated behind me in the audience. He knows every single word of this play. He recites the play along with the actors. I try to sneak a look, nope. No quarto, no folio, no Arden, no script at all in his hands.

His recitation is from memory.

I'm trying to ignore him and suspend disbelief because that's what I BELIEVE theatre asks of us.

Suddenly, in a silence he whispers directly into the back of my head, "exit pursued by bear". Right on cue, an actor with a bear's head runs across the stage chasing the character off and the Prince Georges girl in me wants to hurl my purse into this asshole's face. I refrain. Maybe if he'd been carrying an umbrella the bear could have been shooed away. I'd like to see that.

Why? Am I aware that's coming in the play? YES! But, I AM HERE TO SUSPEND DISBELIEF. I am here to EXPERIENCE THE MOMENT. I'm here to keep my purse in a proper location.

Why do people need to know what's going to happen next at the theatre? In life, yeah, I get that. It's terrifying. We want to know we are going to be happy and not die. We want to know that what we're suddenly smelling isn't leaking gas and that we won't die in our sleep…most likely. But this is theatre, we can afford to kill as many people as we like and they all stand up at the end to bow and curtsy at their curtain call.

It's a PLAY.

It's make believe.

It's shared imagination one night in a room with one specific set of people that will NEVER happen again. It's the celebration of the gift of the moment.

Are we confusing make believe with reality?

Have I killed myself to train and come up with my vision to be trumped by anticipatory people who lack imagination?

What's going on?

Up is down.

Left is right.

What am I doing?

I'm remembering the people who stay seated and take the journey. The quiet ones.

It's the squeaky wheel that demands everything.

[deep breath]
....
We collaborated with an organization called, "Break the Chain". We did a staged reading of a play by Lisa Voss. She wrote one of the shorts for the first Bad Girls Festival. The play we read was called, "Tiny Madmen".

In it, the main character is an indentured slave living in the US. She's accused of stealing her Mistresses earrings and she's cruelly punished.

After the reading we gathered in the Warehouse Cafe for a quick talk back. The reading was on the Main Stage during the day. A time when I could afford it, once.

The women from "Break the Chain" were weeping. We stayed in the cafe for hours and hours. Lakeisha played the main character. The women suddenly told us their stories. Stories of being abducted in Africa. Coerced with a promise from a trusted family friend usually about going to University in America. And then kept below deck to cook and be raped. For years. One woman had gone partially blind because she was kept down in the darkness for so many years. These women were told that if they attempted to run, they would be arrested.

She found her courage and ran when the ship was docked in Baltimore. No green card, no identification, no money. She found out that libraries were free and said she taught herself to read by enlarging the screens so that she could see them.

Another woman said she was kept inside the home and never allowed to leave. It sounded like a McMansion. Her Mistress was a woman who taught Feminist Theory at University IN DC. It made me think of Violet and the whole idea of having a Mistress or a Master and how that was sexualized in our culture. It made my bones shake. This woman was told that the cameras used on people who ran red lights were everywhere in the US. She was told if she tried to leave the home they would track her on cameras.

I couldn't believe this group of women.

....

We met to workshop with them. They ask us what something fun is in our culture. Not a question I ever expected. I immediately remember playing congas and dancing to the Banana Boat song at the House of Ruth with those broken and frayed women. Until I was made a victim as well.

The thing about victimhood is once that label is slapped on you, it's hard to get it off. The only real option is to transform it. As Wendy would often tell me, "It's all just energy, moving".

Another woman leading the workshop started talking to these women and telling them about Madonna and teaching them that Americans (assuming ALL Americans?) VOGUE. She played Vogue and we vogued all over the offices where we were meeting.

That didn't seem right. It felt ridiculous and hollow.

It seemed like there should be more to our culture.

Perhaps, no?

Vogue we did. In exchange, we were shown some African dances that were incredible. In my own head, I decided that Americans were shallow depraved creatures who mostly just liked people to look at them. But, I did not say that part out loud.

There's an obligation for women in the US. There's materialism.

Where's the play?

The question of my life.

If it doesn't exist, create it.

Venus.

The play is at Venus. I'm making the play. This is why it's so hard. It doesn't really exist. People can't see what I'm doing. They can only compare it to what they already know which is classist and sexist and racist.

There I was though, voguing. I swear that everytime one of those women cracked a joyful smile I could hear the crumbling of their forced detention.

Vogue.

………

Doing quick play readings has proven to be incredibly rewarding. It's a good way to see what works on its feet. It didn't take me too long to be able to read a script and tell right away whether it had the "breath" that Sam McCready taught us about. I could tell if it was breathing. And then, connect with it where it was and run like hell through the process to find it in moving three dimensional flesh.

Staged readings give me a chance to work with a lot of different actors. There are only one or two rehearsals and one performance. So, it's low stakes. It's a way to look for compatibility without having to get into contracts and confrontations. It allows me to find my people in a kind and generous way. I like it.

We do at least one public reading a month from plays submitted to me by women all over the country.

………………..

"Rules of the Playground" and "A Chat with Miss Chicky" are two plays read in conjunction with CodePink. The CodePink women are still protesting at LaFayette park. My friend Valerie

sings protest songs alone as the snow comes down all around her in front of the fence where the ten suffragists handcuffed themselves for me. So that I have a voice now. They were pulled off, imprisoned, and force fed.

And now there's Valerie, singing like a nightingale.

"Chicky" was a suffrage play intended to make people laugh. An Edwardian Comedy. Medea of Code Pink shared a spread of food that someone donated. A picnic to try to prevent Dick Chaney and W from contracting our country out for war in the Middle East.

Crazy.

"Rules of the Playground" was written by Carolyn Gage. In it, she describes the rules of war as if on a literal playground. I don't know why, but I spray painted a bunch of trench coats pink and tied the epaulets together with rope. The actors read the play like that.

Unfortunately, a squirrel decided to jump around on them a bit when they were all tied together. So, maybe not the most powerful rendition of that particular script. Maybe when costuming comes in, rehearsals need to be made to accommodate. Perhaps I should find a costume designer?
.....
Carolyn sent me a full length play called, "The Anastasia Trials in the Court of Women".

I met Kerri Rambow for a beer at Fado on 7th Street. I told her about this script and asked her if she'd be interested in directing it. As it happens, she has just been doing very heavy research on the Romanovs.

This was a match.
....
Kerri did such a great job directing that play.

ven*us*

AD Michelle Schupe and Director, Kerri Rambow

Helen Hayes has launched, or relaunched, the Legacy Project.

The objective is to honor the work of Helen by honoring the work in theatre. The biggest obstacle theatre seems to be facing right now is audience. We're losing audience. They're dying and the best hope is to cultivate new generations of theatre goers. This program sends theatre teaching professionals into the DC Public School System. It's titled, "The Helen Hayes Legacy Project".

*Toni Rae Salmi post-performance,
Adventure Theatre*
First, I trained with a woman who would talk to the students about which actors were getting plastic surgery. I'm not sure what that was about. I guess she maybe was making the point that your body and appearance are your instruments?

Can't be sure.

I was able to tour, "How She Played the Game" through the Helen Hayes Legacy Project.

I performed on very nice stages as well as in cafetoriums. I was under contract with the organization until they violated the contract and brought it to an unexpected end.

This gig did allow me to fund some Venus shows. I'm really grateful for that.

I'm constantly being told that I should not be funding plays myself. We do get some donations. But donations are not consistent and I'm on a schedule to keep going and get as many opportunities for women out there as I possibly can.

Tricia is also a Theatre Educator with the program. Sometimes, we are assigned to the same schools.

John Vreeke is our program director. He'd directed some episodes of "Northern Exposure".

He is great to work with as the Legacy Director. Honestly, he's what the program has been needing for a long time.

Some days, I will teach three classrooms at once.

The thing that determines the quality of the visit is always the same.

Leadership.

....

Carolyn Gage outside of the Warehouse Theatre

Carolyn Gage submitted another play to me called, "Ugly Ducklings". This one takes place at Camp Fernlake. A girls summer camp off of the coast of Maine. It has thirteen female characters. The ages range from eight on up into retirement ages.

The play centers around an eight year old who is teased for being gay and attempts to hang herself.

The script is older than most of the cast. No one wanted to touch it until it landed in my hands. Carolyn is having a good ride with Venus. "The Anastasia Trials" has gotten special Samuel French distribution into Universities because of our production and the press it ended up receiving.

I reached out to the Duke Ellington School for the Arts to help with "Ducklings" casting. I taught Legacy programming there as well. They brought in a Toby's Dinner Theatre tour about Ben Carson. It told the story of how rough his life was and how he'd become a famous brain surgeon. How he was a major success story.

Sometimes God laughs.

I cast the kids on the spot because I didn't want them to have to wait.

It was a gigantic cast in a tiny space.

The two main characters were played by Rosalie Fisher and KC Wright. Both of them were straight A students. Both of them had agreements with their parents that if their grades dropped they could not do the show. So, they were doing homework on every break. KC studied for the SATS behind a canoe chopped in half on set.

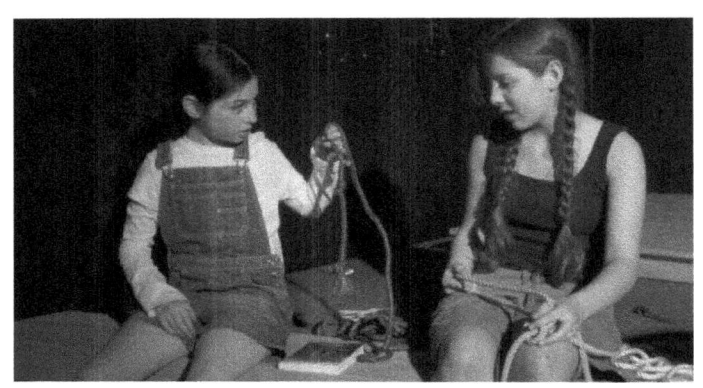

Rosalie Fischer and KC Wright
Lisa Helfert Photography

I told them to think about Jodie Foster and how intelligent she was. If they want to be strong actors, they should be building their brains.

Paul Kelm was my designer and builder. Another student turned professional sent to me by Gregg Schraven. It was a gorgeous design. Carolyn even included Paul's set design in her published script.

"Ducklings" was nominated for an American Theatre Critics Award for the prestigious ATCA/ Steinberg New Play Award, an award given annually for the best new play produced outside New York. It won a 2004 Lesbian Theatre Award from Curve magazine.

....

Improvisational work revealed a lot with these girls during their last rehearsal. The news that none of my girls can take the bus shocks me. I asked them why, and they said strange men will sit next to them and sometimes do things. One revealed that she could no longer stay over at a friend's house because her friend's

Dad had been really inappropriate with her when she was sleeping one night. He exposed himself to her and I don't know what else. She shut down.

I start looking at their parents very differently. I don't know how they're doing this parenting thing. The world seems so horrifying to me. What are these girls going to do? How are they going to grow into healthy women who feel like they have a safe place in the world? By safe place, I mean a place they will not be raped or killed.

There were times during that show that I could hear an audience member gasp.

....

Our production of "Ugly Ducklings" reawakened a more-than-decades old script. The award nomination helped a lot too, I think. Along with Carolyn's verve. It was turned into a documentary. A non-profit called Hardy Girls was created around the play. Through that project "tolerance kits" were distributed throughout the state of Maine's Middle Schools. Carolyn swears we saved lives. I really hope that's true.

*Me and Molly Ruppert
Hugging one of my sheroes
in the final days of the Warehouse Theatre*

Molly Ruppert is one of the owners of the Warehouse. I was working one day, loading some pieces in by myself and visualizing the space, and this man kept following me down the sidewalk. I told Molly about it. She said, turn around 180 degrees on your heels and walk straight at him next time.

Seems counterintuitive.

I did that and it worked!
....

"How She Played the Game's" Althea Gibson died. Of the six Olympians in the show, she had been one of three still alive. Now, it was down to two. Gretel Bergmann was known to be very shy and did not want to meet people or talk about her exclusion from the Nazi Germany Olympics. Then there was Gertrude Ederle. She was 98 and living in a nursing home in Wyckoff, NJ. Wyckoff is a neighboring town of Franklin Lakes. Franklin Lakes is where I spent my summers as a child. My Gram married the Mayor of Franklin Lakes and they had the cheapest house in the wealthiest neighborhood. I spent my summers hanging out with kids who lived in real mansions. Each room had a fireplace, including the kids rooms and office spaces.

It was always strange when they admired my K-Mart clothes.

I could get to Wyckoff. I think that's where Gram's Country Club was. I'm pretty sure I went swimming in that lake in the 70's.

I drove out in my Tracker. It was mostly held together with Velcro and hot glue. The weather was really bad. Rain was going sideways. I turned on the radio and it talked about different counties getting hit by tornadoes. I had no idea which county I was in.

I found the nursing home.

I asked about Trudy. They say, "she's right there looking out the window."

I stepped into her room and said hello.

The first thing I ever heard her say was, "I could swim on that sidewalk".

Trudy is a world class swimmer. She swam the English Channel, beating the records of the five men before her by 2 hours during a storm back in 1926.

Trudy would hold that record for 24 years, until Florence Chadwick broke it in 1950.

Trudy was a gold medal Olympian Swimmer before that. An all around swimming powerhouse. She was the very first woman to swim the channel. She broke 29 U.S. National and World records.

Hard life.

In 1933 she slipped on loose tiles in a stairwell and injured her back. She was told she'd never walk again. By 1939, not only was she walking she was swimming in Billy Rose's Aquacade at the New York World Fair.

She ended up teaching swimming lessons to the deaf kids at the Y in her retirement years.

Playwright Cindy Cooper said she visited Trudy in her home before the nursing home. I think she said it was in Brooklyn. The mailman had befriended her and would bring her groceries every week and check on her. That's just Trudy's personality. Everyone falls in love with her. She's still America's sweetheart, if you ask me. She asked Cindy if she wanted to see her medals. Cyn said, sure. She was pointed up a staircase. She walked into an untouched dusty room covered in medals and awards.

I think they were all sent to a Swimmers Hall of Fame or something eventually.

I looked at Trudy and told her I was honored to meet her and that I would be playing her on stage.

She says, "Well, you gotta do what cha gotta do."

I sit in the comfy lazy boy with the pockets on the sides. The pockets are stuffed with books about her.

The Channel swim was her second attempt. She couldn't afford a third, that's why she swam through the storm. I ask if the people on deck were cheering for her.

She says, "they were doing everything but standing on their heads."

Every once in a while she winces. Her lips pucker up and she makes a quick inhale. And says, "Oh! My rear end.". They bring her applesauce. "Apple sauce". It has her meds crushed up inside. She refuses to eat it and prefers to stay conscious, pain or no, to hang out with me.

Loud feedback is blaring out of a metal headband which is her hearing aid. The water has made her nearly deaf. Her sister worked with an ophthalmologist to create goggles for Trudy to wear on the Channel swim. I stand in the parking lot of Dick's Sporting Goods scratching my head wondering what Trudy would have done in today's swim gear. No one considered protecting her ears. Not even her.

The TV is blaring. I am watching a famous basketball player on the TV screen. He is showing the huge diamond ring he's purchased for his partner to a news reporter. This is national news. He thinks the ring will make up for him raping a 19 year old girl.

This seems entirely ridiculous, nevermind offensive, to me. Here I am, sitting next to an athletic legend, and here the world is. Not knowing about one of the greatest athletes that ever lived sitting in that bed staring out of that window dreaming of, what? Paying someone off for her crimes? No. Dreaming of SWIMMING. Because that was her love and her joy and her reason for getting out of bed.

I'm having a hard time understanding why our culture focuses on pitying men who have committed crimes over women who have exceled.

What do we think is newsworthy?

It seems to me that her passion is so much larger than her pain that she might not even be aware of the rest of the world filled with harsh realities. Or, if she is aware, she'd rather dream of swimming.

Trudy asks if I have seen her Mother or Sister in the hall. I know that they've both already passed away. She has a couple of nieces still living but no one from her younger days. She is the last of her time.

I'm holding her hand now. Staring out the window with her and watching the sideways rain. Ignoring the news blasting louder than the feedback coming from her headband.

I'm holding her hand.

I gave her a gift and a card. You know, just to thank her for living the life she did and inspiring so many people, including ME. She has a teddy bear that she likes to hug. It's late October and she just turned 98 on the 23rd. I was there on the 28th.

I tell her she is 98 and she says, "What?!?!"

I have to keep repeating it. I write "98" with a sharpie on the envelope of her birthday card. I hold it up for her to see.

Me with Gertrude Ederle
Holding the hand of one of my heroes October 28, 2003

She finally says, "How'd that happen?!?"

Then she asks again if I have seen her Mother and Sister in the hallway.

I tell her no but they might be waiting for her and if she wants she can go with them now.

I don't know why I'm saying this, I only know it's what I need to say to her.

I stayed with her that night for about three hours. Then I drove into NYC to meet up with Cindy and catch a reading at the Drama Bookshop.

Before I left Trudy, we held hands again. The nurse who took our photo commented that we looked like we were related.

Trudy looked into my eyes and she said, "you're very kind."

I told her she was my hero (I hold back tears as I'm looking at her) and that she was doing me a favor by sharing her life stories with me. THAT WAS THE GIFT.

She tells me I don't have to sit with her. That I could be doing so many other things that young people like to do. But I was kind enough to take the time.

It heals me a little more. First, an Irishman directly descended from Molly Maguire calls me clever, and now an Olympian hero calls me kind.

I am starting to see myself differently.

I'm beginning to see myself as clever and kind, through the eyes of my heroes.

I began this journey because I could not find a woman that I honestly looked up to fully. I needed to find someone I aspired to be like and that's why I went digging. There were always women in my life that I loved. But, I began to really search for inspiration. Seeking it out meant finding a lot of duds.

Understanding how lackluster some of the women around me were was disappointing.

THIS MOMENT, was the point. A touchstone. A realization that her story was mine to tell now. I could only hope it would be well received. She deserves to be known. She showed up and she took every risk.

Trudy died about a month after my visit. She was born on October 23, 1905 and died on November 30, 2003. She had 60 years on me. That's 15 whole Jimmy-lifetimes.

What will I do if I still have 15 of his lifetimes left to live?

I can't believe I got to sit in a room with her. To chat. To discuss life and what it was like to be in a ticker tape parade? What was it like to be the toast of the town? She talked about the car that she got to ride in and how fancy it was.

I am finding women who inspire me now. I am holding their hands! It's amazing what happens when an intention is set.

Trudy didn't know she could leave. She was wired to stay and fight it out another day. I connect with that so deeply. The only option is to get back up. My Monster taught me that. You either lay down and die or you get back up and fight! THOSE ARE THE OPTIONS! She also constantly told me that I could do anything I wanted to in life as long as I wanted it bad enough.

That's not the same thing as love. I am finding gratitude for my Monster because she gave me life and a place to live. She fed me. A roof over my head, food in my mouth, clothes on my back. For these things she assumed I owed her my life. I'm replacing her now. As gently as possible with true inspiration. With golden hearts and honest spirits. Gently and slowly, I'm edging her out of my own spirit and filling the dark void left with absolute inspiration. I remain awestruck by the fact that a perfect stranger can impart so much love on me in one sitting.

There's a solid truth about the darkness.

It ALWAYS defines the light. I'm beginning to think that's its only purpose.

There are more miracles waiting to be found. I just know it. Those miracles are housed in solid character. So, the pursuit to stage strong characters walks hand in hand with the desire to know them in life.

I'm so lucky

When Jerry Manning was running me through the audition drills, I'd cultivated some monologues by Migdalia Cruz.

What a fierce writer.

She is a student of Maria Irene Fornes. I have her scripts on my bookshelf from Backstage Books in DC. Have had them for so long.

I decided I should produce Migdalia, if she would let me. I got in touch with her agent and read the bulk of her plays.

"Fur" really stood out to me. There's no way I could cast it though. I'd have to put an actor in a cage.

Migdalia is extremely sexual in her plays. She doesn't hold back.

I read, "Cigarettes and Moby Dick". It felt like the one.

I decided to stage it in the attic of the Warehouse.

Intimate.

It was a dingy place where many pigeons used to live.

Bird lice and poo remained in the rafters. I would not let my cast see the space until I had cleaned it up. We rehearsed downstairs in the art gallery spaces of the Warehouse.

Paul Kelm was my designer again along with a woman named Cat.

We had a production meeting at TGI Fridays where I expressed my ideas for staging. Cat said, I don't get it. And Paul responded, I never do at first either, just trust her she always knows what she's doing.

I explain how I wanted the three rooms of the attic to be designed according to elemental influences. The largest room would be the water room, the kitchen and living room would be the fire room, and the little movie theatre would be air.

The design they came up with was pretty brilliant.

The audition process was a lot. By now, we had a system. I left two or three unpublished scripts with the barista/bartender in the Warehouse Cafe. Actors could come by anytime and read them.

There's no way I'd ever audition someone for a script they had not read. Consider it due diligence.

At the audition, actors are rehearsing themselves with their sides in the hallways and digging in.

Monalisa and Laura have never met. The thing about auditions is, you can make connections for life there. This includes the people you are competing against. It's some kind of strange artistic trauma bond.

Jerry Manning called me to the Kennedy Center to audition for the tour of "Lilly's Purple Plastic Purse". I made a friend there. We looked at each other and said, we're competing against one another to play mice. Mice! So, we laughed and decided to become friends. Rhea Seehorn was cast for that tour. I'd directed her in the "Pizacatto Experiment" in one of the Source Summer Festivals. She's doing well in Hollywood now.

Theatre is like a spinning top. Auditions bring you to the center. From there, this centrifugal force just spins you out into your own spiral. It's stunning, magical, unpredictable, glorious.

Monalisa and Laura are up to read a scene cold for me. Only, they've had enough time to memorize it and to do some deep scene work together. They are so connected, it's undeniable. They end the scene with a kiss. Something I did not ask them to do. Something they decided would be right for both of their characters.

That is the level of trust I need to make this show work.

Girls kissing is definitely a theme for Venus. I would like to say it's a lesbian empowerment intention. But, the truth is, I'm trying to get as many women on stage as possible. Sometimes these dynamics include love interests. And sometimes those love interests kiss. In the case of Migdalia Cruz, she's just so sensual and sexual in her work. It requires actors to be free in their bodies. It's impossible to fake that. I never want to put an actor in a position where they are not comfortable. Consent is key.

Mac was in, "Ugly Ducklings". Now she's my assistant director.

It's happening.

We're cast.

We're in rehearsals!

This show is so sensual that it has to have constant trust around it energetically. Monalisa is also the fight choreographer for the show.

The cast consists of three women and three men. The team is stunning from sound design to costumes to stage management, straight on down the line. Incredible!

Ellie Nicoll and Monalisa Arias Lisa Helfert Photography

I'm on a schedule.

Meaning, I have to pay for every minute that I'm in this place. Forget about parking in DC and the scam of parking tickets they load on you that make no sense.

I make a rehearsal schedule. It accounts for half hour blocks of time. We're right above the cafe, so anyone not needed for a half hour can go have a coffee and come back when they are needed. I try to not waste anyone's time on the schedule.

Eventually, we are teched into the attic.

Ellie is playing the Warhol lithograph version of Marilyn Monroe. I place her inside of the shallow scrimmed victorian closet. Paul and Cat have her backlit. Jessica designed the costumes and they are stellar.

The audience is promenaded past Ellie several times during the first half hour or so of the performance. They believe she's a wax figure at about the half hour mark.

Soon after that, on cue, she stretches in the closet and steps through the scrim. I stand in awe of how much she encapsulates Marilyn Monroe. She says, "I'm dryer than dust!" and jumps behind the bar Paul and Cat have built up there and starts making martinis for herself and anyone who will take one.

This is where I met the director of the Kennedy Center page-to-stage festival. He's a Helen Hayes judge. They are all shocked that they are ACTUALLY in an attic. Especially the judge who was accidentally standing in our beach water wearing his very expensive imported italian leather shoes.

As they were leaving he asked me why Venus wasn't a part of the page-to-stage festival. I tell him I don't know. He invites us in that inaugural year and every year to follow for the duration of the festival.

We had a big fundraiser for Venus and Andrea Dworkin was there. She called me on my boot phone as I was driving into the city. I can't believe it. I'm at RFK stadium. I just keep driving around the stadium in circles and talking to her on the phone. She asks if she can come to our fundraiser.

OF COURSE.

Nav from Wild World is a belly dancer now, and she danced at the fundraiser. It was a grand time.

I reached out to Andrea after the event to see if Ellie and I could swing by her place and have some coffee and talk to her about Marilyn Monroe and women's sexuality. As one does.

Andrea Dworkin has written the foreword to the BEST biography on Marilyn that I can find.

Andrea agrees and we are set to go to her home on Saturday April 11, 2009. Mac and I were driving around DC the Thursday before, trying to find some kind of couch for the "movie theatre". My boot phone rang again.

It was Carolyn Gage. She said she had bad news to tell me of Andrea. She said, "this is not to leave the inner circle". I couldn't believe I was a part of anyone's inner circle. Then, she told me Andrea had died that day.

She was 58.

'Feminism requires precisely what patriarchy destroys in women: unimpeachable bravery in confronting male power"
<u>Andrea Dworkin</u>

I can't believe she was in my house.

It makes me think of all of the women I've brushed up against so far on this journey. Amazing women. We've opened for Erykah Badu at Take Back the Night marches. I've hung out in dusty rooms in dingy houses not only with the women of CodePink, but also beside Bikini Kill. Attending their empowerment workshops and reading their zines.

It's a lot to take in.

We are still in rehearsals for "Cigarettes". I am still on a schedule. The bills don't pay themselves.

I'm always on the table for the first week of rehearsals. This means we all sit around the table and go through the script line by line and analyze it. This gets my cast on the same page, literally. Always. I hear a muted voice coming through the wall as we're going through a scene. It sounds a bit like the SNL landshark in terms of tone.

"If anyone can hear me. Hello? I'm trapped. I'm trapped inside of the bathroom and I cannot get out."

It's one of my actors.

I jump up, mostly because I'm on a schedule and he needs to be there for the next rehearsal time slot. I tell everyone, "STAND BACK!". Flashes of Angie Dickenson as Police Woman suddenly play vividly in my mind.

People begin to gather around.

I kick the door with my foot and the door throws ME backwards into the half-wall behind me that frames the steps and prevents anyone from accidentally falling down them. Including me in that moment.

This angers me.

I kick again, much harder this time, and the door flies open, trim falls in from the right side of the door frame. I see a diminutive figure shrinking into a smaller size while wearing a green t-shirt and retreating backwards away from the door in a seeming slo-motion.

This angers me.

I say, "I SAID STAND BACK!"

He replies, "I didn't know you were going to kick the door in."

And to that, I say, "I'm ON a SCHEDULE!"

We get back to the table having not even lost five minutes. We're on track.

At the scheduled 15 minute break, I head downstairs into the cafe.

Molly Ruppert is having an art gallery opening. She's drinking a tiny plastic cup of white wine.

I say, "Listen, Molly. I have something shocking to tell you. Just now my actor was trapped inside of the bathroom upstairs. So, I kicked the door in so he wouldn't be trapped and also because I'm on a schedule."

She tipped her cup toward me and glanced up into my eyes and simply said, "Good."

I thought everything was fine. But, then her son needed to talk to me. He wanted me to know that Slim was still trying to fix the door. And that NEXT TIME, I needed to come and get him so that he could "get his tool box and take the door off of its hinges properly."

To this, I called his name and he looked at me a little stunned by my volume. I followed this up with a simple question, "Have you fixed the lock?"

"Well, no. We haven't gotten to that yet."

"Here's the deal. If you fix the lock so none of my people ever get trapped inside, I promise I will never kick the door in again."

That was that.

I'm experiencing low-grade fury almost all of the time now. It almost comes with its own humming sound. I have to pay to do a whole lot of work. I'm not GETTING paid. "The work IS the reward".

I'm so sick of being criticized for needing to get more "butts in seats" that I decided for this particular project there will be NO seats!

Audience can sit on set pieces we weren't using for various scenes.

Fuck this noise and GOOD LUCK!

I was told Adam's Morgan was too hard to get to. Well, here we are between four different metro stops in a completely different part of town.

What's the reason now?

Could it be that the world hates women?

I'm starting to think the world hates women.

Migdalia is coming down to see the production.

I'm a nervous wreck.

I'm driving the Tracker held together with hot glue and Velcro. My exhaust pipe wiggles.

I parked in the Union Station parking garage.

I got to the florist inside of Union Station for validation of my parking maybe too soon. First hour is free. I spent the only money I had on flowers for Migdalia. Her train is running late.

Really late.

I'm remembering a Helen Hayes Legacy gig nearby. I'm remembering walking into Union Station for my lunch break and being interrupted by a man with a heavy accent. He's saying, "Hey! Hey!"

I look up at him.

"Why aren't you smiling?!?"

What?

He became more agitated.

"God has made this glorious day just for you! YOU should be SMILING!"

Holy hell. I'm thinking about staging in a specific space. This does not require me to smile. I wish I would have said, "ya fool!" but I did not.

I see her! I welcome her. I cannot believe she's here. I give her flowers and tell her, "my car is this way".

She has brought her New York City dramaturg and director along for the experience.

My Tracker can definitely fit four.

Tightly.

They are fussing with their baggage.

I have FIVE minutes left now until I breach the one hour of free parking mark. I have spent my money on flowers. This has to happen NOW.

I load them in. Somehow.

Kindly.

Their luggage is shoved in the shallow back.

Gently?

We are out of there with a minute to spare.

Whew! That could have been really embarrassing.

I take them to their hotel, which she has paid for.

I get over to the cast. They know she's here. I've told everyone in town she's here. They all decide to come to the show that Migdalia attends. I guess they all want to see her or something. It's so packed.

I walk her up the steps and she says, "this is actually an attic".

Yes.

She feels, rightly so, that she should be produced by big houses with proper budgets.

She's skeptical and she's hot because it's spring with a quickly approaching summer and we are in an attic. She takes off her sweater.

I'm watching her walk through the production and experience the show.

Promenade.

Everyone is watching her and pretending not to be watching her. It's a little creepy.

We all go back to Ellie's apartment because it's so close. Monalisa and I play guitar. One of the actors decides he needs to sleep in silk pajamas so Ellie lets him wear hers and stay the night. I eventually went home. But many of the actors stay up all night with her.

People continue to be so blown away by that show.

Tricia tells me she and Denman talked about it on the metro ride home. Denman created the sound design. Tricia tells me how exceptional and important the work is.

It makes me proud. It makes me glad I was so particular with the staging. I really was particular. The cast was ideal.

"Directing is 90% casting."

One of my playwrights offers to fund her show. I've never done this before. But, at this point I'm spent and really out of money and energy. So, I take her up on it.

This was an important play. Meaning the subject was really vital. It was about the fight for DC statehood. The cast was gigantic. Cat came onboard to design and build the set.

It's interesting. I'm feeling free in choosing these works and having the space to create them. But, I'm also somehow a part of an industry that wants to pretend I don't exist.

My intern from the Bad Girls festivals is assistant directing beside me. I've got a world class stage manager too.

I'm onboard for this because the world is going madder by the day and I've produced enough plays by now to know I can pull off anything.

I have found some incredible talent for my stage and the message is really powerful. I staged a riot. Monalisa jumps in to choreograph. It's beautiful.

It's in slow motion and "We Shall Overcome" is playing. I mention to my lighting designer how much I love the bricks in the loft of the Warehouse Mainstage and she lights them into a rich texture which creates a perfect backdrop. I have many areas on the main stage that are playing spaces in the proscenium layout, including the loft. I use every single nook and cranny. Lots of levels here.

The Warehouse really is an expansive place of magic. Alan and I would spend a New Years eve or two there. One year, a woman with a tiny key chain tarot deck asked if she could pull a card for us. We said, sure. She looked at us with wide owl-eyes. Her right hand lifted with fingers spread and palm making a slightly concave shape. She began to make little swirling movements in the air with her right hand and said, "So much love. So much talent. Be careful who you allow to be around you." And then, she was gone.

We do a promo with a radio station.

This is such a gift. I think back on all of the collaborations.

I tried to work with the Washingtonian women. I was born in the city. I belong here. I keep telling myself this over and over. But, I was raised in Prince George's County. I was only born in DC because there was not a hospital close enough in Maryland on October 10, 1966.

I remember being asked to direct the DC citywide version of V-Day. This was interesting. I'd seen the "Vagina Monologues" read at the Studio Theatre and I'd gotten a signed copy of the script from Eve Ensler.

It was not a dynamic show at the time. It was just her on stage wearing reading glasses and sitting at a table with a microphone and index cards.

I wanted to think it was a feminist version of "Krapp's Last Tape".

But, she just read a lot of transcribed interviews she'd gathered about vaginas.

I almost fell asleep.

All of the sudden, "The Vagina Monologues" started popping up everywhere. It reminded me of the plays that were given University distribution after we'd done them.

Good for her! I thought.

Of course I'm going to direct the City Wide V-Day performance.

So many meetings in Georgetown. Lots of running to feed the meter for my car parked blocks and blocks away.

Nothing ever seems to get accomplished in these meetings. The administrative assistant has interesting hair and takes a lot of notes. I can't imagine what she is writing. We're talking in circles saying absolutely nothing for hours and hours. But, the parking meters don't care about that. cha-ching!

I'm not allowed to use professional actors.

What??!?!

I'm holding the big binder with all of the text and all of the guidelines.

It tells me they want the performances to be "pedestrian".

So, I'm not ALLOWED to hire professional actors?!!

No.

A bunch of professional actors want to do it. They are willing to do it for no pay. They are willing to pretend they are amateurs.

What?

Hours of meetings and they give me approval to allow professional female actors to work for free.

In the meantime, every production MUST have a hired tech crew.

What?

All of the technicians they are hiring are men.

So.

Women work for free and men get paid.

Anyone?

Is anyone seeing this?

I have no budget for a set and the venue is not secured.

I am going to take a tour of the Lincoln Theatre.

Many meetings are held discussing this.

I'm told it's a go.

Until the next meeting when it's not.

I'm introduced to my co-director. NEWS!

What?

She's best friends with Chelsea Clinton. She directed V-Day last year in Japan. She used a lot of satin textiles.

Okay.

We have no budget.

She's always wearing a pashmina. I'm sure Chelsea has one to match. Powder puff pink, swooped around her fourth chakra and swaddling her in a privileged hug.

What?

I think my Prince George's fin is popping up.

At the table where we meet, women are talking about giving as much money as possible to a chosen nonprofit. It has to be a desperate nonprofit. One whose women are about to lose their tits to dysentery, or something.

Something that makes their checks look like the honest white saviors that they are.

I ask the obvious question: "What does theatre have to do with this? Why don't you just mail them a check?"

Silence.

Apparently, the administrative assistant wants to see all of us wearing red leather skirts as we enter the lobby. She wants to see her Uncle sitting center in the third row screaming "vagina" over and over again.

This is the vision.

That's why we were doing the show.

Huh?

I blasted off a long email explaining to them what I thought theatre was and expressing to them that they were doing a great disservice to everyone with their underestimation of the power of theatre.

They decided we might perform at the entrance to a restaurant. A theatre was too expensive. They wanted that money to go to the cause.

I quit the project and suggested they just mail checks.

I didn't mention that I was running my own nonprofit and working for free myself. I was losing money on the parking meters alone!

I thought I had it to give.

I didn't have it to give.

I went to events that ended with women getting out their checkbooks and writing big numbers to younger women they were weirdly lusting after. The whole thing really skeeves me out. I thought the male gaze came from men. NO, Ma'AM. Those eyeballs can bulge out of any head. ah!

The Universe was sending me into a looping spiral. It was up to me to decide whether I was ascending or descending.

Suddenly, the call came from the Sewall-Belmont House.

They would like Venus to perform.

What?

Okay.

Linda J. Lumsden will be there doing a book signing. Her book is called, "The Life and Times of Inez Mullholland". It's about a woman of wealth and privilege. I bet Inez would have worn a pashmina if they existed. Soft pink. She admitted openly that her beauty is what earned her so much attention. She was a proud martyr of the suffrage movement. She rode a white horse with the movement as it progressed through towns and cities. Her doctor advised her to rest. She would not stop. She died prettily of pernicious anemia out on the front lines of protest. I think she was napping on top of or beside her pristine white horse wearing her white robes of justice when she passed. A martyr indeed.

Well.

I don't really have any suffrage plays on the ready. I DO have this monster truck trailer park musical.

I get the standard: Sure sure. Fine fine.

I could do whatever I wanted to do.

Okay.

I recast the thing and I put myself in it as Step-Off girl. I'm playing guitar and wearing pink sponge curlers.

I'm freaking out.

What an elegant place.

I know what I'm about to do.

Michelle is my stage manager for this. This is her third project with me.

I'm about to sing about VIBRATORS!

I tell Michelle. I'm about to sing about VIBRATORS!

Michelle tells me that if vibrators were readily available during the time of the Suffragists every room in the Sewall-Belmont House would have had one. She tells me, the women who lived here would have partaken and I'm just honoring them in a different way.

Oh, my God. I'm about to sing about vibrators.

I'm tuning my guitar.

I'm trying to tune my guitar. I'm tuning my guitar backwards because all I can think is how I'm about to sing about vibrators wearing sponge curlers in a historic house that has one of only three feminist libraries in the entire NATION.

One of the male actors I've hired to be in the show is watching me. I noticed this. He gave me a nod.

Huh?

Then he starts to speak, "you want me to…"

What?

"Tune your guitar for you?" His face is lit up with a gigantic grin.

What? Do you play guitar?

"No, but if you can do it…"

WHAT?!?! I do not have time for this.

File it! File it away for later.

It's time. It's time for me to go down there and face the women-of-pashmina.

It's time for me to entertain the women-of-pashmina.

I will meet their sprayed helmet hair with pink sponge curlers.

It's time.

It's time.

Ahhh…

It's time.

Why is the floor bricked? Who bricks a floor. Why isn't it level?

Was it inspired by cobblestone? Why is it brick? I'm befuddled over this floor.

There are elderly people here, they could fracture a hip.

The wine glasses are so small. I never even knew they made plastic cups that small.

What are these intended for the church? Is this some kind of communion?

It is.

I'm about to violate a feminist communion.

I have to make them laugh.

Have to.

Make them laugh.

They are reluctant to laugh.

There's a mother/daughter coupling. They are here for the book. We've all got a signed book by now. The writer is so relieved. So sophisticated, understated, intelligent. She probably has more than one of those microscopic cups of wine.

I can hear Wes from the Scandel Bus Tours announcing, "the more you drink, the funnier we get!".

This isn't a bus.

It's a historic building.

A place deserving reverence.

They have the desk of Stanton and Anthony downstairs. The one the Declaration of Sentiments was drafted on. It's next to a statue of Joan of Arc.

This is not a bus.

Ahhhh…

Here we are.

We're doing it.

Everyone is doing their thing.

We are met with a mixture of shock and stoicism.

Do other people even exist?

Here comes the song.

I'm gonna have to play it.

Curlers are out and thrown in my guitar case.

There's no way to stall.

X always said, "hesitation is death in the theatre".

I'm strumming. I'm singing. I have two grown men waltzing together. The mother/daughter duo is waiting patiently to leave. They sit upright. Rigidly. I don't think either of them has ever just plopped down in a bean bag chair. What kind of life is that?

They watch and listen as I sing the words of Kim Moore:

"I just need my gals and myself
A shrink to preserve my mental health
Fulfilling career and parties to cateeeeer.

  (this is it! This is the moment. Do Not Hesitate.
   HESITATION IS DEATH!!!!)

And, I'll still get my lovin from a

(thump guitar three times)

Good Vibratoor!!!!!"

The mother of the mother-daughter team loses her pashmina. Her hair moves a little.

She releases a sneeze-laugh the likes of which I have never experienced in my life. A sneeze-laugh is an involuntary thing. It's a bodily function expressed when the soul can no longer pretend. It's a blurt with spit and blanched monosyllabic doppler sound.

Her daughter daintily giggles beside her.

My work here is done anyway. I'll take one sneeze-laugh over a million chuckles any day of the week.

Back at the Warehouse Theatre we're making headway. The first week of attendance is light but week two is good and week three looks to sell out.

I'm down 7th Street having a pre-show late lunch/early dinner.

The call comes.

It's THE MAN, from the Warehouse.

He says, "I have good news and I have bad news. What do you want first?"

Good?

"The good news is no one was hurt!"

Hurt? Why would anyone be hurt?

"The bad news is, there's been an explosion?"

What?

I jump up from the table and run about 12 city blocks up to the theatre wearing my boots with my phone clipped to them and a dress. As I approach New York Avenue I can see that there are about seven Pepco trucks covering the entire block extending around the corner on 7th Street. The construction on the new convention center has come a long way. The block is lit with the twirling yellow lights from the tops of Pepco utility trucks as the sun begins to go down sooner than seems astronomically possible on this day.

Something about the salt that they put on the road to melt the ice dripping down. Usually a sewer cap goes hurling into the air from the explosion. But that didn't happen this time.

There was an electrical explosion akin to a lightning strike. Smoke came out of every outlet.

The dimmer packs for the lights were fried beyond recovery.

No light. No electricity.

THE MAN asks me what I would like to do.

What?

I call every single member of the cast after I call the playwright and crew.

I begin every time with, "I swear I'm not making this up, there's been an explosion." And, I end every exchange with, "What would you like to do?"

I don't want to ask anyone to work through this mess. But, it's the final week of performances and we've worked so hard. They've waited so long to have sell-out audiences. I cannot take that away from them. It's a conundrum.

Unanimously, we decided to do the show.

UNANIMOUSLY.

THE MAN heads home for the day. I'm talking to the Pepco guys. Just another hour. Probably another hour. Maybe one more hour or so.

Hours tick by.

At some point I'm in the dirt floor cellar of the Warehouse staring at a bunch of round breakers and pretending I know what I'm saying while simultaneously NOT imagining the beginning of every horror film I've ever watched.

Nothing.

The playwright arrives first. She's baked cupcakes for everyone.

Cupcakes?

The rest of the cast begins to arrive. The crew has arrived.

Nothing.

We go onto the Mainstage lighting the way with only our brick cell phones.

Spontaneously we all lay around the stage and begin singing, "We Shall Overcome".

Out of nowhere, every light comes on over the house. Lighting a ghost audience. Perhaps the Mollies have hung around?

No light on the stage. Nothing anywhere else on the block. Just over the empty seats of the audience. Like some kind of promise.

Audience is beginning to arrive.

We found two plugs that work. We find two lamps and plug them in. We light candles.

I can't watch it.

It's a full house, Thanksgiving weekend.

I stay in the cafe and ask Denman for a shot of Jack Daniels. He pours. I sip. He nudges his hand toward mine. He says, "aren't you supposed to throw that back?" I tell that straight edge to shut up, I'm sipping and that's the best I can do. He chuckles at me.

People come out at intermission.

People leave after the show.

I'm not doing this again.

I'm not renting "shared" space.

In fact, I don't want ANYONE touching my stuff.

My drummer friend K asks if I think the GodDesS might be trying to tell me something.

I'm not producing theatre again until I can lock the door and hold the key. When I come back, nobody better have touched my stuff either! And if the street explodes and it's my job to deal with Pepco I BETTER own the DAMN building!!

I've seen the Douglas Development signs all over the city. I've stalked properties with my polaroid. One man became very verbally confrontational after I took a photo of the building he was standing in front of. He did not want his image captured. I should have asked for his consent but I was just trying to capture the building he was sitting in front of for my HUD scrapbook of spaces I'd like to save.

I looked at the Old Wonderbread Factory, the Howard Theatre. So many spaces. I called HUD and asked about gray fields. I confronted them. They said I had a strong personality.

All of the pieces were there, but they were not for me to pick up.

SO SO SICK OF THIS SHIT!

I can see Alice standing there with her sandwich bag full of cut apples saying, "Don't you quit. Don't you dare quit."

I'M OUT!!!

[flourish: MT12]

Girls and boundaries
Two words that are never supposed to go together
Say yes
Pick up slack
Do the work
That IS the reward
They sip
In cups made on the fancy half
Of the Dixie factory
They sip
And judge
And approve
Or disapprove
Never really moving
Unless it is to leave
There it is
That slack
Just slithered out on the floor
Flatulent Ouroboros
Impotent Ouroboros
Sad little circle

PICK IT UP
Keep it goin
NO
She says, NO

That's not allowed
She can't say no
If she does say NO
We can never admit
We've heard it
Our way or
The Highway
She drives
Past cars left
On the shoulder

Deborah L. Randall

Some Storm that was
Bumper Cars on the Parkway
She flies

Screaming to herself
The lyrics of Pat Benetar
Or Joan Jett
Or someone
Maybe not
Maybe no lyrics
Maybe just screaming

Into the abyss
Home of the Ouroboros'
Endless
Belching
Pit

The slack attached
To something deep
And dark
And never ending

She screams some more
Waiting
Just waiting
For the tailpipe of her
Velcroed car
To fall away
For the hot glue holding everything together
To melt away

Instead
Her fear goes
It leaves her
That's what happens when the worst thing
Is real
No
More
Fear

Just a lot of

venus

SCREAMING
And
DRIVING
On
To what though?
She doesn't know.

The Next.

Chapter 12:
"TAKE WHAT YOU CAN USE AND THROW THE REST AWAY"
-BUD STRINGER

Objective: Create Structure (so everyone can fly)

Venus has a permanent home! It's a little storefront on a tributary street off of Main Street in Laurel, MD. The Venus Theatre Play Shack is located at 21 C Street. I came up with a brand-new, three-pronged vision for Venus. This space allows us to break off one of those pieces and launch BabyPlay. It's not the full vision so the sign won't read Venus Theatre yet. That will happen when the time is right. I think BabyPlay will be a win/win all around.

> My CV has resumed:
> BabyPlay
> Heartfriends
> Heartfriends Product
> "How She Played the Game"
> "Molly Daughter"
> Arts District Battle

Laurel Board of Trade
LADEC
An All-Female "Measure for Measure"

Mission: Follow a Path Laid By My Very Own Jane

One of my prior side-hustles was teaching for Gymboree. Jane was my boss. She had a British accent and a trusting nature.

Chip-chip-talley-ho?!?!? Who says that with any kind of professionalism? JANE! She's so perfect she has lip liner and eyeliner tattooed onto her face. She just watched me teach my training classes and I was climbing all over the equipment for the babies and she starts clapping her hands and smiling ear to ear and sing-songingly chanting as she bounces, "chip-chip-talley-ho, LOU!"

She's decided my Gymboree name will be Lou because she already has at least one Deborah and it's just easier on the paperwork to use my middle name. Probably easier to track complaints too.

I really love this job. I get to sing songs and wear socks while I work!

I decided I would take that part of my new business plan, the BabyPlay part, and bring it to C Street. That's why I padded everything and now dwell inside of a pallet of primary colors.

BabyPlay coincides well with the Heartfriends Musicals that Alan and I created. We even have a product line for Heartfriends as well as CD's for sale of all of the original music from all three shows.

Aunt Ginger came out with the whole family to see, "Juanita the Walrus Goes on a Shopping Spree"! It's incredible to have audiences filled with three and four generations all clapping and laughing and singing.

It's AMAZING!!

I LOVE THIS!!!

John Palmer Claridge was a Helen Hayes judge. Small world. He told me that even though it was for children he could still identify my writing. That was a big compliment and really encouraging.

We made it in the Style Section! That's a relief!!

The press and upper management at the Helen Hayes Awards aren't considering this real theatre work. They say it's not serious enough. When I create serious work in DC they say it's not family-friendly enough.

I don't know where to file their contradictory nature.

I've been following every rule. I'm not allowed to use the same costume or prop pieces from one show to another. It's stupid and wasteful but I'd like an audience so I'm following every rule.

I've pulled two solo shows into the space in the evening and I'm running four classes in the first part of the day.

I'm meeting with Karl Brendle in City Hall at least once a week. He's the City Planner. He encourages me to keep going.

I'm a director on the Laurel Board of Trade.

I'm a chair on the Laurel Arts District Exploratory Committee.

It's a lot to juggle…

OMG! I just performed "Molly Daughter", my solo show for one audience member and that audience member is a Helen Hayes judge. He saw Jason Miller's play, "Nobody Hears A Broken Drum" on Broadway, or off broadway. Anyway, that's the first play in the anthology and my play is the last. He sat through my entire performance and stayed to speak with me afterward. He told me it was one of the bravest things he'd ever witnessed. I'm not sure what he means.

I'm performing, "How She Played the Game" in the back of the room, but hardly anyone is coming at all. Helen Hayes Awards are telling me they'll stop sending judges because we don't have enough professional lights.

I spoke with them directly about production value before I signed on and was assured it would not be an issue. They are like some underwater creature that's constantly changing colors and patterns depending on any given environment.

I'm still me.

I don't care about them. This is fun. I'm bringing theatre into Prince George's County, the place that introduced and first taught me. This is my dream. Besides, every time I think I should quit something amazing happens.

I read about the Guerilla Girls in NYC. They print messages on Avery labels. Then they volunteer to usher for plays on Broadway. Play's that don't put many or any women on stage. At intermission they go to use the bathroom and plaster every stall with all of these specific sexist facts about the company.

They say that any woman who creates theatre should keep going. At least that's the message I'm getting and that's why I'm going to keep going.

Karl said I should go to Annapolis to represent Laurel and make the case of turning it into an Arts District so I did! I was the only person there from Laurel. I took the mic on a pitch challenge and won the room. It was so awesome! I wish someone had been there to see it.

We are going to present an all-female Measure for Measure!

Swirling hellscape.

The toilets back up after two flushes. This is a cast of 14 women. They've taken to driving to McDonalds on every break to pee. One of them is breastfeeding so I've made sure to have a microwave so she can heat things up when her husband brings her baby for feeding. I also have the rocking chair that Pappa Dave built in the basement for breastfeeding.

I love "Measure for Measure" so much. It's a great script. It says everything I can't seem to find the words for these days.

I'm costuming the whole thing to keep costs down. All of the female characters are in long gowns and veils. All of the male characters are in tights with their legs exposed.

We only have three platforms and the "All She Cares About is the Yankees" steel apparatus that Laura and Paul built. We use it. I have invited people to bring their own bottle along with a packed dinner.

I'm really proud of this show.

The levels of the platforms delineate the social strata. That's it. And, in warm ups, actors that play lower class characters cannot bring themselves to even step up onto the top platform. It's fascinating.

Someone that used to be a big support to me showed up to tell me he could have done a better job directing than I did.

Thanks?

I swear, there are swirling vats of jealousy all around me.

AHHH! We're set to open on Thursday.

I heard a sound and ran down into the basement. A pipe burst and was waterfalling through the electrical panel. Raw sewage dripped down from the ceiling into the basement over the electrical box.

I called a plumber. He brought his boss.

They told me that whoever installed the pipe installed it backwards, as if water moves uphill. So after two flushes everything backs up. Until it burst. I had to come up with over a thousand dollars to fix it. Two days before we were opening.

I called the slumlord and told him we could roll that into one and a half months rent. He said it was all my fault. He told me I had children flushing toys and clothes down the toilets.

WHAT?!?!?!

Nothing about that is true!!

He said if I don't pay the rent on time, he's changing the locks. Rent's due the day the show opens and I guess money grows on trees.

Am I back at the Sofari Sogoodi???

Alan sells some equipment and I drive over to the office early on the day of returning to black box work for the first time in years. I was expecting a celebration. Once again, shit.

The landlord's wife is at the desk in the front office. She's very kind and she says hello to me. I went to say hello back, but I just burst out sobbing. She pointed me into his office with a deeply concerned look on her face.

I walked as quickly as I could into his office and just laid the check on the corner of his desk sobbing uncontrollably. I couldn't even speak. I tried to say something but a huge sob came out of me instead of words and I left.

That fuckhead!! He's not shutting down my work.

Throughout all of this Tricia is studying herbology at Thai Sophia. She's been running NuTricia workshops in the back of the theatre.

She keeps telling me that I have a SPACE! She keeps reminding me that's the dream and I have it. She tells me I have a PhD in LIFE. I thrive outside of the box according to her.

She asks to use my actors as her guinea pigs. For her class she has to read tongues. I have no idea why. But my whole cast shows her their tongues.

We use the wall backstage as a blackboard.

One of my actors keeps threatening to call "Actors Inequity!".

We all just keep going.

Laurel decided to declare itself an Arts District and announced that publicly even though they never did fill out the form for the state.

I was so sad to get the phone call.

Jane with the makeup tattooed on her face committed suicide.

I thought there was more joy in the world. All around me, I find sadness. Except when I'm building a show. That's when I feel heaps of joy and promise.

I'm just gonna keep going.

Interestingly enough, as soon as I stopped staging Heartfriends, the DC theatre bureaucrats and the National Press (which honestly feel like the same organization) decided the main focus should be children's theatre.

What can I say?

I'm consistently ahead of my time.

[flourish: MT14]

It's like
It's like
It's like
Being birthed
It's like
Coming out
Of a dank darkness
And swirling down
Through that tunnel
That brings us

Here

Disoriented
Experiencing gravity
For the very first time
The Weight
Of
Everything

It's like
It's like
NOT
Jumping to any
Conclusions
This place is new

Give it time
Let them
Get to know
YOU

It's like
It's like

What

Deborah L. Randall

The

Ever

Lov

Ing

Hell?

Chapter 13:
UMBRELLA ERA

Objective: Understand times are changing and pay attention to the shifts

The Inaugural Fringe Festival happened in DC in 2006. I was happy to be the MC of the opening party and Monalisa played guitar. A huge shift hung in the air.

There was a $700 fee to participate. This fee included performance space for five performances, box office, and marketing. For more money, it was possible to purchase more marketing.

Inaugural Fringe: I MC'd the roll out, produced a different solo play on all five different performance nights. Including, "Molly Daughter"

Second Fringe: Collaborated with Alan and Monalisa to create a Rock Opera riff on "Lysistrata" called, "Lysistration".

I was told how much money Venus could make by the person in charge. If the extra marketing package was purchased, I could sell out every show. There were 40 seats (max, de-

205

pending on the space), $20 a seat. That's $800 potential five times. That's $4,000 Venus could make!

Most spaces had no air conditioning.

I gently explained that the cost to participate would add up to over $4,000 for only five performances. This was very different from the 16 show requirement of the Helen Hayes Awards.

There were nine people in the cast who needed to be paid. If I paid them only $200 each, that would be $1,800. The remaining $2,200 minus the initial $1,000 investment becomes $1,200. This total would need to cover the cost of the musical director, stage director, costume designer, costumes, prop designer, props, sound designer, sound equipment rental, set designer, set pieces, lighting designer, travel, and parking. Although the lighting board was preset, that design would be "provided" in the one tech rehearsal offered.

Also, with only 15 minutes to load in and out I would need a tight crew on the Venus side. That's how the "tech bucket" came to be for "Lysistration". Every single person on the project would have a job. A full sound system and drum kit and stage design would be loaded in and struck each night within 15 minutes. Often the performance before ours ran over and tapped into our set up time. Especially when it was an amateur operation. We'd see them shaking hands with friends in the house when they should have been loading out. Actors need their egos. Sometimes, it's a grueling thing to behold.

I explained to the person in charge that the best case scenario would be a break-even.

I puzzled over why, much like with V-Day, all of the artists were expected to work for free so the producer could scoop up the money?

I had entered the "Umbrella Era". Perhaps the warning was symbolically embedded in the staging of "A Winter's Tale" years earlier.

Corporate thinking entered and revealed itself as a beautiful umbrella that would keep the vulnerable safe from the elements.

Sometimes I sit in my back garden just as the storm begins to roll in and I watch my Gerber Daisies bend in the wind. I marvel at how strong that makes them.

Now that everything can be done online, most especially at the box office, the money is tracked electronically and optimized. Every performance in the festival seemed to be about generating money. None of the work was juried or curated.

The Fringe Festival in DC was an umbrella for theatre makers that would take away the nasty numbers work and allow them to create freely. The Helen Hayes Awards would divide themselves into two tiers, separating the significant theatres from the insignificant ones. That is to say, the theatres with big budgets from the theatres with small budgets. There would even be a Women's Theatre Festival that would boast a budget of a half a million dollars and feature on the cover of American Theatre Magazine.

All of this fell under its own umbrella called "progress".

Only each one seemed ill-advised and uninformed. Each one seemed like a census box being checked so that "WOMEN" would sit down and shut up or "SMALL THEATRES" would be given a place no matter their level of work so they could be ignored. It felt like we were nuisance children with alcoholic parents. Like we had to tiptoe around them, become codependent with them, and hope they still loved us after they tried to destroy us. It felt so familiar to me.

The overall message as a woman and as a small theatre was the same. "Here's your present, aren't you so grateful? Now sit down and shut up."

Still, I thought for certain that there were lessons to be learned here. That there must surely be so much I didn't know yet. Larger budgeted theatres were staring me right in the face, there must be something that I had not yet understood.

Hm.

I decided to stay open to the lessons.

Mission: You Already Know What You're Doing. DON'T STOP!

Being at Fringe is exciting because there's a big tent on New York Avenue where everyone drinks and watches cabaret performances. Yes, we ARE back at the Warehouse but it's not my problem if the lights go out or the ceiling leaks anymore. This is a huge relief and I still very much feel like I'm at home in the cafe.

At the same time, I get to rehearse in MY OWN ROOM!!!

"Lysistration" is allowing Alan and I to play so much. Monalisa and Jeni and Tim and Ellie are in it along with a handful of my other actors. It was so much fun reading this at the Kennedy Center for page-to-stage.

Gregg said we had to sound check with him. He had to be sure our song, "Rat Shit" did not disrupt "Shear Madness". That's always gonna make me laugh. He told me he wanted my work to sink into the fibers of the carpets there.

Ever since my orgasm pill monologue I've felt oddly joyful and at home at the Kennedy Center. I feel like it was built for me and for my work.

I had to go through some incest recovery when a memory came back to me about my Father. I've written it into "Lysistration". Monalisa has taken my words and put music to them. She sings this song so beautifully. It's called, "Home". I'm just throwing incest out there.

During curtain call the other night when we were singing our song, "Love Anyway" (screwed and frayed? Love anyway.), we were back on the Warehouse stage and all of these women in the audience stood up and danced and sang with us. I was completely transformed. It's the same stage as "Daughters of Molly Maguire", the same stage as "A Little Rebellion Now", and I'm completely transformed AGAIN on this stage.

So many years have gone by. So much has happened. It's all a blur.

Lysistration was an opportunity for me to flip the script again. I took permission and did just that. The investigation of the lysistration inversion provided an effective device. I was able to write about the aftermath. Men just waiting for a bus suddenly poked with the inversion device. That meant anytime moving forward that they began to have an erection it would invert and impale them. I thought I was making an obvious point. Once a woman is violated she has to deal with it for the rest of her life. So, I flipped the script and made that the case for the men in my world.

One audience member absolutely lost it. He was enraged. He called me a man-hater. He couldn't see that I was holding up a mirror.

That's how I knew the play worked.

My board has nudged me to agree with them that Venus should participate in the Women's Voices Festival.

I'm told it would just be wrong for a Women's Theatre Festival to exist and not have Venus be a part of it. By now, the developers have completely taken over DC. By now, the Fringe Festival owns buildings.

Bricks and mortar are not theatre. People are theatre. At least that's the advice I was given at the Women's Museum of Art that fateful night when I decided to begin this journey.

We are producing two plays in the WFV. We have already produced FIFTY plays that empower women!

It will be good to see what a half a million dollars can do in the way of marketing.

THE BIG SEVEN are featured. These are the "real" theatres in DC. Arena Stage, Signature Theatre, Shakespeare Theatre, Woolly Mammoth, Ford's Theatre, and two others. Anyway, there's only one female artistic director in the BIG SEVEN line up.

We go to the meetings. We are essentially laughed at. Some angry little man in a bowtie who works at Ford's Theatre snaps at me when

I make a suggestion. He asks me what I think I'm going to do with HIS money. At the Shakespeare Theatre a director tells all of us about Suffrage Plays and that we should be producing them. (ya think? I wonder why the Shakespeare Theatre hasn't been producing them. A little Edwardian Comedy could really spice up their season, if you ask me. Which, by the way, NO ONE did.)I cannot count how many Suffrage plays I'd already done at this point.

Carolyn Gage in the lobby of Venus Theatre holding her award

In conjunction with our 50th play having been produced, we thought it wise to create the Venus Theatre Lifetime Achievement Award.

Carolyn Gage received the first award. In her acceptance speech she turned the tables and thanked me. I never expected to be compared to Eva La Gallienne, Henrietta Vinton Davis, or Minnie Maddern Fiske. Carolyn pointed out that before "Carousel" was a musical it was a drama called, "Liliom". The lead was played by 23 year-old Eva La Gallienne. She was so traumatized after performing the role on Broadway that she was institutionalized. This makes the point of embedded misogyny and blatant sexism in our field. Carolyn ended her acceptance by saying, "Wherever Deb Randall sits, that's the head of the table."

[jawdrop!]

This is something that is still very difficult to take in because I know there are, and HAVE BEEN, many women doing this work who have, like me, been largely ignored.

The Women's Theatre Festival is happening and there are various lectures. I'm not invited to speak. I ask them about it and they say I am welcome to attend just like everyone else. I tell them I should have been invited to be on the panel. They disregard me.

Our production is one of only two to launch the festival but they have buried us at the bottom of their website. I ask about this and am told it's alphabetical, there's nothing anyone can do.

On one of the lecture stages, one of the men claiming to be expert at this declares that plays by women are not being produced because they are not being written. I'm seeing this peripherally on Twitter.

I can't believe what I'm reading.

He then goes on to say, there's no "pipeline" for women's plays.

Now, I'm livid.

How lazy. How incompetent. How ABSOLUTELY ASININE!

Women don't work in pipelines, ya nidgit!!!

Women have been writing plays at least as long as men have and anyone who calls themself a professional should be able to get their hands on scripts written by women.

I did!

Even if they are out-of-print, they can be found.

What an entire ASSHOLE!

There's a surprise. At first I'm invited. But then, I'm disinvited. ONLY playwrights.

Except the AD of Arena is allowed. She sits on a stool center stage. A staging that says she's the savior that has done all of this work to solve the woman-problem in the world of theatre.

Okay.

We're at the Wharf now. One of my playwrights has flown in from Tennessee to be here for this. I picked her up at the airport and dropped her off at the front door of Arena Stage. My other playwright has driven in from Baltimore.

I drive over to the fish market and park and watch the construction while they gather inside across the street.

I remember waiting tables at Philip's Flagship. It's now leveled. Completely gone. As if we never hustled our asses off waiting on everyone from teenage drug dealers to Oprah.

There's so much equipment. So much construction. It's quite a sight to take in.

My playwright texts me so I drive over to pick her up.

It was a photoshoot.

A big surprise. They are all going to be on the cover of American Theatre Magazine.

Huh.

Okay.

Good for them.

This is not my festival.

One of my board members goes to a meeting and they ask if she's the one with the boutique in the lobby. I've boasted about inviting women artisans in to sell their wares in our lobby. They are laughing at this as it is just so far beneath them. Very smug. I bet that bowtie yippy-man wears a pashmina.

She tells them, no. She's not me. She then tells them that she WORKS for me. Interesting phraseology. They shut up.

The big rollout party is happening at the National Museum for Women In The Arts. The very location Venus was greenlit by a room full of GodDesSes I respected more than just about anyone. It seems like incredible serendipity. We are told to wear "festival-attire".

Laura Matteoni Schraven and me in festival-attire

Laura, the board member who "works" for me is my date, and Alan is showing up later after he gets off work. A couple of our actors are attending as well.

I'm wearing a corset and a fascinator.

It feels like everyone else is wearing polo shirts. Not very festive.

Nelson Pressley is here from the Washington Post. He's written a piece on women in theatre and sent out their best photographer to do a shoot with me. They put me on the cover of the Style section to say that women's theatres have been left in the dark.

Irony abounds.

Life and theatre both exist in tension.

Standing next to Nelson is another Artistic Director. He and one of the BIG SEVEN artistic directors will both be chased out of town in the years ahead because of accusations of sexual assaults and overall inappropriate actions.

The important people take the stage. They are all older, mostly gay white men, with the exception of two women, one AD and her assistant.

OH!

One of the men is having a birthday. There is cake and singing and we are focused on HIM.

As they speak one by one representing the BIG SEVEN on the little platform stage, mostly congratulating themselves for the wonderful thing they've done here, people begin drifting over to me as I stand in the back.

They are upset.

I'm not sure why.

They say things like, "why aren't you up there?", "You've BEEN doing this". Molly from the Warehouse comes up to tell me she's about to snag the microphone away from them and hand it to me. I can see her pure intention and pull her back and ask her not to. I wish I could count how many Cafe paninis and noodles she's served me over the years of making the impossible happen in some nook or cranny of her building.

Alan went home early and I took Laura to Ben's Chili Bowl for the first time. We had a blast.

I sent communications to two of the AD's just to do some damage control.

One was the woman, the other was the birthday boy. I let them know who I am and what I've done. I explained to them that people are asking me questions that I cannot answer. They want to know why my work has not even been mentioned. They want to know why I've been excluded and I honestly don't know what to tell them.

The birthday boy is loving and kind and says he meant no harm or disrespect. He sends lots of love and encouraging words.

The female AD snaps at me and gives me a lecture. She asks me if I've picked up the brochures from her lobby and whether I've done my due diligence of passing them out.

This PISSES ME OFF.

I wrote her back immediately.

I tell her that printed advertising like that only has about a 2% effectiveness rate. I tell her, unlike her, I do not have a staff that can just run around and pick up things for me because ALL of our budget goes to artists, rent, and production.

I don't know why people think they can bully me.

OH!!

SEE!!

I used to think I was always catching up to what I'd missed due to my ridiculous childhood. But now, I see that growth is a choice and there are people I hold in the highest regard who are now actively doing everything they can to erase me.

They must think I'm an idiot.

We are in the final week of the second show and Missy who cuts hair a few doors down tells me she's got a couple of boxes for me that FedEx dropped off.

The Asshole-Supreme has sent us TWO CASES of brochures for the final week of production. Laura decides to carpet our display window with them.

FOCUS!

I wanted to see what a half-million dollar budget could do. I'm told they spent half of that budget on the rollout event. ONE NIGHT. ONE QUARTER OF A MILLION DOLLARS!!

Holy shit and HAPPY BIRTHDAY!

Wow, did they let us EAT CAKE!

They say the other half is in-kind donations. Or some such thing.

It was interesting to see how people I'd never met before in my life were visibly upset on my behalf.

It's interesting for me to note how acclimated I have become to being treated like my life's work has added up to nothing.

I'm interviewed by various online publications. I can't even remember the names of most of them.

I tell them simply, watch.

Watch to see what the BIG SEVEN produce in the years ahead. You'll see for yourself whether this was a real shift, or a grab for money and attention on the backs of women.

Just watch and see how many female playwrights they produce in their seasons to follow this or if they will simply have another highly funded "FESTIBAL!" to check off whatever boxes need checking on their patriarchal white privilege consensus form.

It was amazing to see the show that Arena Stage produced immediately after the festival. One of the very examples Carolyn indicated in her speech.

"Carnival".

"When he hit me it felt like a kiss!"

I see this clearly.

I wonder if anyone else does.

[flourish: MT15]

Contemplating the elements
The air blew through
In its passing
It lifted the lacy edge
Of a tablecloth

Wanting to escape
Into a torrid love affair
With the air
She was trapped
In her location

Normally folded and flung
Into a linen closet
Lovely
Cedar
This was her day to be free

As the air blew through her
She felt alive
Finally
Flung open and free
Excepting

Excepting the weight
That had been put upon her
She knew she was
Utilitarian
But she had beauty too

Just for the sake of it
Beauty
Blowing through
Lifting the edges of her UP
Into the elation of what could be

Laughter surrounded her

Play
Objects flew by
And that kite just kept going UP
She yearned to be an object

Freed by the flow
Of life
Just
Flying
UP

If it had just been one thing
Holding her down
Maybe then
She could have understood
Her calling

She was nothing less
Then expansive
In the sunlight
In the breeze
Liberating her entrapment

Wanting to
Liberate
The things that held her down
Were there for a reason
Mostly

There was the awkward thing
Also new
Always the awkward seemed to be new
And the familiar thing
Rigid and predictable

So much glass
Porcelain
Heirlooms
In
Waiting

She had purpose

Utilitarian purpose
Largely she made it all seem
Beautiful
And soft

Billowy and free
She laid over unfinished wood
Unhewn
Saw horses that could no longer be
Used

Put out to pasture
At the Sunday family picnic
Where it was okay
When they rocked
Neither plumb nor level
Utilitarian
She tickled their surfaces
Lit them up with joy
Retired now they could
Laugh and
Rest

She, however
Waited all week for
Her time to sophisticate
The unwashed
Family

Still playing
They hardly noticed her
Still
The breeze came and lifted
The edges of her

Telling her
She was exactly where she belonged
Reminding her
She could be lifted
She could fly

New touches tapped on her
Not heavy

Deborah L. Randall

Colorful leaves
So she knew
Her time was running out

She'd be in that dark place again
For a season or two
Taking the place of the
Green and red
Embroidery in the linen nook

To be fair,
Green and Red waited longest
And were only used a few times
Each year
At best

She should be grateful
She is advantaged
Adored
Assumed, yes
But present also

It was never enough with that one.

Chapter 14:
FOCUS!

Objective: REALLY Discover What You Can Do With A Little Bit of Money and A Room Of One's Own

After staging an all female "Measure for Measure" I began to take submissions for new plays.

With a consistent roof over our head we could now stage four full productions each year.

One Jimmy-lifetime would include 16 new scripts.

This new count began in 2009. It does not include roughly 40 scripts that had been workshopped, read and performed through Venus Envy and the years of Venus Theatre Company before moving into the Venus Theatre Play Shack. It doesn't include summer camps or empowerment workshops. So, it's been a little difficult to add it all up.

The math is solid moving forward. It's going to be a lot easier to count with a room of our own.

The schedule works!

First Jimmy-lifetime producing new full length works at the Venus Theatre Play Shack:

2009 - **Retro-Classic Series**
1. "not such stuff" by chris wind
2. "Homokay's Medea" by Julianne Homokay
3. "Why'd Ya Make Me Wear This, Joe?" by Vanda
4. "Helen of Sparta" by Jacob M. Appel

2010 - **Guest Directors**
5. "Zelda at the Oasis" by Pat Lin
6. "In the Goldfish Bowl" by Kay Rhoads
7. A Haunted Tour of Laurel in conjunction with the Laurel Museum
8. "Play Nice!" by Robin Rice Lichtig
9. "Looking for the Pony" by Andrea Lepcio

2011 - **Guests and Tours**
10. "The Last Reading of Charlotte Cushman" by Carolyn Gage
11. "Hypnotic Murderess" Steven Levingston
12. "Lou" by John Carter
13. "Hitchcock After Dark" An immersive choreographed haunted river hike
14. "The Stenographer" by Zoe Mavroudi

2012 - **BOLD HOPE**
15. "A Girl Named Destiny" by Rand Higbee
16. "Punk Rock Mom" by Allyson Mead
17. "Devil Dog Six" by Fengar Gael
18. "Claudie Hukill" by Sean O'Leary

Kennedy Center Page-to-Stage Reading participants:
"Lysistration" by Deborah Randall
"Another Manhattan" by Claudia Barnett
"Devil Dog Six" by Fengar Gael
"Claudie Hukill" by Sean O'Leary

<u>2012</u>
UMBC - Alumna of the Year 2012
The City of Laurel - Proclamation from the Mayor and the City Council that November is declared Venus Theatre Month in the City of Laurel until the year 2020

Second Jimmy-lifetime producing new full length works at the Venus Theatre Play Shack:

   2013 - **Lucky Thirteen**
     19. "Following Sarah" by Rich Espey
     20. "Grieving for Genevieve" by Kathleen Warnock
     21. "Gift of Forgotten Tongue" by Fengar Gael
     22. "No. 731 degraw-street, Brooklyn, or Emily Dickinson's Sister" by Claudia Barnett

   2014 - **Fierce Fourteen**
     23. "Ding, or Bye Bye Dad" by Jayme Kilburn
     24. "Light of Night" by Cecilia Copeland
     25. "We are Samurai" by Daria Marinelli
     26. "Virus Attacks Heart" by Shannon Murdoch

   2015 - **Feral Fifteen; Feminist Fables**
     27. "God Don' Like Ugly" by Doc Anderson Bloomfeld
     28. "Dry Bones Rising" by Cecila Raker
     29. "Witches Vanish" by Claudia Barnett
     30. "Raw" by Amy Bernstein

   2016 - **Sweet Sixteen; Groovy Young Things**
     31. "Fur" by Migdalia Cruz
     32. "Garbage Kids" by Jayme Kilburn
     33. "Rock the Line" by Kathleen Warnock
     34. "Soft Revolution: Shafana and Aunt Sarrinah" by Alana Valentine

Kennedy Center Page-to-Stage Reading participants:
   -"Witches Vanish" by Claudia Barnett
   -"Rock the Line" by Kathleen Warnock

Participated in the Women's Theatre Festival:
   -"Witches Vanish" by Claudia Barnett
   -"Raw" by Amy Berstein

Venus Celebrates 50 productions
Venus Gifts First LIfetime Achievement Award to Carolyn Gage

Third Jimmy-lifetime producing new full length works at the Venus Theatre Play Shack:

2017 - **To a T!; Love Notes To a Friend**
    35. "A Collection of Suffrage Plays" by various Edwardian playwrights
    36. "Tunnel Vision" by Andrea Lepcio
    37. "Aglaonike's Tiger" by Claudia Barnett
    38. "The Ravens" by Alana Valentine

2018 - **Grief**
    39. "Living and Dying with Tricia McCauley" by Deborah Randall
    40. "The Speed Twins" by Maureen Chadwick
    41. "This Little Light" by Jennifer Faletto
    42. "Running on Glass" by Cynthia Cooper

2019 - **The Final Season on C Street in Laurel, MD**
    43. "Jane App" by Deborah Randall
    44. "#solestories" by Renee Calarco
    45. "The Finger" by Doruntina Basha
    46. "The Powers That Be" a Rock Opera by Deborah Randall and Alan Scott

2020 - **PANDEMIC STRIKES**
    Landlord attempts to raise rent by 20%
    The world feels very dangerous
    Theatre is now on a two-dimensional world stage playing out the terrible scripts of misogynists and fascists

Kennedy Center Page-to-Stage Reading participants:
    -"The Ravens" by Alana Valentine
    -Special guests in from NYC with Vanda
    -"Living and Dying with Tricia McCauley" by Deborah Randall
    -"The Speed Twins" by Maureen Chadwick
    -"This LIttle Light" by Jennifer Faletto
    -"The Powers That Be" by Deborah Randall and Alan Scott

Part Four

Chapter 15:
FIRST JLT IN THE HOUSE-THAT-LOVE-BUILT

First Jimmy Lifetime

2009 - Retro-Classic Series

"not such stuff" by chris wind | direction Deborah Randall |costumes Brittany Graham| cast Ophelia played by Julia Heynen| Portia played by Carol Vandegrift| Kate played by Heather Whitpan|Miranda played by Tiffany Garfinkle|Juliette played by Angela McLaughlin|Lady Mac played by Chameeka Joy Bradley|Regan played by Tina Renay-Fulp|Marina played by Lisa Hill Corley|

"Homokay's Medea" by Julianne Homokay|direction Deborah Randall|costumes Brittany Graham|set design Joseph Musumeci|carpentry Matt Kulp and Stephen Webb|set painting Ali Daniels| cast Medea played by Toni Rae Brotons|Jason played by Christopher Mancusi|ensemble Bethany Corey-Ekin, Dane Peterson, Jessica Preece, Rebecca Herron, Carol Vandegrift, Phil Amico, and Michael Burgtorf|

"Why'd Ya Make Me Wear This, Joe?" by Vanda|direction Deborah Randall|costumes Brittany Graham|stage management Deborah Randall|running crew Christine Stein Lively| cast Charlie played by Brittany Graham|Aubra played by Allison Harkey|Philip played by

Dane Peterson|Joe played by Christopher Herring|Emily played by Georgia Mae Lively|Grandma played by Janie Richards|

"Helen of Sparta" by Jacob M. Appel| direction Deborah Randall|-fight choreography Christian Sullivan|set painting Alli Daniels|costumes Brittany Graham|cast Helen played by Julia Heynen|Menelaus played by Christian Sullivan|Paris played by D. Grant Cloyd|Cassandra played by Rebecca Herron|ensemble Ellie Nicoll, Phil Amico, and Mary Burke-Hueffmeier|

"We are such stuff as dreams are made on..." Shakespearean anthology purchased at a card shop while I was not doing theatre, but still dreaming of it. Later used in this image as a promo for an all female M4M.

The Retro-Classic year was an opportunity to bend the cannon. It was such an adventure to romp through what maybe used to be viewed as rigid and turn the expected on its head. "not such stuff" was breath-takingly gorgeous and that was in large part due to the character work of the actors on that very simple stage. The simplicity and discipline of the writing coupled with character executions that took my breath away every night. "Homokay's Medea" was a large cast for the space but the actors worked brilliantly together. At the time Julianne Homokay was working as a writer on the Craig Ferguson show and it was so wonderful to explore her LA humor. Vanda brought us,"Joe". What an incredible exploration that was. Another brave cast doing powerful stagework. By the time we produced "Helen of Sparta" at the end of the year I'd been completely liberated in my staging thanks to the designers and actors slamming it out of the park all year long. I remember waking Alan up in the middle of the night because I was laughing so hard in my sleep dreaming about rehearsal that night. Lots of energy in our little space. And lots of friends showing up to help us land each project.

Christian Sullivan and Julia Heynan
C. Stanley Photography

This was such a powerful season.

Jeri Marshall
C. Stanley Photography

2010 - Guest Directors

"Zelda at the Oasis" by Pat Lin| direction Lynn Sharp Spears|set, costumes, lights, and painting Lynn Sharp Spears|stage management John Nunemaker|cast Zelda Fitzgerald played by Mundy Spears| F. Scott Fitzgerald by Davis Hasty|

"In the Goldfish Bowl" by Kay Rhoads|direction Deborah Randall|set Joseph Musumeci|construction Matt Kulp| fight choreography Christian Sullivan|lights John Nunemaker|stage management John Nunemaker|costumes Brittany Graham|cast Phyllis Penn played by Allyson Harkey|Sylvia Washington played by Jeri Marshall|Cherry Pie Muldoon played by Lauren Uberman|Shawna Devine played by Maya Jackson|

"Play Nice!" by Robin Rice Lichtig|direction Lee Mikeska Gardner| set Joseph Musumeci|lights Kristin A. Thompson|sound Neil McFadden|costumes Marilyn Johnson|cast Isabelle Diamond played by Kelsey Painter|Matilda Diamond played by Robin Covington|Joanie Calliope played by Nayab Hussain|Luce Diamond played by Jay Saunders|

"Looking for the Pony" by Andrea Lepcio|direction Catherine Tripp| set Catherine Tripp|costumes Brittany Graham|original musical score Lucas Lechowski|cast Oisie played by Rose McConnell|Lauren played by Rebecca Herron|ensemble Louise Schlegel Wood and D. Grant Cloyd|

Kelsey Painter
Darla Photography

Much like the Bad Girls III Festival, I was advised to bring in more directors and so I did. The benefit was the same. So much more texture and diversity in styles and approaches.

For my part, "In the Goldfish Bowl" was a glorious challenge. The actors were so well cast and deeply committed.

One of my favorite performances on any of my stages over the decades was Jeri Marshall's portrayal of Sylvia Washington. Sylvia was a woman sitting on death row guilty of murdering her baby. The way that Kay penned that character coupled with the way Jeri played her was absolutely crushingly dynamic.

It's performances like that that make me feel bad for not being more successful at getting the work of Venus into the mainstream. Because nothing could touch her performance in that production as far as I'm concerned. I'd put it up against anything anywhere. All of the actors in that show were stunning. But, Jeri shook me to my core every single night.

Our choreographer Maria Cotto, came on board and created "Hitchcock After Dark". She had dancers placed throughout the river path in River Park which is half a block away from the space. Each young dancer represented a character that had been killed in a Hitchcock film. Our concept was to bring them all back from the dead at once to haunt one collective leading man who happened to be the tour guide. We played "The Birds" by an open fire with hot cider down in the pavilions in the park by the parking lot.

Hitchcock After Dark Ensemble
Maria Cotto, choreographer

2011 - Guests and Tours

"The Last Reading of Charlotte Cushman" by Carolyn Gage|direction and performance Karen Shields|

"Hypnotic Murderess" by Steven Levingston | direction Deborah Randall|performance Kelsey Painter|

"Lou" by John Carter|direction Deborah Randall|performance Kathryn Kelly|

"Hitchcock After Dark" An immersive choreographed haunted river hike concept Deborah Randall and Maria Cotto|choreography Maria Cotto| dance ensemble Maria Cotto, Abigail Yaffe, Taylor Lipka, Maria Kelly, and Erika LaMere|pedestrian ensemble Amy Rhodes and her children, Mary Burke-Hueffiemeir and her children|

"The Stenographer" by Zoe Mavroudi direction Deborah Randall|set and lights Amy Rhodes|costumes Marilyn Johnson|props Deborah Randall|cast the Professor played by Frank Britton| the Girl played by Amy Rhodes|

Ann Fraistat
Curtis Jordan Photography

2012 - BOLD HOPE

"A Girl Named Destiny" by Rand Higbee|direction Deborah Randall|stage management Thomas Johnson|set Amy Rhodes| lights Kristin A. Thompson|sound Neil McFadden|costumes Marilyn Johnson|props Deborah Randall|graphic design Laura Schraven|fight choreography Christian Sullivan|sketch artistry Alexander Gevshanow| cast ensemble Ann Fraistat and D. Grant Cloyd|

"Punk Rock Mom" by Allyson Mead|direction Deborah Randall|assistant direction Jaki Demerest|stage management Melynda Burdette|front-of-house Mary Burke-Hueffmeier|costumes Marilyn Johnson|lights and set Amy Rhodes|sound Neil McFadden|props Deborah Randall|graphic design Laura Matteoni Schraven| cast Jamie played by Deborah Randall|Joan played by Ann Fraistat|Aster played by Queen Suyat|ensemble Alex Zavistovich, James Waters, and Chris Williams|

"Devil Dog Six" by Fengar Gael|direction Deborah Randall| front-of-house Mary Burke-Hueffmeier|costumes Marilyn Johnson|props Deborah Randall| lights Kristin A. Thompson|set Amy Rhodes|sound Neil McFadden|choreography Maria Cotto|graphic design Laura Matteoni Schraven| cast Devon Traymore played by Kelsey Painter|ensemble Deborah Randall, Alex Zavistovich, Matthew Marcus, Andi Dema, and Jason Glass|

"Claudie Hukill" by Sean O'Leary|direction Deborah Randall| front-of-house Mary Burke-Hueffmeier|costumes Marilyn Johnson|props Deborah Randall| lights Kristin A. Thompson|set Amy Rhodes|sound Neil McFadden|graphic design Laura Matteoni Schraven| cast Pearl played by Alyssa Sanders|Clara played by Harlie Sponaugle|Tierney played by Katie Zelonka| Kit played by Rebecca Korn| Sam played by Rick Coleman| Rob played by Chris Williams|

Me playing Punk Rock Mom
Curtis Jordan Photography

Jaki Demerest was the AD for "Punk Rock Mom". A series of events and circumstances led to me jumping back on stage after a decades-long sabbatical. I'd been so worried about creating opportunities for other women actors I'd almost forgotten that I myself am a woman actor.

Ann was cast to play my daughter. After that, we'd be bonded in everything moving forward.

OH!

I've found home. I love this. I love acting so much. I love building this woman, I love the music, I love the cast, I am entirely living in love and joy and floating on clouds.

I mean, I'm still directing and it's still a lot of work, but I really love this cast and this project.

My dream has come true.

The reviews raved. That did feel good because although I'd done about eight solo shows, it had been about a decade since I shared the stage with other actors. Now we are being covered by online reviewers. The upside to that was being able to get pull quotes and exposure from the comfort of my desk at home.

Next up was Fengar's play. She'd crafted a play that featured race horses. It was an out-of-body coming of age show. I jumped on stage again. In the process, we took a lot of field trips to the race track. It was about a mile away. We met a jockey and took tours. It was completely immersive.

The sound design, the lights, the stage! Everything about this project was exceptional. At the time, Randy Kroop had her little generation-old boot factory across the street. This was the second time she contributed hand made boots to the costume design. The first was the all-female "Measure for Measure".

In Fen's play, Maria has us galloping as the horses we clearly are. I was joking with Neil that there was a live sound design on stage being made by our feet and also his sound design. He told me that was an accurate assessment.

Kelsey Painter and Matthew Marcus
Curtis Jordan Photography

I walked into a tack shop on Main Street. I told the owner working there that someone is choreographed to ride me like a horse. I explained that I needed a girth and some stirrups. Without blinking he pointed over to a box of 'this-n-that's' on the floor and said, "You should be able to find some things in there." Clearly, this happens more often than anyone would suspect.

venus

I do find all of the parts I need.

He stitched the whole thing together on the spot. At rehearsal that night I was saddled up and figuring out how to not separate internal organs with this thing. This is before I learned about myofascial tissue. Tissue I was clearly abusing for this production.

I join Matthew Marcus, Kelsey Painter, and Alex Zavistovich in a race horse ensemble.
Curtis Jordan Photography

There were only two women in the show, and four men. This is the only time I've ever had more men on stage than women. It suits the racetrack culture and makes a valid point.

At the end of the play, the horse I play, Crown Ruby, wins the race. The play is titled, "Devil Dog Six". Originally, Devil Dog won the race. But in a developmental reading in NYC two women asked Fen why the female horse didn't win. And she went back and changed the ending.

We ended this first Jimmy-life in our very own space with Sean O'Leary's play. By this time I had been vying to turn our part of Laurel into an Arts District. I was chair of the Laurel Arts District Exploratory Committee. And I'd been a director on the Board of Trade too.

None of it panned out well. I assume people understand the value of theatre when clearly people DO NOT understand the value of theatre. They just want to know if I can get them free tickets to the musical national tour coming through town. People!

The City of Laurel is using us to attract developers. It's the same thing that happened in DC. The theatres attract the developers and then the developers price the theatres all the way out of the area.

Still, I'm in my glory. All we ever have is the moment at hand and I'm loving it.

Sean's play meant getting another child actor on stage, which felt good. I want girls to know there are many diverse ways of producing theatre. This is a play about a coal town losing its beloved to a dam break. It's moving and it's powerful.

It's also a little cursed.

We have just come out of a racetrack play where the dressing rooms smelled like Tiger Balm at any given minute. We had a solid half hour dancing warmup led by one of my actors who was from the middle east. It involved laying on the floor and pounding it with our hands and clapping in the air and jumping around to lovely music.

Not a single injury during "Devil Dog Six". I was so afraid of injury during that very physically demanding show.

Now, doing a living room drama, all hell's breaking loose. My oldest actor fell down the steps. I had to borrow a zero-gravity chair from the acupuncturist next to the Meat Market. Geez. Our first ever incident report. The entire back wall of the set collapsed too. I was sitting in the lobby and just heard the crashing. The stage manager L stuck their head out of the booth and gave me a long and piercing stare. That's when I heard all of the crashing. The only way backstage was to go outside and around the building. I'd have to run around back. Run I did! I burst out through the front door and ran around the building, because that's the only way to get backstage. There was a singular actor left onstage, Katie, and things had not stopped crashing once I opened the back door. Plates and dishes and kitchen objects were twisting and tumbling down over three shelves, glass pitchers were falling off and pouring into the power strips. Next up in the staging, Katie was supposed to come into the kitchen that had just crumbled and bring out a snack to be consumed on stage. Everything is covered in shards of glass by the time she starts to make her cross. I couldn't believe she was making her cross and not running off of the stage to get in her car and drive home never to be seen by us again. There were broken plates well into the vom. This was backstage but unmasked, so it was visible from the far side of the ally audience. Audience on that side were watching the destruction. But the people on the red couch side could only hear it happening behind and beside them.

Surround sound.

Katie Zelonka
Curtis Jordan Photography

I was texting Amy from backstage telling her we were in crisis. She was in Baltimore, I don't know what I was thinking. I grabbed the Little Debbie sealed snacks and opened one and put it on a clean glass-shard-free plate. Katie made her way down the vom, eyes glazed over. She didn't see me right away. Her wheels were turning wondering what to do next. I whisper. Her now UFO-sized doe eyes catch my gaze.

"Take this!"

She does.

The play goes on as I SILENTLY pick up and sweep the area so none of my actors get hurt.

We are given a lot of awards by online sites for a lot of these productions.

Suddenly, the work is being covered and winning awards. But, it's assumed that we are a start up. That we are another Company that grew out of a Fringe festival. I was producing festivals before Fringe was even a glimmer in its Daddy's DC eyes. It's puzzling.

It felt like parts of reality suddenly just disappeared. On the one hand, yay! Theatre seems to be happening everywhere now, or almost everywhere. That's a dream come true. On the other hand, do I play along and pretend I'm younger and less experienced than I am? My silence is beginning to feel like consent.

I watch the pendulum swing through me, nearly giving me a concussion. I can only be glad to still be standing.

The good news was all of the press attention we were getting from online reviewers. At first I was resistant. I had no idea I'd develop relationships with the reviewers who took the time to come out and cover us. It changed everything. I, and Venus, owe a debt of gratitude toward all of those revieweres. Joel Markowitz, with DC Metro Theatre Arts, told me every single time we announced another production how valuable my work was. How it was unmatched. He brought in Amanda Gunther who later went on to start her own online presence site, TheatreBloom. Lorraine Trainer steered the helm of DC Theatre Scene. At the Laurel Leader Melanie Dzwonchyk watched and reported on all of our decisions with writers such as Patti Restivo, Katie V. Jones, and Gwendolyn Glenn. Gwendolyn won a national literary award for her coverage of, "In the Goldfish Bowl".

Suddenly, I came to understand that the reversal of things in the industry came with opportunity. As the newspapers were losing ground and becoming syndicated, that meant that the Baltimore Sun was now picking up stories from the Laurel Leader.

Without these critics and their coverage, we would have stayed stuck in the white collar controlling grasp of hierarchical privilege. In other words, we would have been entirely ignored. It is the passion of these believers in new works, believers in the black box, believers in the work of women that created our longevity. Without them It absolutely could not have happened and we at Venus love and adore them all forever.

Another incredible thing happened. I was awarded an Alumni of the Year Award for Visual and Performing Arts at UMBC. This was so significant to me because I almost didn't finish my course of study due to financing. I had to laugh knowing there's no way I'd be able to afford to go there now.

As part of this award I had the great privilege to dine with Freeman Hrabowski in the top floor of the library surrounded by windows that overlooked the lights of Baltimore.

We had great conversations that night. He looked at me and told me I was "impressive".

It was a lot to hear from a Civil Rights icon. It was a lot to take in.

Then he gave us a tour upstairs and we looked down on the campus. Half-joking he said they needed more than blue lights on campus at night. I didn't know what he meant. He explained that the blue lights were "rape" lights. They were emergency lights where women could go and pick up a phone if they were being assaulted or just didn't feel safe.

While I appreciated everything, this shook me up a little. It left me wishing I had more or better words. I was happy to be included with the entrepreneurs and give a class talk. Happy to revisit the newly renovated theatre rooms and spaces. Gone was the grunge of the 90's. What's that German saying about grunge holding art together?

Chapter 16:
SECOND JLT IN THE HOUSE-THAT-LOVE-BUILT

Lucky Thirteen is our first venture into video screens in the alley space. Espey's play has each character holding her cell phone and texting and the audience gets to peek at their screens on the walls of larger screens in our theatre. This is the second production of the play. The first was done on a proscenium. I've got actors running behind the audience on both sides and Neil has live video footage. It's nerve-wracking because it's new. But, it's also really exciting.

Katie Zelonka
Curtis Jordan Photography

venus

James Jager
Curtis Jordan Photography

Second Jimmy Lifetime

2013 - Lucky Thirteen

"Following Sarah" by Rich Espey|direction Deborah Randall| front-of-house Mary Burke-Hueffmeier|lights Kristin A. Thompson|set Amy Rhodes|sound and videography Neil McFadden|costumes and props Deborah Randall|graphic design Laura Matteoni Schraven| cast Sarah Gardner played by Kelsey Painter| Kat played by Ann Fraistat|Maddie played by Katie Zelonka| Julia played by Czarina Joy Flores|Kenya played by Tricia Homer|ensemble and puppeteer James Jager|

"Grieving for Genevieve" by Kathleen Warnock| direction Deborah Randall| front-of-house Mary Burke-Hueffmeier|costumes Marilyn Johnson|props Deborah Randall|lights Kristin A. Thompson|set Amy Rhodes|sound Neil McFadden|stage management L| assistant direction/Genevieve understudy Melynda Burdette|graphic design Laura Matteoni Schraven| cast Delilah Peck played by Ty Hallmark|Angel Peck played by Kelsey Painter|Danni Peck played by Deborah Randall|Genevieve Peck played by Karen Costanzi|

"Gift of Forgotten Tongues" by Fengar Gael direction Deborah Randall| front-of-house Mary Burke-Hueffmeier|lights Kristin A. Thompson|set Amy Rhodes| sound and videography Neil McFadden|videographer Kristen Anchor|costumes and props Deborah Randall|graphic design Laura Matteoni Schraven|choreography Maria Cotto| cast Fernelle played by Kelsey Painter|Celia played by Kathryn Elizabeth Kelly| Claude played by Matthew Marcus|Dr. Weaver played by Deborah Randall|Felix played by George Tamerlani|

"No. 731 degraw-street, Brooklyn, or Emily Dickinson's Sister" by Claudia Barnett| direction Deborah Randall| front-of-house Mary Burke-Hueffmeier|costumes and props Deborah Randall| lights Kristin A. Thompson|set Amy Rhodes|sound Neil McFadden|stage management cast| fight choreography Paul Gallagher|graphic design Laura Matteoni Schraven| cast Kate played by Ann Fraistat|Charlie played by Matthew Marcus|ensemble Amy Rhodes, and Deborah Randall|

My character starts a plastic food fight onstage with my stage sisters Ty Hallmark and Kelsey Painter.
Curtis Jordan Photography

Lucky Thirteen was filled with permission to play. We explored worlds that went from a girls private school, into a very dysfunctional Baltimore family of women, on to mutagens and a mad scientist, and ended in a twisted steampunk aesthetic that landed us all in a Nelly Bly insane asylum. This year took us on an incredible journey. It proved to me that we can create any world we like in our tiny 17' blackbox. When we choose a world then build it and occupy it, the audience takes the journey with us. For "731" we had no stage manager or crew or even front-of-house. So, the four of us ran everything. We were all shocked at the power we felt having complete control over the entire show. It was the right ensemble to do it. This year was a wild roller coaster ride and I wouldn't change a thing.

ven☾☾

Ann Fraistat and Matthew Marcus
Curtis Jordan Photography

2014 - Fierce Fourteen

"Ding, or Bye Bye Dad" by Jayme Kilburn|direction Deborah Randall| front-of-house Mary Burke-Hueffmeier|costumes and props Deborah Randall| lights Kristin A. Thompson|set Amy Rhodes|sound Neil McFadden|stage management Deborah Randall| graphic design Laura Matteoni Schraven| cast Hamiere played by Kelsey Jane Hogan|Boomer played by Amy Rhodes|ensemble Tina Renay Fulp|

"Light of Night" by Cecilia Copeland direction Deborah Randall costumes and props Deborah Randall| lights Kristin A. Thompson|set Amy Rhodes|sound Neil McFadden|stage management Deborah Randall|fight choreography Paul Gallagher|intern, special fx make-up Katherine Drake|graphic design Laura Matteoni Schraven| cast Stephanie played by Katie Zelonka|Isabelle played by Davin Ralston| Jim played by Elliott Kashner|

"We are Samurai" by Daria Marinelli|direction Deborah Randall| costumes and props Deborah Randall| lights Kristin A. Thompson|set Amy Rhodes|intern Allison Lehman|graphic design Laura Matteoni Schraven| cast Elias played by Catherine Benson|Regan played by Daven Ralston|Rocky played by Patrick Gorirossi|Josephine played by Ann Fraistat|ensemble Mary Burke-Hueffmeier, Amy Rhodes, and Elliot Kashner|

"Virus Attacks Heart" by Shannon Murdoch|direction Deborah Randall| costumes and props Deborah Randall| lights Kristin A. Thompson|set Amy Rhodes|sound Neil McFadden|stage manage-

243

Deborah L. Randall

ment Deborah Randall|graphic design Laura Matteoni Schraven| cast Beatrice played by Karin Rosnizek|Jamie played by Joe Feldman|

Amy Belschner Rhodes
Curtis Jordan Photography

Fierce Fourteen began with speed dating, then we jumped to abduction in a locked basement. From there we went full on environmental promenade with Samurais only to land the year with a sensual two-hander that explored mortality and sensuality.

I tried once again to dance with the commercial industry but once again, I got my symbolic teeth kicked in. Turns out doing all of this work with a budget of under $50,000 a year meant no matter how well the work landed, it would now officially absolutely not be taken seriously.

Here's what I wrote on Facebook...
Rolling world premiere May 2014. Disqualified by Helen Hayes Awards. Venus production was not listed in NYC program and this qualification was articulated in the winter of 2014 months after the production closed. We were disqualified via a post production MailChimp survey generated to disqualify us. After inquiry we were informed that the procedural process of rolling world premieres was determined by the National New Play Network standards. In an attempt to join NNPN we were informed that our operating budget was below their membership requirement. This ended a 13 year professional relationship between Venus Theatre and the Helen Hayes organization. A relationship that included almost ten years of going into D.C.P.S. as a theater educator with the legacy project. Fi-

nal nomination list of the Kilroys http://www.ceciliacopeland.c om/press. html Published in January 2015 http://www.indietheaternow. com/Play/light-of-night

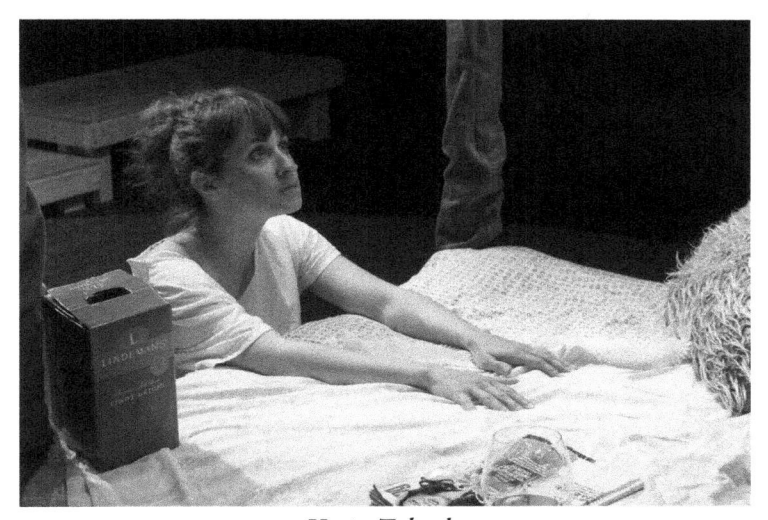

*Katie Zelonka
Curtis Jordan Photography*

Daria's play followed that. It's the first time I'd ever received a submission in landscape format. There were many columns. With scenes happening simultaneously and characters speaking at the same time. The play required six different performance spaces.

Adam S. Lowe Photography

It is perfect. A promenade play. And the audience gets to choose what is primary and what is secondary action.

I have a really strong cast of four. I've added three more characters. Silent Samurai. Mostly for safety. I want to have people who can roam around and keep everything safe.

Rehearsals are a blast! Jasmine loves this show most. She sometimes runs around the building.

When I gave Catherine a note she thanked me. I couldn't believe it. I actually needed confirmation that she just thanked me for asking her to reenact the Samurai wars using only the meows of cats while incorporating the audience as much as possible.

Then, I asked Amy who was playing her flute in this show if she could play the song "Memories" from "Cats" the musical on her flute and she just started playing it on the spot. It was hilarious.

During our final dress rehearsal, this man was at the top of the street shopping at the Meat Market. After he put his groceries in his car he followed Amy down the street as if she were the pied piper. Then he drifted into the final dress rehearsal. He couldn't believe what he was seeing. He kept looking at Ann. We turned the back area of the theatre into her character's apartment and he kept pointing at her saying, "she's crazy! She's NUTS!". He went out back to watch some scenes back there and he was really rolling with the show, compelled to check out as much of it as he could. All of the sudden he just blurted, "MY GROCERIES! I have to go home."

He left quickly but came back to see the show with a friend, which was amazing. I got to sit at the front desk and just listen to all of the scenes play simultaneously. When one scene would get ahead or behind another scene I could hear the actors adjust on the spot. It was flawless.

What I didn't plan on was the weather. It was really hot. All of the Helen Hayes judges came to one show and it was almost 100 degrees. I had ice-soaked wash clothes for them to put on the back of their necks. And then, an electrical storm rolled in. One of my actors wore a metal plate on his head and he let me know by saying, "It's a good thing I'm the only one walking around with a metal plate on my head!".

We moved all of the outdoor bits inside and it really became an entirely different experience.

Daria came to watch. She's unlike almost every other playwright I've produced. She watched my staging in silent areas and did not watch many of the scenes that she'd written. I asked her why she did that and she said she already knew what she'd written and she wanted to see what we'd come up with.

Daria Miyeko Marinelli, playwright

It was her birthday so she and I stayed after and drank Saki. I thought we were going to do notes with each other. Notes consisted of each of us saying, "I like your work" to the other and then we drank saki and gave one another tarot card readings. She was trained by a seeming expert of Tarot.

After she laid my cards down she looked alarmed. She said this can all change. Let's pick this spread up and put it away so it has no more power. There would be trauma in the years soon to come and it seemed like she saw it in the cards that night.

I gave her relationship advice in her reading.

I join actors Joe Feldman and Karin Rosnizek to welcome playwright Shannon Murdoch in from Australia

Shannon came into town next. She flew in from AUSTRALIA. I saw her in the parking lot outside of Tampico near the train station. The first thing she said was, "How is it still fucking Thursday?!?!?"

I can't really believe she's actually here.

I love the poetry in this play and I love the way the timeline jumps all over the place with no apology.

Two-handers are a whole lot of pressure on actors. This was really sexual too, so that always adds to the pressure cooker.

But, the experience was good. We even had a show on Thanksgiving. Ellie and Tricia came. We ate a lot of food after and just hung out. There was so much bonding this year.

It was really lovely.

ven☾☼

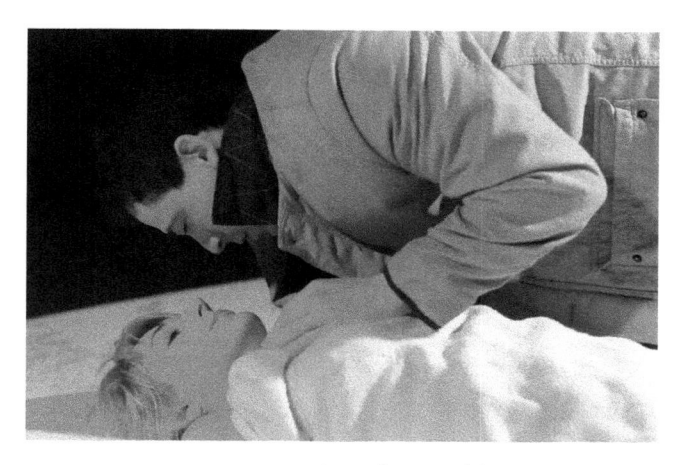

Karin Rosnizek and Joe Feldman
Curtis Jordan Photography

2015 - Feral Fifteen: Feminist Fables

"God Don' Like Ugly" by Doc Anderson Bloomfeld|direction Deborah Randall | costumes and props Deborah Randall | lights Amy Rhodes| set Elizabeth Jenkins McFadden| sound Neil McFadden|stage management Deborah Randall|construction Deborah Randall and Amy Rhodes|graphic design Laura Matteoni Schraven| cast Esme played by Catherine Benson|SJ played by Ann Fraistat|Bessie played by Nancy Blum|Stranger played by Gray West|

"Dry Bones Rising" by Cecila Raker direction Deborah Randall costumes and props Deborah Randall|set and lights Amy Rhodes| sound Neil McFadden|mask work Waxing Moon Masks| FX Vanessa Q Laveque|stage management Deborah Randall|construction Deborah Randall and Amy Rhodes|graphic design Laura Matteoni Schraven| cast girl played by Ann Fraistat| boy played by Erin Lee Hanratty|Golum played by Allison Turkell|

"Witches Vanish" by Claudia Barnett direction Deborah Randall costumes and props Deborah Randall|set Deborah Randall|lights Kristin A. Thompson|sound Neil McFadden|mask work Waxing Moon Masks| energy work Noreen Javornik|stage management Deborah Randall|construction Deborah Randall and Amy Rhodes|graphic design Laura Matteoni Schraven|ensemble Lakeisha Harrison, Tara Cariaso, Vivian Allvin, Jenni Berry, Leticia Monet|

"Raw" by Amy Bernstein direction Deborah Randall costumes and props Deborah Randall|set Elizabeth Jenkins McFadden lights Amy Rhodes|sound Neil McFadden|mask work Waxing Moon Masks|-construction Deborah Randall and Amy Rhodes| stage management Deborah Randall|graphic design Laura Matteoni Schraven| cast Wilomena played by Katie Zelonka|Eliza played by Allison Turkel|Harriet played by Jenni Berry| Jamie played by Becca Korn| Chuck played by Patrick Gorirossi|

Catherine Benson
Curtis Jordan Photography

Our first playwright, Doc hails from England. Her husband, John, is a pilot. They are flying in for the late tech, photo shoot, and the show opening. Luckily, I have Amy around most of the time now and she is able to pick them up from the airport and drive them in.

Doc kept telling me how she wanted to see her character Esme's butt wiggling under the hood of a car. She couldn't wait to see it. There's no way I'm putting one of my actors under the hood of a car. It's way too dangerous. Amy and I have built the set, Elizabeth designed it. Elizabeth says she doesn't need a whole car. She just needs half of a car. Or maybe, a part of a car.

My Stepgrandmother died. I'm estranged from my family because I tried to stay connected to them for 40 years and the toxicity just got worse and worse. By that I mean, the last time I went over to my

Monster's house. Her voice pitched up into that old familiar tone that was always the precursor to her assaulting me physically when I was small and vulnerable. It usually came out of nowhere when I was having a good day. That pitch flew out of her mouth and onto me once again, on a summer afternoon in 2008. I'd long since stopped working at the plumbing shop with her. When I did, her hand went numb because all of that fury suddenly had nowhere to go. Something snapped inside of me this time. It was as if my body somehow remembered every attack it had endured from her throughout my lifetime. As if previously tucked away under my ribcage, I felt the pull of it all coming out and it affected my breathing. The adrenaline made me feel powerful.

This happened once before when I was 16 and she asked my Stepfather to help her flip me over on their bed so she could beat my ass. They both tried and then I have no memory of what happened. I snapped. When I was aware of what was going on again I found myself on top of her, looking down into her red-spitting face, restraining her on the bed by her wrists. Exactly what she'd been trying to do to me. I found him cowering by their closet doors. They were each twice my size at that time.

This last time in 2008 though, was a deeper snap. I could see myself but I was outside of myself. Sounds were distorted. There was a monster voice in my own head and it started talking out loud to her. It started asking her how it felt to be the weaker one now. And, I swear it wanted to throw her all the way through the brick wall. It wanted to see and hear her skull crack against the flagstone under our feet that my Grandfather had laid on her patio right before my 7th birthday.

I kicked my sister's bedroom door in. Flashes of new dresses on the bed blurred through my mind. So many times after coming home from school there'd be a Fashion Bug ensemble waiting for me and no word spoken about the violent night before. These details slurred by with a list of everything they'd ever bought for me and an echo of "HOW DARE YOU!". Money spent needed to be shown as a wise investment. Instead of feeling grateful like I was supposed to, I became more enraged with fury. They tried to buy me instead of owning up to abusing me.

Luckily, Alan was with me and calmly said, "I think we should go now." I heard him although sounds were somewhat muffled beyond the metal-shearing pitch of my lifetime Monster. I heard her shrilly screaming at me, "GET OUT!!!" Very similar to the way she was screaming "GET OFF OF ME" that time when I was 16.

I drifted, body and soul in a side-stepping weave down the driveway with Alan to his car and we left.

I knew I could never go back. It would be dangerous for them if I did.

I suddenly and seemingly out of nowhere understood elder abuse. The body remembers. The rage she'd unleashed on me during my formative years was still in me. It wanted a turn at bat. That primal part of me felt fully justified.

I want nothing to do with that kind of violence.

I know I have choices, and I know I have angels watching over me and guides seeing me through. I know I'm not just living for me, but for Jimmy too. I know this life is a gift and I can't waste it on the violent and insecure.

I cannot afford to be put in that situation again. I cannot afford to see them or to be at that house. I offered to meet with them somewhere neutral if we had a third-party professional overseeing things, but they said no.

It seems that in my family the ones who seek therapy are labeled mentally ill. That label makes us damaged goods to never be respected or listened to again. Erased and disregarded. Failures.

On the other hand, the violent and untreated never seek therapy because to them, if you need help you are weak and unloveable. This is why, in my family, the people who visited my cousin in prison could not find the time to attend my college graduation.

Progress, joy, success, none of these things are real to them. They will convince anyone that good things are not happening. They will fixate on the failures and make them all last a lifetime. The eyes of alcoholic Aunts are green where they should be white. When they die far too young, everyone talks about how loving they were, after tailgating in the funeral home parking lot. Treatment was never on the table. There was never a problem. Because if there had been a problem then that would mean they lost the game of Family. And, BY GOD, they won because look at how many people are crying now!

It's a strange moment of evolution. Those who demand pity and play victim are not the ones fighting for dignity and forward movement. True victims never want to stay in that darkness. Chronic manipulators trade on it.

Somewhere Darwin must be laughing. And I guess because of that unwillingness to grow through admitting the truth, I never saw my Mother again.

My boyfriend from High School is messaging me. Only I think it's really my Mother using his phone.

I ask him where I can get a part of a car. He runs a towing business.

He tells me, "Crazy Rays".

It's five miles from the theatre. CRAZY RAYS! It's a huge lot of broken down cars and car parts. There are things embedded in the mud. It reminds me of my Grandfather's house from my youth.

I've visited Crazy Ray's about four times, always with different people. I took Amy once. And then her husband came another time. That's when I SAW IT!

It was a 1971 light blue Volkswagen Beetle with white interior. The EXACT same car that Jimmy's Mom had. The one we rode all the way to Ocean City in standing in the back and making up a puppet show back there laughing nonstop and slightly annoying our mothers.

I remember when we stopped for gas in that car on the way to the beach, she would get a free flower sticker. People decorated those cars with stickers and paint and hippies didn't wear underwear.

Crazy Ray's takes me back.

Amy's husband advises that I should apply for a job in fast food.

The climate changes quite a bit with each Crazy Ray visit. I go to Crazy Ray's in the mud, snow, and also navigate frozen icy ground. Tricky, because all kinds of metal shrapnel is sticking up in unexpected places.

I take pictures of the Bug. I posted about this online.

There is a funder and wonderful audience member I simply call Scooter-Lady. I was amazed to see her pull up in front of the theatre on her scooter, wearing her helmet and her business suit. It was glorious to find out that she'd scooted her way up from DC. She decided to donate $500 for the Beetle. She wanted to see if I could get a car inside our space. Oh, YES I CAN!

We also have Teddy and Margaret. They are an older lesbian couple. Teddy drives a red sports car and likes to drive to the theatre with the top down.

We have Elizabeth who drives in three hours each way from Norfolk, VA. We have some people from town who come to see everything we do. Sometimes Broadway actors will take the bus down and ride back up to do a show that same evening.

The location is perfect. This is incredible.

I tell Doc to stay at the Comfort Inn on the corner.

She reports back that a member of the staff of the hotel has gotten into a farting contest with a homeless person trying to make the best of the free continental breakfast.

This has been the biggest tech weekend crisis of my life.

Saturday went along just fine and so did Sunday morning. At the dinner break though, one of my actors locked themselves in one of the bathrooms and started wailing and sobbing. We managed to get them out and take them downstairs into the dressing room. I thought their Mother had died.

I recognized the trauma response right away. Professional intervention happened. The actor insisted they needed to leave and was in no position to stay and work. I'd later find out that what followed after that was pretty dark. It was downright terrifying.

I always give my actors the Monday after tech off so they don't get sick for the run. This means we have Tuesday and Wednesday dress rehearsals and then we open on Thursday.

Thanks to Scooter Lady, and the help of a lot of friends, I managed to get an actual car on the stage.

A neighbor loaned me a red pickup truck to haul the Volkswagen Bug down Route One. An historic site as far as I was concerned. The first day was too icy. So, I borrowed it a second day. I hired a man named Carlos to cut the car in half on the lot. On a diagonal as instructed by our incredible set designer Elizabeth.

On the second day the people of Crazy Ray's drove their forklift to the very back of the lot where the car was. They tied old seatbelts in a big loop through both windows and lifted BlueBird up with the strap over her roof. I watched her come dangling toward me. Suddenly I realized I had taken no measurements.

The red truck belonged to Eric. He was the Dad of two of my summer campers. His wife Draga was so kind as to lend me his truck for this. We'd heard he'd been diagnosed with stage four colon cancer. So, the following summer we created Butterfly Camp. I wanted the girls to have some kind of symbol of life beyond life. At one of Eric's fundraisers, I won a raffle to get a tattoo. Something I was sure I would not win. So, I still carry Eric's energy with me on my right shoulder, to be specific.

Eric is watching over me, Jimmy is here too, I've got so many spirit guides, I'm sure it will be okay. It has to be okay.

They dropped BlueBird in the bed of Eric's Truck and she fit snug as a bug. They asked if I'd brought any pressure straps. Nope. Didn't even think of that.

So, the staff at Crazy Ray's decided to cut out more seat belts from the car and tie them all together. I was sure it would be fine. I floored it and hit the breaks a couple of times on the lot, and it seemed okay.

I turned onto Route One. I made a left and headed back to the theatre. Suddenly I saw what looked to be a State Trooper giving a ticket to someone driving northbound.

Don't make eye contact.

Pretend everyone else is hallucinating.

I have no registration for this truck.

Much like when we arrived home from touring, "The Voice Inside the Vessel" to the lower east side of NYC, after I'd pulled off impossible feats, only to realize I'd forgotten my keys to let myself back in my house when the mission had been accomplished. I turned around on C Street when the thought suddenly arose in my head. How am I going to get this thing inside? The doorframe is 34" wide.

Puzzling.

But first, how am I going to get this thing off of Eric's truck?

Alan had arrived and that was good. Randy appeared from her boot factory across the street and handed me a wrought iron bar and told me to use it for leverage.

As if the heavens opened up, a woman wearing a black trench coat riding a bicycle with a blue mohawk just stopped in the middle of the street next to us and laid her bike right there in the street. Then a group of men jumped out as they were pulling BlueBird off of the truck and began pushing her back in, undoing our work. I stopped them and they explained they thought it was junk we were trying to trash.

Fools.

That's when the car was pulled off of the truck and placed in front of the theatre. On the sidewalk.

How was I going to get this thing inside?

Alan stayed with BlueBird and I drove Eric's truck home and got my car. Alan brought Jasmine to me at the theatre and I pulled the "Hypnotic Murderess" set out of the basement. It was a down mattress and blanket and pillow.

I called Rob at Public Works. He always picks up immediately.

"Rob? I need you to do me a favor."

"What have you done now?"

"There's a car on the sidewalk. Please don't take it!"

"How much time do you need?"

"I just need 24 hours. In all the years I've been here, we've never gotten this much attention. People are stopping and getting out of their cars in the rain."

"Well, put a sign on it. Hey, put some flyers on the seat."

"Okay. I'll have it off of the sidewalk by 6pm tomorrow."

I love how Rob is never shocked by what I'm doing.

About one hour after that, we had rehearsal. The actors had to step over the car to get in the front door. They doubted me!

They thought it was never coming inside.

People always bet on the wrong horse when it comes to me.

Rehearsal goes pretty well.

Jasmine and I spend the night at the theatre staring at the car on the sidewalk through the plate glass window.

I remembered my physics class. There's a formula for torque. Things can be twisted.

I'm communicating my situation on Facebook and my friend Bill declares that he is coming and that the car WILL be inside of the theatre by nightfall.

It turns out you can completely break down a VW Beetle with one ¾" socket wrench. Solid bolts. Which is why I'm willing to put my actor under it. The hood is essentially a trunk. Solid. Those hinges were built for war.

Bill shows up and I have my socket wrench ready. Alan comes back with an industrial dolly that he moves all of his music gear and equipment with. The woman in the trenchcoat with the mohawk comes back with her husband who is about 7' tall, also wearing a trenchcoat.

The rain has stopped. I used paper towels to wipe BlueBird down last night.

Bucky, the mechanic who works in the alley popped in with a simple, "WHAT ARE YOU DOING?" I can't explain this to Bucky.

It's in. Bill took the doors and the hood off. We laid her on her side on top of Alan's dolly and we torque-twisted her through the door.

What a journey!

I felt so ready to have a playwright from England arrive.

And then, that tech hit. I talked to the actor a few times. She was in a state.

I grabbed the baseball bat. I contacted one of my actors who was also a detective and an expert on domestic violence. She told me to expect the "honeymoon" phase next. He'd probably show up on opening with flowers. I explained that I'd already told my actor if I saw him anywhere near my theatre I would, without hesitation, crack his skull open with a baseball bat.

I was instructed that I should not have said that.

Truth is truth and I'm still on a schedule.

On Monday I'd been convinced that the show would go on as rehearsed.

By Tuesday, I'm ready to pull the show.

Honestly, it's not worth risking someone's life. Nothing is.

On Tuesday, I was just leaving Target. Picking up last minute prop backups. The call came. They could not do the show. The playwright was landing that afternoon.

Of course I support this decision. I can't have anyone feeling unsafe on my stage.

I call Ann. She's already played my daughter and she was incredible in "A Girl Named Destiny". "731" was a symbolic bloodletting bonding our sisterhood. Ann picked up the phone.

"Hi Deb. How are you?"

"Not good, I'm not good at all."

"What's wrong?"

"I have a playwright on an international flight in the air right now and one of my actors just dropped for reasons I totally agree with. I'm in a tumble."

"Oh, God! Is there anything I can do to help?"

"Well, you want to come and read her character in so we can have this dress rehearsal? It also happens to be our photocall. So, if you could just help keep things moving, that would be incredible."

"Well, can I read the script?"

"Of course."

"I'll email it to you when I get back to my office. Can you meet me at the theatre at 6?"

"Deb? It's 5:10 now."

"OH, SHIT!"

"I can meet you there. Can I read the script?"

"Yes, I'll have a printed copy ready for you when you arrive and you can give it a read as I explain things to the cast."

"Okay, I'm on my way, see you soon."

"THANK YOU!!!"

I called Amy to ask her to please stall the playwright and her husband after she picked them up from the airport. Take them to dinner or something.

Time bends.

Ann is there, the photographer is there, the cast is there, I'm talking fast.

We were ALL worried about the health and safety of our actor that had to drop.

Once Curtis the photographer is ready, we need to go so we don't fall into late hours in case we have to stop and go back and shoot things."

Ann asks me one question, "Can I read the script?"

I don't have time to explain the blocking to her.

"I need you to get into costume for the camera."

The cast envelops her and transforms her. The costume fits her perfectly.

She's reading the script for the first time during the run of our final dress as she plays each scene. I'm in the booth running lights and sound and shouting stage directions at her through the scrim.

There's a moment when Catherine as Esme gets inside of the car and Ann places her hand against the windshield. The windshield is original from 1971 without a chip on it. Esme put her hand up to meet Ann's. Ann reached toward her. I gut-sobbed in the booth.

It's a GORGEOUS MOMENT.

Curtis is shooting it. When you look at the production shot, you can see Ann's script on the hood of BlueBird. She had not yet finished reading the play at this moment.

Ann Fraistat and Catherine Benson
Curtis Jordan Photography

Ann is playing a stranger coming into a strange place so the whole thing completely works.

Doc and her husband arrive and walk across the stage to the far side as this moment was being discovered. I had no control over anything. The only thing I could do was navigate the currents.

Ann falls in love with the play. The cast falls in love with Ann.

Ann arrived at 5 on Wednesday. She wanted to be very clear that she will be holding her script for opening. Of course, of course. BUT. Since we have this hour before the rest of the actors arrive, let's put you out there. I'm on script anyway running lights and sound. I'll read in all of the characters and shout out any stage direction if you get caught. Hold your script but don't look at it, just call for line and let's see where we're at.

"Okay, but I'm definitely holding the script for the opening."

"Of course."

Ann is running her own dog walking business. So, she spent all day Wednesday on the line learner app walking dogs, picking up their poop, and running her lines. She said the dogs were looking at her in a funny way because they couldn't figure out who she was talking to.

NOT ONCE did she call for line in the entire first act. NOT ONCE.

She was entirely off book in one day. I've never seen anything like it.

I haven't slept much.

It's opening.

I climb into the booth. We open this thing that has no business opening.

I'm almost falling asleep. I hear Catherine as Esme onstage going "play play play" and the sound of her pushing the cassette deck buttons over and over jolts me out of the worried director role.

AH! That's my cue. I'm watching the actors as a director and forgetting that I have to run sound.

In the lobby afterward I was asked if the stuck cassette was a part of the staging. Nope. And then, I was told how much the audience loved it. One critic said it was some of my best work.

How is that even possible?

How?

Catherine Benson
Curtis Jordan Photography

Words invoke energies. Feral Fifteen tried to kick my ass. We went from getting a car in through the front door and landing one of our strongest productions to date to staging an essentially hasidic poem about the end of the world and a golem savior. Then we conjured the Wyrd sisters from Shakespeare. Finally, we staged a vengeful cow making a documentary on how absolutely effed up humankind had become before blowing up the farm that took her babies. Feral indeed.

Lakeisha Harrison, Vivian Allvin, Tara Cariaso, Leticia Jones, and Jenni George
Curtis Jordan Photography

Katie Zelonka
Curtis Jordan Photography

Ann, and Amy, and I had given "Witches" a read at the Kennedy Center's page-to-stage festival. It's the only time in all of our participation there that we received a standing ovation for a reading. I remember as soon as we were out of the audience's view, I collapsed. All of the energy in my body had been sucked out.

There's no way I could represent the spectrum of womankind with three white women. We went on a casting spree. The cast was exceptional. The work was hard and dense. It's the only time I've ever seen Neil have to stop and cry while creating his sound design.

At the reading I played drums and Amy played flute between the vignettes as Ann read the names of over 80 women lost to matricide never to be recovered.

For the show, Neil recorded all of our actors reading the names. Tara came on board and made some incredible masks as well. Lakeisha came back to Venus and did an incredible job.

It ended up being a five woman cast. I had two shadow crones. Tara executed this crazy mask idea I'd had. The faces would be the tops of the actors heads so they could walk upright as one look and then bend over to reveal a bent body and cronian face.

This is how I handled the "cauldron-problem".

Claudia had been told this play was unproduceable because it required magic things to appear out of a huge cauldron. She was told that no small theatre would be able to do that and no large theatre would take the risk.

I staged two previously unscripted crones to become the cauldron. More Spirit-Mechanicals. They would sit on the floor facing each other and holding arms and then creating a cauldron and then magically they'd stand upright and "poof!" their cauldron would be gone.

I remember Tricia came to that performance. I remember seeing her in the lobby afterward. She looked at me and said, "Can we go someplace?" I said, "yeah".

We walked up Main Street to Oliver's Tavern. It's the same place I won the raffle at Eric's Fundraiser for my tattoo. There was an 80's cover band playing. They played the Outfields, "Your Love". Tricia completely zenned out. I took a picture because she was so zen in a crowded bar. I laughed at her. She said, "I love this song. I really love this song."

She closed her eyes and took it in. We blew off a lot of steam that night. She had me laughing so hard I woke up feeling like I'd had a 3 hour ab workout. We talked about everything.

Tricia McCauley
"I love this song. I really love this song."

During the "Witches" tech, THREE men were found guilty of murdering young girls and dumping their bodies in landfills in Juarez. These practices had been going on since the 80's and suddenly during our tech week in 2015, three men were found guilty. It was a wild feeling.

2016 - Sweet Sixteen; Groovy Young Things

"Fur" by Migdalia Cruz| direction Deborah Randall| assistant direction Amy Rhodes| costumes and props Deborah Randall|set and lights Amy Rhodes|sound Neil McFadden|stage management Lydia Howard| fx Lewis Shaw| fight choreography Lewis Shaw and Mallory Shear|construction Deborah Randall and Amy Rhodes|graphic design Laura Matteoni Schraven| voice over artists Wendy Nogales|Joe Feldman| cast Citrona played by Deborah Randall|Michael played by D. Grant Cloyd|Nena played by Karin Rosnizeck|

"Garbage Kids" by Jayme Kilburn|direction Deborah Randall| costumes and props Deborah Randall|set Amy Rhodes| lights Kristin A. Thompson|sound Neil McFadden|stage management Lydia Howard|fight choreography Mallory Shear|construction Deborah Randall and Amy Rhodes|graphic design Laura Matteoni Schraven| cast Scuzzy played by Deborah Randall|Belly played by Jay Hardee|ensemble Amy Rhodes|

"Rock the Line" by Kathleen Warnock direction Deborah Randall|assistant direction Marni Penning Coleman|costumes and props Deborah Randall|set Amy Rhodes| lights Kristin A. Thompson|sound Neil McFadden|stage management Jenna Lawrence|fight choreography Mallory Shear|construction Deborah Randall and Amy Rhodes|graphic design Laura Matteoni Schraven| front-of-house Lydia Howard and Karen Costanzi|construction Deborah Randall and Amy Rhodes|graphic design Laura Matteoni Schraven| voice over artists Marni Penning Coleman and Nancy Blum| cast Nancy played by Rebecca A. Herron|Lucy played by Myrrh Cauthen|Candy File played by Amy Rhodes|Joanne played by Tamieka Chavis|Kelly played by Lida Benson| Leslie played by Deborah Randall|Mickey played by Patrick Gorirossi|

"Soft Revolution: Shafana and Aunt Sarrinah" by Alana Valentine direction Deborah Randall| costumes and props Deborah Randall| set and lights Amy Rhodes|sound Neil McFadden|dramaturgy Pat-

ven*us*

rick Gorirossi|stage management Deborah Randall|construction Deborah Randall and Amy Rhodes|graphic design Laura Matteoni Schraven| cast Shafana played by Nayab Hussain|Aunt Sarrinah played by Meera Narasimhan|

Grant Cloyd attempts to draw a map in the sand for my hirsute character
Lisa Helfert Photography

I need a cage!

Laura is making incredible graphics for the set. Amy and I have decided to resurrect the steel structure platform. The one that was built for, "All She Cares About Is The Yankees" then used in the all female "Measure for Measure". It's been downstairs in storage. We decided to attach the steel steps that Cat welded for "A Little Rebellion Now".

It feels like home.

Migdalia writes sexually and does not hold back. Citrona is a hirsute. Grant has to wheel me on stage in a bag. I've knitted a body suit out of black fuzzy fur. It's my ode to the Guerilla Girls!

My reliance on kneepads is very strong.

The sound design Neil has put together, once again defines a heartbeat in the play.

Amy has lit the set in an economical and great way. She uses the steel on the steps to create a gobo effect. We've got sand on the stage we have to manipulate and I'm going to need to stab someone at the end of the play. That's after I spend almost two hours literally locked in a cage.

The internet has made so many things accessible. I put the call out. I need a cage! Rob with the city can't help me here. He doesn't have a cage large enough to hold ME.

I met this man who is clearing out his set and prop stock. He creates props and set pieces for commercials. There was some insurance commercial that needed to put a lion in a cage. He still had the cage hanging around and needed to get rid of it. It was green.

Fine by me.

He had to chop it down because apparently, we couldn't fit a lion on our stage even if we wanted to.

The fight choreography for the stabbing is intense.

Drew comes back and is onboard to do the fight choreography along with one of his newly trained. He's built a knife for me to use.

He's taught me how to stab her convincingly without hurting her. I just feel like I'm back. This is what I do. I'm in my body, I'm becoming text, I feel so alive.

He tells me the play is weird. Which is good.

Lydia, our intern is holding down the lights and sound and overseeing us. She is kind and brilliant and understated. She is my favorite type of artist.

I trust her completely, which is essential. Especially essential when I'm playing a homicidal deeply abused monkey woman living in a cage.

I'd performed with Migdalia's words in my mouth before. That was just for audition pieces though. Two minutes at a time. Playing an actual character in a full length play felt like a feast for my artistic soul. Jasmine was confused that I was inside of the cage and she was outside of it at rehearsals.

I was in Shangri-La.

Grant and I matched, note for note. Even when the new front-of-house person kicked the lobby door in for late seating and destroyed the tension of our opening scene one night. I had to trust him completely. I was locked in a cage and he had the keys. There was also a spare set hidden inside with me but that was just in case of fire or some life threatening emergency. I adore having scene partners that I trust with my life.

This was the case with "Fur".

We opened to audiences not used to seeing anything like this. For fun, I chose to stage a section of one of the scenes TeleMundo-style with lip synching and overdubs created by two actors I adore, Wendy Nogales (the original "Juanita the Walrus" and "A Little Rebellion Now" news reporter) as well as Joe Feldman, an actor that is such a joy to direct. The expertise of Neil's recording and mixing made all of this come together and work.

Wendy Nogales and Neil McFadden.

One critic sat on the red couch in the front row. After we came back up from the dressing room after everyone had left, he'd twisted and pressed his feet so hard into the floor he'd managed to dig down through every layer of paint to the stripped wood. It was like looking at the cross section of a freshly cut tree. I could recall each production with every layer of exposed paint.

Tricia came with a couple of friends. And of course, Tricia being Tricia she needed time to swing around in my cage. She commented that it was difficult because the bars were squared steel and not round. I told her, it was hard enough finding a cage to hold me, I couldn't be particular with the steel selection. Plus, it was good enough for a lion, so…

When Migdalia came down to see the show I couldn't believe it. She called me one of her Citrona's. We were in the grocery store shopping for refreshments. I couldn't believe I was standing in the grocery aisle being called a Citrona by the GodDesS of creation herself.

I remember driving her to the train station and feeling like I was floating even though I hadn't really slept and I was more exhausted than I could express.

That show was a dream come true for me.

Jayme's second play follows. This is the year I did the second plays in what felt like a possible trilogy of work by both Jayme Kilburn and Kathleen Warnock. It felt like touching the bones of souls getting so close to their worlds.

Jay Hardee and I check our tags Curtis Jordan Photography

Jenny Walls lives in town and she ran the day center for the homeless at the time of our "Garbage Kid's" production. She allowed us to come into the center and share lunch with the people there.

Visiting homeless people was an incredible experience. I feel like we absorbed something of that experience into the fibers of our production. A smell or something.

Once a script is chosen I want to see how far we can run with it. A play needs three productions to find its identity. It's always my goal to be one of those three productions.

I so often forget how terrifying the work I do can be to actors.

Amy and I turned the stage into an actors playground. We hung a tire swing center stage and created a junkyard sliding board.

I remember Jayme coming in to watch it.

I was glad we were producing in a small town. Jayme was traveling with her dog. She was stuck in traffic. She called me to say that she could make it to the theatre in time but she wouldn't have time to drop her dog off with a friend. She asked if she could leave her dog in the lobby.

No.

The entire space is only 17' wide. I've had Jasmine in tech rehearsals and even in the lobby you can hear every little step.

I hopped on the internet and put out a call to the Old Town list-serv. A woman immediately offered up her yard at the top of Main Street. Jayme was able to drop her dog off. The woman had her grandchildren over. They got to play with a dog in the yard for a couple of hours.

The woman refused to let us pay her anything. She wouldn't even let me buy her a candy bar.

It feels like Venus is a part of the fabric of this town now. We even have a block on the Laurelopoly board game.

Next up is Kathleen's play. We read it at the Kennedy Center. I felt so good about the casting. A larger cast for my tiny stage. About half of the Kennedy Center readers were not available to do the show. And, Kathleen wanted me to replace an actor.

She indicated that it would be better if I played the role.

It was another big year for me. Three really big roles in a row. I felt like I was in paradise.

Each time I've created a character that is close to the bone of the playwright it has brought a real feeling of sisterhood. A metamorphosis of sorts for me to become versions of them.

I don't know. It just feels like exactly where I'm supposed to be.

We were excited to use the VW Bug in "Rock The Line". That partial car became a company member. I cast Amy as Candy, a drug-addled antagonist. During the first week of rehearsal Amy asked if I thought her character would have a mohawk.

Yes.

Definitely.

The next day she showed up with half of her head shaved.

Amy Belschner Rhodes
Mike Landsman Photography

The whole concept of the show is about a group of friends who follow a rock star around. They wait in line all day. You see their personalities.

I think I've seen it all when all of the sudden a sound cue changes my life. Or, as Stephen Covey would have said, a paradigm shift.

In the staging I didn't think much about it because it required no fight choreography or blocking. It was a sound cue. Another brilliant Neil design.

The sound is a group of guys in a car, they throw a bottle at us and call me a dyke and speed off.

I know this. I'm directing the show. I chose the script.

But, every single night that was the most violent moment of the show for me. And we are jumping off of platforms and pinning each other to the wall.

As a heterosexual woman I have experienced a lot of things. But, not that. Once inside of the scene, it was a kind of terror that was new. That I could just be standing there and a group of hateful people would throw a bottle at my head and laugh after they just tried to kill me.

It made me freeze every single time.

There were lines to be spoken after that. It's like with Kathleen's first play we staged. A fist fight on the floor and then, "I'm hungry." and an invitation to go get something to eat. Like nothing violent just occurred. I understood that based on my own life. But this was a different version of that. This was the version where I could only be the target, never the aggressor. And, as a woman I definitely understand that. Usually it's because there's a sexual attraction so it has a rapey feel. Never in a way that is just benign sexually. Uncharged. It's pure hatred without a sense of personhood at all. As a heterosexual woman my market value is how fuckable I am according to the patriarchy. I see that. I feel like I can dip and dive through that, although it may still kill me one day, I still can try to hide when I need to. As a lesbian, that's impossible I discovered. You're viewed in a different kind of hostile way with no way to hide from it. You are a threat that needs squelching.

This is the value of playing a character unlike oneself. It's an empathetic meditation in motion. It's life altering.

The long chapters in Melville's "Moby Dick" go through all of the descriptions of sea life. It's a book within the book. Being a woman is a book within a book. That was Migdalia's point. Here I am trying to explain the difference between two types of women, hunted in different ways. Both still hunted.

All I can say is I discovered a new kind of terror on that stage. One that required me to keep moving and tune out of my kinesthetic awareness if I wanted to stay alive.

Which is the opposite of my own experience where I have to be hyper-aware.

Marni Penning Coleman jumped in to do the voiceover work for Patti Roxx. She voiced the icon all of the characters were waiting to see.

It was an incredible lineup!

Neil, Me, and Marni

I costumed that show too, and I'm so proud of my design. We were all in leather. This meant we finally purchased a heating and cooling unit for the space.

It was an $8,000 purchase. Huge investment! If you stand in the right spot now, you can feel the cool air on the stage.

Myrrh and Rebecca Herron
Mike Landsman Photography

This year ends with a playwright from Australia.

It's a two-hander. I can't cast it to save my life.

I love reading scripts blind. I don't look at who's written it, I just read the play and pay attention to my own visceral experience. This one grabbed me.

The entire play centers around a hijab.

The artist in me LOVES this play. The producer in me cannot understand how an entire play can revolve around a single fairly small piece of fabric.

I think Nayab should play the aunt but we can't find a niece. Nayab suggests she play the niece, which sounds good. If only I can find a middle eastern actor to play her aunt.

Nayab was in "Play Nice!". Then, when a Stage Manager dropped during "Looking for the Pony" Nayab jumped on the boards and was the self-appointed captain of Team Awesome. I know when Nayab is involved, whatever needs getting done is about to get done.

I push the performance dates back a few weeks.

At last, thanks to Nayab, Meera signs on to play the aunt.

We are one week into rehearsal and so excited for the election. We can't wait until tomorrow to hear that Hillary has been elected.

We are about to have our FIRST FEMALE PRESIDENT OF THE UNITED STATES!

…

…

Nayab picked up the Georgetown cupcakes as promised.

Trump won.

People are tweeting about setting women on fire in Walmart if they are wearing hijabs.

I'm terrified for the safety of my actors.

TERRIFIED.

There's not a baseball bat big enough to crack this many ignorant skulls.

How will I protect them and keep them safe from Islamophobia? In the play there are monologues about 9-11. Powerful monologues. At the rehearsal table, Nayab has shared how terrifying it was for her in the days after. A time when I thought the country had really pulled together.

She tells me about many of the things she's had to tolerate.

Meera begins to wear a hijab in rehearsal. Saying she wants to wear it as a show of solidarity.

And then, she goes to the woods. For a week. Because the world suddenly became a terrifying place.

By the time we opened the show, it had only been rehearsed for two weeks. Half the time of usual productions with at least twice the amount of intensity.

We're all pushing it through.

We've decided we're going to land this thing.

The Washington Post is coming out to cover it.

Out of nowhere we are on the cover of the Style Section in the Washington Post again.

Proudly standing between Nayab Hussain and Meera Narasimhan

Meera is telling everyone about the show. Houses are selling out. I have to put the piano bench in the theatre so more people can sit.

The staging was challenging.

How do we capture this experience through the voicing of an Australian playwright, dealing with Muslim issues, coming out of Pakistan here in Laurel, MD?

I didn't want my audience to be stuck in the given circumstances. I didn't want to clutter the setting with an explanation. I decided food was the answer.

Meera would always arrive an hour early. I had an electric skillet backstage. She cooked with spices I did not know existed. The entire theatre was filled with amazing scents by the time the audience arrived.

We had a wall of projections. By now Neil and I had clean communication on the Q-Lab software and could project full length films on the walls of Venus. This show had lots of video. Lots of projections. Gorgeous projections. Meera's character liked to pretend she was on Nigella's cooking show as Nigella. I put a crockpot on the stage. She added various ingredients at different times during the show.

Meera Narasimhan and Nayab Hussain
Curtis Jordan Photography

After curtain call, I moved the crock pot into the lobby and pulled out bowls and spoons. Usually the audience stayed and ate with us. That's when the conversations started. One woman told me that she'd just driven back from Williamsburg with her daughters. She said they were arguing through all of the hours of driving. But now, she told me, she suddenly understands what her daughters were trying to tell her.

So much communion in that lobby over that crockpot.

Later, I confessed that as a white hetero woman maybe I shouldn't have staged it. Maybe the playwright shouldn't have written it. There's so much chatter going around about appropriation.

Nayab told me that in her culture, there really isn't much theatre. She told me that if we hadn't told the story, it would not have been told. Not in this way.

This year helped me to understand that I'm not stuck in a rigid box.

It really is about connection. I believe that EVERYONE should have access to theatre. It's the alchemical process that has the power to change everything. But, it must be experienced live and together. This project threw me all the way inside of that experience during one of the greatest reveals of political terror I'd ever experienced in my life.

There is beauty in expression. Time and time again I am swept out to sea by these artists who dare to do and say things they are not supposed to be doing and saying all through the lens of love for life, love for the craft. It's the most amazing thing.

I think about my original quest to find my gender identity. Maybe gender pride is a better term. Maybe by gender I mean all people. All equal. All having the exact same right to express themselves. I thought I was just dreaming it up in my head. Until the scripts appeared. The actors showed up and delivered.

Now, I am entirely changed.

Transformed.

All of these experiences and the creative people who have decided to make them appear have shown me who I am.

THEY are Venus Theatre.

All of them.

I took Jasmine to the beach for a quick reset. She tried gyros on the boardwalk and now that's her favorite thing. I shopped for the nieces and nephews because I only leave to come home on the 23rd of December.

While I was away, I found out that Donna Kaz/Aphra Behn had written her memoir, "Un/Masked". Guerilla Girl has unmasked herself and spoken out about being raped by William Hurt. That's among the bravest things I've ever read!

The Guerilla Girls kept me going under the fluorescents in the playing space before it was even a theatre.

I find her email and write to her to tell her that her work is what encouraged me to keep showing up. I tell her I would like to give her a Venus Theatre Lifetime Achievement Award on behalf of all of the women in theatre she has helped over so many years.

She agrees! We picked a date in February of 2017. She's coming to tour her book, she'll give a presentation on the stage. I'll roll out the season. All in the same night.

Whoa!!

Tricia texted me.

Happy Solstice.

She hates the dark days and for many years we spent solstice together sitting on the floor of her shared apartment having left our shoes at the top of her steps. Cardboard filing boxes were turned upside down and put into a circular formation on the floor with place mats on top. She didn't have a table big enough. For some years, just a buffet spread appeared on one table and we crammed in to connect. Always, twinkle lights. Always wine. Always a candlelit sharing of what we wanted to release and what we would like to carry on into the new year. The lighter days were now promised.

She loves to celebrate the return of the light.

We're texting back and forth. Brian is there with her. We exchange emojis and I tell her it's modern day hieroglyphics. She apologizes that she couldn't come to the beach with me, that she missed the last show. She tells me all the time how I thrive outside of the box.

I almost texted her about Donna Kaz/Aphra Behn. But, I decided to wait until I see her face to face. It's so unlikely that this connection has been made. I want to see her facial expression and then stay up all night with a bottle of wine while she explains my star charts and how synchronicity abounds.

On Christmas Eve Tricia posts a memory on my FB wall. It's a photo Alan took of the two of us at one of her Solstice/Christmas Eve gatherings. The only caption she writes is, "aw".

Me and T.
One Christmas Eve
Alan insisted on snapping this photo

On Christmas day, Alan's Mom is in the hospital. We go to visit her and I show her all of the pictures of the ocean I've saved on my phone.

The day after Christmas Alan and I decided to go see the new Star Wars movie.

Someone has been writing weird things on my Facebook wall under the photo Tricia has shared. It's a strange name. I don't recognize it. Must be a troll, those fools are everywhere. I ignore it.

One of Tricia's college friends jumps on and tells me that it's Tricia's brother. He changes his screen name and now I see. Tricia never arrived on the West Coast to see her family. She wasn't on the plane. She never showed up to Christmas dinner with the Stage Guild.

I tell her to calm down. T probably crashed out. She'd missed that dinner once before.

Her friend says they are meeting the police at her apartment. A newsperson will be there. Can I go over?

NO!

Absolutely not. Everything is fine.

I can feel Tricia with me telling me, "Everything is fine."

We come out of the Star Wars movie, and still no T.

I start panicking. Alan and I start driving around the city looking for her car. Marshmallow. Stupid little car.

They find parts of her phone on a sidewalk somewhere.

More people are driving around the city looking for her.

I'm up well into the night. All kinds of people are coming at me.

An animal communicator is getting a reading, do I want to share it?

I ask her brother, do you want me to share this?

He tells me that, why not? Anything that might help find her.

So, I post that this is very controversial. Do not read on if you are feeling upset. I scroll scroll scroll before I cut and paste. This woman is telling us that Tricia is barely alive. That she's being moved around the city. That there's a big chair.

The police put out a bulletin. We share it on twitter.

One old theatre critic is communicating with another old theatre critic who is out walking his dog. In real time he says he thinks he sees her car.

RIGHT NOW.

Some guy smoking a big blunt is driving it.

It has her bumper sticker on the back bumper, "Plant More Plants". That's her bumper sticker. That's HER CAR. Where is SHE?

He says something to the driver. The driver becomes hostile toward him. The music is blaring too loud through T's speakers and this guy peels away.

I can't take it.

I want to believe that we will all be laughing about this in the morning.

I shut everything off and go to bed. I can feel Tricia telling me to go to bed.

The next morning, I turn my phone on. It's flooded with comments. The first thing I see is "I'm SO SORRY."

And, I turn my phone off immediately. It's like standing on the edge of a deep pool knowing you're about to be pushed in. Stalling for seconds longer to stay dry. Just a few more seconds before finding out whether or not this is going to drown me.

I sit on the couch in the living room. Alan is in the shower.

He comes down the steps.

I say his name.

He looks at me.

I say her name.

He says, "NO!" and he starts wailing.

I am frozen.

Friends are asking if I can talk to the press. I feel like this is an opportunity for a last act of friendship.

I meet the press at the theatre. I think it was two film crews and a couple of radio shows.

Alan does a lot of the talking. I still cannot process what is going on.

I'm sure she's fine.

Things are moving so fast.

One reporter tells me she wants people to know who Tricia was in life. She encouraged me to take the opportunity to talk about HER and not the way she died.

Died.

Tricia is dead.

Dead.

Murdered.

Raped.

Then murdered.

Then tied up with her own seatbelts in the back of the smallest car the world has ever seen.

He drove around with her back there for three days.

I'm still trying to figure out how to stay dry. Every time I go to speak now all I can do is sob uncontrollably.

Carolyn calls. Many people are trying to check on me. I'm sure I should be dead and Tricia should be alive. There's been a big mistake. I'm the one with a violent childhood. She didn't know about that kind of pain.

Another friend had to go to the CVS parking lot to identify her body.

None of us will ever be the same.

Her rapist and murderer was inside the CVS with her credit cards buying things when the police found her car. He's had two passengers over these days at least. One appears to be a prostitute he paid for with Tricia's money. With her raped and tied up dead in her own backseat. This is absolutely incomprehensible.

This is the worst script I've ever read. Make it stop.

I can't breathe.

I can't think.

I shouldn't exist.

I find myself going through the cabinets in my kitchen. Looking at all of the expiration dates on all of the cans and bottles. I can hear Tricia commenting. I can hear her laughing at how old some of these things are. "The 90's, Deb?" [laughter laughter laughter]. I see things moving in my home.

I'm not sure what's real.

I decided to clean out my coat closet. It's so long overdue.

I'm taking trash bags filled with I-Don't-Know-What to my car to donate at a later date. It's dark. Alan has a late show. I hear this voice shout, "RUN!". So, I ran back inside and locked all of my doors. I think about crawling under the dining room table just until Alan gets home.

I'm holding Jasmine. Crying into her. Petting her.

How many Jimmy lifes did Tricia live?

11.05

That was supposed to be me.

I decided I will build an altar for her in the kitchen.

I grab a bunch of her Leafy Head products, pictures, memento's, plants, candles. I add journals to the mix. In one journal, every day I write down things she said to me. I never want to forget the things she said to me.

In another journal, I write down my memories of her.

I need a fountain pen.

It's New Year's Eve now, 2016. I write on FB that I will never know another year with her in it so I think I will stay up all night.

Someone I've never met starts checking in on me every 20 minutes. She wants to know what I'm doing, how I'm doing. Another woman tells me about essential oils that will help me and Jasmine too. So much support is flying at me, I cannot decipher it.

I can't read anything else about what's happened to her.

The Washington Post interviewed her rapist and murderer and told his side of the story. He said they were dating and she invited him to take all of her things.

I couldn't…

I can't…

She kept her home and her car immaculate.

It was filthy and on National News. She doesn't want THAT!

As soon as I saw her car on the news, the only thing that I could really focus on was how filthy it was around the driver's door handle. She would have never allowed her car to become even slightly dirty, much less filthy.

I asked her. I ASKED her in the summer if she was safe after that intern disappeared on her block.

She promised me she was safe. She said only certain people make the news and she was furious about that. She told me about her neighbors. She went through her neighborhood routines with me. I was sure she was going to be fine. This reporter told me that they weren't going to cover it nationally until they saw her headshot. Once the producer saw how beautiful she was they decided to run with it. A news reporter excitedly told me I might be on "Good Morning America" tomorrow.

NO!

NO! NO! NO!

I DO NOT WANT TO BE ON GOOD MORNING AMERICA!!!

Fucking press!!!

I've been staging about the dilemma of being a woman MY WHOLE LIFE!

What good did that do?

I can't think.

I can't function.

I can write poetry and watch the room spin around me.

That's it.

Build a bigger altar.

She's gone.

He took her.

He took her because he felt like it.

This cannot be real.

Chapter 17:
THIRD JLT IN THE HOUSE-THAT-LOVE-BUILT

Third Jimmy Lifetime

2017 - To a T!; Love Notes To a Friend

Plays from the Methuen Collection Edited by Naomi Paxton direction Deborah Randall| assistant direction Patrick Gorirossi| costumes and props Deborah Randall|set and lights Amy Rhodes|sound Neil McFadden| stage management Lydia Howard|front-of-house Myrrh Cauthen|construction Deborah Randall, Lydia Howard, Patrick Gorirossi, and Amy Rhodes| graphic design Laura Matteoni Schraven|ensemble Allison Frisch, Jean H. Miller, Erin Lee Hanratty, Christine Jacobs, Emily Sucher, Deborah Randall, Myrrh Cauthen, Lydia Howard|

"Tunnel Vision" by Andrea Lepcio direction Deborah Randall| costumes and props Deborah Randall|set Amy Rhodes| lights Kristin A. Thompson|sound Neil McFadden|stage management Deborah Randall|fx Paul Kelm|construction Deborah Randall and Amy Rhodes|graphic design Laura Matteoni Schraven| front-of-house Myrrh Cauthen|cast Jill played by Katie Down Hileman| Olexandra played by Kyosin Kang|

"Aglaonike's Tiger" by Claudia Barnett direction Deborah Randall| costumes and props Deborah Randall|set Amy Rhodes| lights Kristin A. Thompson|sound Neil McFadden|masks Waxing Moon Masks| puppets Matthew Pauli|choreography Alison Talvacchio|stage management L| front-of-house Myrrh Cauthen|construction Deborah Randall and Amy Rhodes|graphic design Laura Matteoni Schraven| cast Aglaonike played by Ann Fraistat| Tiger played by Matthew Marcus|Ericho played by Deborah Randall|ensemble Katie Down Hileman, Katie Zelonka, Amy Rhodes|

"The Ravens" by Alana Valentine direction Deborah Randall costumes and props Deborah Randall|lights and set Amy Rhodes|sound Neil McFadden|masks Waxing Moon Masks|choreography Alison Talvacchio|fight choreography Deborah Randall|dialect coach Erin Lee Hanratty|stage management Deborah Randall|front-of-house Myrrh Cauthen|construction Deborah Randall and Amy Rhodes|graphic design Laura Matteoni Schraven| cast Kira played by Suzanne Tirado|Nina played by Erin Lee Hanratty|ensemble Alison Talvacchio and Ashley Kissandra|

I'm looping.

There is this tapping sound and very bright light. And also, complete darkness.

I'm in fifth grade. Sitting at a desk in a classroom run by a woman who talks about driving to Amish Pennsylvania to get fresh eggs every weekend. She tells the same story every Monday and we all look at her like we've never heard it before. Like, this is the great enlightenment.

The way she says "freSH" feels fresh too. Like she's managed an extra s and added a soft c to the word.

She turns all of the lights out and does not tell us to put our heads on our desks. That's how we know.

I look around at the other kids and they usually seem pretty rested to me.

I'm having a full conversation with myself inside of my own head. Next weekend I will go to my Dad's house. Which is never really his house. It's my Grandmother's house and he lives with her again, between marriages when he lives with his wife.

I wonder if we will go to Pennsylvania next weekend? If we do, I know we won't purchase any Amissscchhh Eggs. We might go to Dutch Wonderland and sit on a stationary bench while the little house we're in spins around us. Because it feels like I'm sitting on a stationary bench and this little place I live in right now is spinning around me.

Whatever happens it's bound to be better than the weekend I'm coming out of. The screaming of my Mother always frames my time at home. She likes it when I make her look good. And having friends over does that. Being popular does that. Being pretty does that. So, I'm working on making her like me.

I've decided.

I'm not going to learn. I'm turning all of that off.

I'm too tired.

I'll learn when I'm older and have more energy.

I'll learn when I start eating breakfast in the morning. I'm too tired before lunch to know much of anything now.

The teacher rolls in the movie machine.

"Mulligan Stew."

We've seen it before but I think this might be a different series. It's a nice reprise of Saturday morning cartoons on a Monday morning at school. Feels like magic.

There's a snag.

We've seen the opening song in all of its glory, but there's a snag.

And then a burning. Followed by a gigantic screen of pure white light.

The reel is alone now, slapping through the machine.

That's me now, looping. Not able to project my story. Trapped in the darkness desperately projecting light with nothing in between.

X always said, "there's no such thing as a transition.". You're either present or you're in the mud. I don't know what the mud ever did to him but man, did he think the mud was the worst possible place to be. .

Click click click click click

Suddenly, nothing really works even though it's all the same.

Everything is different now.

I'm a grown ass woman.

Like always, I try to educate myself on any subject I don't really understand, after a substantial brekkie. I research online, I ask questions of people who may have some information.

I'm already crying all day every day. But now, I cannot see. I cannot feel. I have gone entirely out-of-body. I can see myself from the ceiling on the floor moving through the motions of life. I can feel Tricia watching me. She's so fast. How did she get to be so fast?

She's throwing up rainbows and learning the ways of her spirit movement now. Ways I do not understand. Ways I cannot understand.

All I can process is that she's so fast and I'm so slow. She needs to slow down and I need to speed up. I'm pinned by grief. I'm almost frozen. Encased in slowly drying concrete. I'm about to crumble and disappear here so I can join her there and still be connected to her.

She gives me three words. I grasp those.

Artistry.
Levity.
Discernment.

I have three descriptions that I've gathered through my journey. Remember remember remember...

An Irish man told me I was clever, an Olympian told me I was kind, and a Civil Right legend said I was impressive.

Clever.
Kind.
Impressive.

Artistry.
Levity.
Discernment.

I think I can hold onto these six words. I'm sure they mean something.

Alan is desperately terrified. He's not sure if I'm going to live through this. I'm not sure. No one knows.

Jasmine is with me 24/7.

I am maintaining an altar for Tricia. I am writing poetry on Facebook.

I don't feel safe leaving my house.

Many of my online friends are social workers and therapists. They tell me about EMDR. Eye Movement Desensitization Reprocessing Therapy.

Alan tells me to do whatever I need to do. He tells me not to worry about money going out-of-network. He'll cover me.

Somehow.

So many friends are recommending so many things.

I am really out-of-body. I'm going through menopause but I don't know what that means or what it's doing to me because I can't feel anything except sliced through heart and soul.

I'm hearing Tricia talk to me so I think I might be mad now.

I have PTSD, as I'm going through menopause, while I'm having full on days spent communicating with my now dead friend.

While these three things are happening, political dynamics are really amping up too.

People are publishing articles about Tricia. Mostly men. Talking about how they all had a crush on her. What does that mean? It hurts them that she was raped? They can feel it in their collective penis?

What does that mean?

I'm so fucking confused all of the time.

Nothing makes sense.

My soul is screaming a shrill piercing sound that only certain birds can hear.

No one is talking about how she was an entrepreneur. Some of her friends and interns gather up all of her remaining lotions and potions under her "Leafyhead" business name.

T and I bonded over being women running small businesses. We stayed up late at night consoling one another about the sexism we were facing on a daily basis. The classism. How could we both be producing such good stuff and also be completely ignored? It was always mystifying. Some days she could not talk because the temperature and the weather was right for making her lotions and potions and she had to get to work while the air was good. Sometimes she would have to wait out weeks in the swamp of DC until optimum humidity conditions permitted her to create.

I'd just purchased a bunch of stuff from her older stock with her older label. She'd gone through a redesign.

We went to Jailbreak Brewery and she would selectively speak to men with beards and give them a ¼" dram of beard oil, a tiny sample. I would tell her that half of the place contained men with beards and ask why she just didn't pass them around the room. She would tell me that she had to be selective. She had to speak to individuals she felt a connection with.

Discernment.

That's her. Dinner parties too. There's only so much room. Yes, she loved everyone but to be invited was a real gift.

Discernment.

In our talks she told me about the men she'd dated and how they could become real assholes. So, it was shocking to see so many of them at the microphone touting their love and admiration for her. The more they spoke the more I could hear her telling me which kind of asshole that one was. The whole world was shocked at this crime against humanity.

Once her product was mentioned after she was killed, it sold out in record time.

What is it about human nature?

Morbid.

If she'd seen those kinds of sales when she was alive she could have really launched her business to the next level. Do we have to be raped and killed to be seen?

It's December 31, now. Laura has invited me over for her New Years eve gathering. I haven't left the house. I go over with Alan. People are trying not to cry when they look at me.

It's a lot like Jimmy all over again. When they see me they really see the ghost of them. I'm not sure if I actually exist anymore. I can hear her with me.

I'm a feral ghost.

Kindness and caring surrounds.

I brought one of the games with me from the beach.

We play this silly game all night. I couldn't talk. So, this was good.

People are talking to me but I'm still not really sure what they're saying. It's like when I was in school and supposed to be reading a story but my Mother had been screaming at me the night before and all I could do was stare at letters on the page.

I saw mouths moving but I could not really understand. I just played a silly game and tried to laugh with my friends. As someone was talking to me I heard and felt Tricia strongly.

Crying.

I had a full conversation with her in my mind while other people were telling me things.

She wanted to know why no one could see or hear her.

I had the distinct impression she'd been going around knocking on the doors of every single friend she loved, and no one was answering.

I told her that I was here. I could hear her. And there was a place in my heart for her. A canopied bed full of luscious pillows and high thread count sheets. I told her she could snuggle into my heart at any time. I felt her climb in. I told her that people were in pain. They were stuck in terrestrial existence. The pain of losing her was too great for them to feel her now.

She cried, that she was right here. Saying that it happened to HER and not anyone else.

I acknowledged her and told her that her rhythms are different from the rhythms of us "humans" here. She was free and we were stuck. It didn't make much sense.

We both seemed to need time to make this adjustment.

Whatever time is.

It's the next morning. New Year's Day 2017.

I'm spending it online. I'm watching so many of Tricia's friends talk about feeling visited by her last night. I am elated.

She did it.

They did it.

Love never dies, it just changes shape. We terrestrials have to make a real commitment to remain fluid if we want to stay connected. If we allow ourselves to lock up with grief and pain and stop moving through it, we become stuck.

The big trick right now is to keep moving through the quicksand that wants nothing more than to swallow us whole.

I have to release all judgment.

Any way anyone can get to the other side of this drowning pit of terror seems fair game.

We exist in a dichotomy.

Tension makes life.

The real puzzlement here is that we each must take this walk of recovery alone because we each have a specific way we need to move through it. Also, we make the journey together.

Alone together.

Together alone.

The loose film bit is still tapping on the running projector threatening to burn a hole through the machine and take us all out in flames. It's just like the fireman warned with their mobile house that they set on fire outside of the school when they taught us to stop, drop, and roll.

The trick for me is to not incinerate myself.

The journey for me is to understand that I'm not the film of the story running through the machine, I am the light. I shine and whatever story is running through me is not my identity.

First rule: show up!

Whatever story has been put on to Tricia is not her identity.

I know her.

I love her.

These things never stop. To connect and to love is the purpose of life as we live it. I can see it. I can understand it. I can feel it. Everything else is fertilizer for the soil. The trick is to let all the rest go.

"Give it to gravity." It will become useful again there.

Gravity is a feminine energy and it always wins. It's silent and it's invisible and it always wins.

I have a season to create.

I will dedicate it to Tricia.

I will launch more suffrage plays because she gave me her xeroxed copy. I will honor her at every turn. I will live for both of us as I lived for Jimmy and me. For my grandmother and my ancestors who did not have the opportunities that I now have.

I will live four times or more in each moment.

I don't have time to be stuck.

I MUST keep moving.

Aphra Behn is coming into town. I've sounded the alarms, or horns, or whatever needed to be sounded.

Tricia discovered cleavers when she was studying plants in Ohio. Once she did she made a wreath of them and wore it on her head as she waded through streams and learned about more and more of her little green "friends" singing their hellos to her from the ground.

ven*us*

I need to make fairy wreaths.

I run into Rainbow Florist on Main Street. I buy a bunch of green stuff. Laurel. I bought Laurel.

I set up my station in the lobby. Molly Ruppert Arrives with a stack of Aprha Behn's books. By now, her son owns a bookstore and they step right up to offer their help. Chosen family. Joe is the manager across the street and he's been having a lot of success with Sip, his coffee/wine bar. He lets us use the other side of the place. He's reserved it for community events.

Donna Kaz/Aprha Behn is signing book after book. People are appearing to meet her.

Eventually we all travel across the street back to my theatre. Meera is there. People are showing up. Holding me up.

Actors I've directed over the years are appearing. Organizations we've allowed to use the space to pull women together are appearing. It's a smearing blur but I know what's going on.

Sharing my Laurel Fairy Rings with Toni Rae Salmi

At the theatre, I give Aprha Behn/Donna Kaz her Lifetime Achievement Award from Venus. I tell her and everyone there about sitting in that same room under fluorescents and wanting to quit. I tell them about reading about her. And how a decade before I met her, she kept me going by showing up to live her own story. That's the power we have. When we each step into our truth, we pull others up without even realizing it.

She then takes the stage and gives her presentation about her book, about her life, about her surviving her relationship with William Hurt.

We have a raffle. She brought all kinds of Guerilla Girl products with her to auction off.

She tells me that she's sold the most books so far at this event, even though the others may have happened at larger venues.

Giving our second Venus Theatre Lifetime Achievement Award to Aphra Behn (Donna Kaz)

Dear Deb Randall and Venus Theatre,

I applaud you for keeping the voices of women alive for so many years. I salute your bravery in producing season after season of work by women. I admire your perseverance, your style, your grace. I acknowledge your struggle and the struggle of all the women who have gone before you and remain behind via the love that refuses to die. I promise to keep fighting, to keep enduring and to keep advocating on behalf of women in theatre. We are theatre. We are.

THANK YOU VENUS!

I feel the connections firing off.

I announce the season at Venus. I begin to talk and only tears appear. I'm surrounded by a sea of support. I explain how every show is a celebration of Tricia.

I am literally and figuratively surrounded by these women in what feels like a safety net that will NOT let me fall.

I'm wiped out. Things make me really tired now.

I'm going to keep going. I've fought too hard to have a space. Tricia has given NuTricia workshops in this space. She's told us about the terrible effects of white powders, sugar, flour, and salt. She explained that anything refined brings inflammation to the body. She explained that all disease begins with inflammation.

One of the last times we hung out she showed me her reading glasses hidden at the bottom of her purse and told me she'd just been given a clean bill of health by her doctors. For some reason I was compelled to give her a tiny turtle from the Crystal Fox that night. I told her I wanted her to know that no matter where she was or how she was feeling, she was already home.

At another fundraiser she brought dirt and seeds and had people planting things to take home.

She sat in every seat in the theatre. I can hear her laughter in the walls.

I can remember her writing in chalk all over the back walls. I can remember her scraping the tongues of the actors in my "Measure for Measure" cast. Another cause for them to call "Actors Inequity".

We'd meet in the lobby before we'd go thrifting or, as she always called it, frolicking. She showed up when her phone stopped working. I tried to give her mine. She insisted on writing me a check. I still have the check. That didn't work anyway. I sent her to Best Buy and she sorted everything out.

I have to fight for the Venus space because I feel like she's still here in this space. Besides, it's one of the only times in my life now that I know who I am. Where I am. What I need to do. I can function here.

I can't even function going to the grocery store.

I didn't want to go to the grocery store but I needed to go so I did. When I came out I couldn't remember where I parked. Just then, something fell out of my pocket. I heard it hit the ground.

It was one of her lip balms. A lemon one. I didn't realize I had it in my pocket. I bent down to pick it up and when I went to stand up again I saw my car, to the right, in the direction the thing had fallen. I had been headed in the wrong direction. I thanked her.

The first show is a collection of Suffrage plays.

I cast seven women, which has become the maximum number of actors I will work with on any show.

The space is too small for more than that anyway. From a sociological perspective, eight is a group. Anything under eight functions as individuals. It's true of small audiences too. Just need eight or more to feel the group energy. Under eight and it's like death on a stale saltine.

Seven actors means I can guide, lead, and manage. Eight or above means mutiny.

Seven.

Two older women and five twenty-somethings.

And then at the end a final piece where Myrrh, and Lydia, and I jump on stage.

I've decided to craft this piece a little like "Noises Off". The idea being this cast has just been at the Women's March. They come in wearing their pink pussy hats still all amped up. Some are late. They are trying to do what they've rehearsed but some women may not show at all. So there's a generalized sense of chaos and excitement on the verge of panic. We chant between vignettes. "Show me what democracy looks like, this is what democracy looks like."

One of my big goals here is to get the pussy hats on the same stage as the suffrage sashes.

It's such a powerful image.

Frustrating too.

We should be further along by now.

There seems to be this assumption that we've "arrived". That all of the freedoms women have have just always been there. There seems to be little understanding that women won the right to vote by one single man's vote. I once read that this man reached into his coat to find a note which simply read, "Make your Mother proud." That's what caused him to change his mind.

That's how it happened.

Perhaps an oversimplification, but I like that story.

I'm listening to young women now talk about the women's march. I'm watching their energy amp up. The rage and excitement combine into a palpable indestructible force shield.

I can see Tricia in that. I know she would have been there marching. I understand that perhaps we are both generals now. Generals of the Love Army. Each on either side of the veil, almost touching.

It comforts me to know we are Generals in the same battle still.

Two of the women in my cast are older so I offer to pay them more money. I feel I owe older women. I was raised to respect people older than me.

But, maybe they aren't really that much older than me at all.

They are not demonstrating the leadership skills I'd assumed.

Things are wobbly.

Myrrh is holding down the front. Lydia is there, in the booth, they are both willing to jump on stage with and for me. This makes me really excited.

My rocks to the right of me, Lydia Roberts and Myrrh

At the end of notes the other night I look up to see the cast looking at each other and some have tears streaming down their face.

Dear Lord.

I ask what is going on.

I've gone over the planned rehearsal time by one minute.

They are all on a schedule.

I drop what I'm doing and send them home.

One of the older actors is giving notes to some of the younger actors and I'm standing right there.

It's the animalistic part of human nature to assume dominance when the leader is wounded. I know this is true but I still can't believe what I'm hearing.

I ask the actor to not overstep her role. She tells me she can't work in these conditions and she drops out of the show two weeks in.

[flourish: MT18]

2017. 6-March. Grateful (and angry)
Two days ago
An actor resigned
via email
Making the point
She didn't like
Me communicating
With her
via email.
Making the point.
Two weeks into
a 3 1/2 week process
I felt T with me
Meaning I could be
Going
mad
or maybe

Deborah L. Randall

I'm just going
angry
When this happened
Mid-day on Saturday
She let me know
That it would
be resolved
By noon on Sunday.
I called so many
friends
Thank you
For being on the other end
Thank you
I started stitching
Mostly because
I could no longer think
There's no way
of being more clear
There's no room
For petty arrogance
or
condescending classism
or
self-hating sexism
or
whateverthefuckisgoingonwiththisbitch
I was stitching
and
then sobbing

venus

crying

saying

I spent no time at your

altar today

she told me

straight into

my heart

she told me

Let my

altar

Be your

artistry

I woke up yesterday

With a new idea

I could solve this

in-house

With existing cast

More comedy

More roles

for women who

actually

WANT them

I made calls

To see

If I was asking

too much

If they were

game

The final

yes

came

11:20 am

We are set to

open

one week from

Thursday

yeah…

Seeing that

My artistry

Is her

ALTAR

Sacred space

Respect it

or

Be gone.

I have already staged the concept in my head that Lydia and Myrrh and I go out with scripts in hand to perform the final short because of the Frayn concept that the world is conspiring against this cast.

So, for the second to last short, I replaced the actor who dropped with a pLaNt.

It's a perfect nod to Tricia.

I call Amy and we go over to the silk flower store. We choose the perfect silk fern.

The actors will shuffle around and pull the plant in.

Scuttlebutt.

They'll place it on a stool and put one of the hats of one of the characters on it. The character in the play is writing and trying to tune everyone out. The lines are so perfect. "Don't talk to her when she's in one of her moods."

Things like that.

The pLaNt does have some lines. So, I have Myrrh sneak up the vom with a script and attempt to hide behind the fern unsuccessfully to read the lines out entirely unrehearsed.

The plant has more talent than the actor who dropped.

It's the funniest part of the show.

I'm now laughing WITH Tricia.

[flourish: MT19]

2017. 18-March. We Begin Again.
Today we open officially for the year.
Just two weeks ago an actor dropped
out of four roles
Today we open officially for the year.
Last night a few people from town showed up
Attended our final dress
I cried.
These people have come to see everything
ever
staged
at
Venus Theatre Play Shack
Gratitude runs deep
I told them it was a final dress

Deborah L. Randall

We were holding to open
They insisted on paying
No concessions
They had a cup of water
And ate a granola bar
Left from rehearsals at the front
Coins dropped into our
Piggy bank
On top of the fridge
I cried.
Then it was revealed to me
That one of them lost their Mother
That day
From a nursing facility
She finally drifted
Home.
I couldn't believe he was at the theatre
He said
It's only memory
Every play
I see
Stays with me
Inside
He said
The first thing I thought about
After she died
Was
Looking for the Pony
A play staged at Venus

venus

More than
Five years ago
an Andrea Lepcio piece
that chanted 1440
Because it insisted
That all we ever have
Is the moment
1440
of them each day
Dive deeply
Play.
He said
They stay with me
Each one
He said
Keep going
He said
It's like you said
In the face of sadness
The most defiant thing we can do
Is find a way
to
laugh
We sang together
On the stage
After the show
Will the circle be unbroken?

We're having a little frolic in my mind and soul, T and me.

The first week of the run went well. The Washington Post is coming on the second week. We were on the cover of the Style Section twice last year. A pretty unheard of accomplishment.

Instinctively, I know there's only one way to go, and that's down.

I met a new reviewer for the Baltimore Sun, David Strum. He did a feature on us last year as well. David is a Professor of English.

At the end of the show, I let the audience choose the ending, this is determined during pre-show announcements. 1. A regular curtain call. 2. A song the audience sings with us, "Will The Circle Be Unbroken". 3. The audience joins us on stage to dance our feet off to "Bad Reputation" by Joan Jett and the Blackhearts.

It's Thursday. Show tonight.

I'm heading in. I've got this.

I just saw something on the news. A young woman who looks a lot like T. She lived less than five blocks away from T. She was just in town temporarily on a special project for the Corcoran. They found her bound and raped in the townhome where she was staying. Stabbed to death.

It's not Tricia. It's another woman. It could be any of us, I guess.

I'm at the theatre now.

I'm not okay.

The entire cast has arrived.

I'm not okay.

Gasping in my chest.

I can't remember my tools from therapy.

Earthsuit. In EMDR I've learned to imagine a protective suit. I've given it its own oxygen supply. Even the air is safe.

When I wear it I can see myself diving down through the pavement.

It lives under the hood of the VW bug in the lobby. Jimmy and Tricia help me put it on. They want me out in the world. I want to be gone like they are. But I'm here and how many more women are going to be tied up raped and killed while the world pretends none of this is really happening?!?!

A sound comes out of me.

A primal sound.

Myrrh is walking toward me.

She grabs me and holds me tight.

I sob.

Uncontrollably.

Again.

I sob so hard I can't breathe. I can't speak.

Myrrh tells me I have to go home.

I tell her, "no".

I'm supposed to show up.

First rule, show up. I have to keep showing up. I can't quit.

She tells me she's got this and that I did show up. She tells me that I will show up again tomorrow. But today, I need to go back home and rest and take care of myself.

So, I do.

From this moment forward, the actors form a kind of support system for each other out of their own necessity. I have an Assistant Director on this show because I know I'm not okay. They are all deciding things without me because they know I'm not okay.

They tell me they are not comfortable with the last scenes with me and Lydia and Myrrh. They feel they are under-rehearsed. Which is exactly how I want them to feel. But, I see this cast is young and they don't know how to trust me. There's no way I can convince them because now I have been officially diagnosed with PTSD. Which means, I could drop out on them even though I never want to be that person.

For the record, I don't think anyone ever wants to be that person. Life keeps happening.

Every production must have trust and respect. Losing one or both of those will kill a show. So, without talking to Myrrh or Lydia, I cut us all out. This was to the great disappointment of my creative team and likely the reason the press wasn't too glowing on this one. It was an incomplete project.

Still. Venus was still standing. That seems like an accomplishment.

We landed that project only two months after losing, T. It's a miracle!.

[flourish: MT20]

2017. 27-March. No Sleep. Math.
It's been a few days since
I've slept
They call it a
War on Women
But I call it math
Sex Trafficking
Each woman
Is worth
$200,000 a year
One pimp

venus

Plus five slaves
Makes a
Millionaire
The Orange man
Fills the screen
Pussy grabber
One woman
Sometimes sold
Twenty times
A
Day
Most lucrative
product
Better than
drugs
Restitch
Repackage
Resell
Redeem
$200,000 annual
So
No sleep
Math.
Creates a culture
That says
Woman=
Product
Hair+Nails+
Shape+Clothes=

Marketability
No value
On the going market
No need
To live
So
No sleep
Math.
We all walk
In the concentric circles
The labyrinth
In vertical motion
She breathes
But
no
air
She's
Worth
The thickness
Or thinness
The darkness
Or lightness
The penthouse
Or car seat
Depending
on
the
Numbers
Nothing personal

Columns in a ledger
So don't get
Emotional
Collateral damage
Comes with
Profitable
Business
No such thing
As humanity
No sleep.
Math.

I wonder if I should have rolled out this season at all. Maybe I should just hang it up. This not knowing when the floor is going to drop out under my feet is making me what X would call, "anticipatory and way too sentimental". Hesitation is death and I trust nothing right now. All I can do is keep moving so I don't lock up and freeze. I have to keep going. It's the only way I feel like I know who I am or where I am. I have to keep going for T. I just have to keep going.

At the cast party one of the young actors can't stop crying. I ask her why she's so upset.

She says, "I didn't know".

You didn't know what?

"I didn't know that you could just do this." I think she meant, make theatre like this.

Instead of a traditional cast party I filled my car with pLaNts from Meadow Farms and each person repotted a plant for Tricia and we filled the display window with this new growth.

Deborah L. Randall

[flourish: MT21]

2017. 10-March. Helium.
Laughter is helium
and the theatre rent is due
That's why the rule is
When you help
When you contribute
When you invest
You become a part of this
Conversely,
When you judge without knowing
Change without growing
Martyr yourself all-knowing
You can say goodbye to me
Laughter is helium
and the theatre rent is due
17 years paying rent
Sometimes I wonder
Why I've always been so insistent
On playing by the rules
Tricia used to tell me,
"you were born to operate
outside of the box.
It's what you do."
So
Instead of falling into that dark depression

I stage laughter
Because
Laughter is helium
and the theatre rent is due
And because
When I'm in that room
Building a world from my brain
There is no sense of being lost
or sad
or helpless
I am free
In love
In laughter
playing
And I know so deeply
That's exactly where she wants me to be.

I loved sharing the song or the dance at the end with our audience. I wonder why we don't sing or dance together much at all anymore.

It healed me.

Dave from the Sun met his wife at the theatre to cover us. He loved it!

They each had a beer and they each danced their butts off with everyone else at the end. I couldn't believe I had a critic and his wife cutting the rug. That's the power of Tricia though.

That's the power of me.

US.

Two Generals in the Love Army.

What I didn't know was that Dave had been given a terminal diagnosis. He covered every show up until he was gone. He seemed to be on the edge of his seat every time.

He put us on the cover of the local paper.

We are all only ever just moving through.

Another audience regular (former leading man) was Arthur who came on a walker or sometimes in a wheelchair. I always made space for him in the front row. I had a special chair for him. He stayed after each show religiously. I could tell it made his day when he talked to us about his glory days as an actor at the University of Maryland in the 70's.

He would pull up in his car and park out front. Somehow he'd pull his walker out all on his own and then get himself inside. With him it was clear that once an actor always an actor. I wanted to make sure he knew we cared about his stories. His moments in the light. He never missed a show, sitting in his front row seat.

I didn't know these moments were sacred. I was still too busy sticking to my schedule..

Fleeting, sacred, precious.

I just thought I was pushing through and trying not to kill myself.

I'm so glad we didn't have reactionary suicides resulting from the rape and murder of T. There could have been a whole terrifying chain reaction. I'm so glad there wasn't.

It was cold and icy on the day of her memorial. The Stage Guild held it at their space downtown. Tricia was a company member with the Guild for so many years. I saw her in "Anna Karenina" back when they were performing at the Catholic Church. She called the Stage Guild her "theatre family".

The memorial meant her parents were in. Her brother and his partner were there.

I saw so many people.

A blur of people.

Her old partners.

There was a slideshow. Things were said.

Her father told me that if I saw him hesitating or struggling, I should remind him to "breathe". Which is what Tricia always said.

He was stuck behind the podium and I screamed, "BREATHE!" from the house and then ducked down.

Someone was trying to hack my FB account. People had been asking about her memorial but we had to keep it a secret.

The last thing any of us wanted was more press.

I was invited to the after-party, the repass after the repass.

Her parents and her brother wanted those closest to her to come back to their VRBO house and hang out for a while.

I didn't know how any of us were doing this.

I told one of her exes that I wasn't sure how to go forward without her. He told me that I just needed to live.

Okay?

I parked a few blocks away in one of DC's underground garages. I was three to five levels underground. I noticed that it was steep coming up and out of there.

I don't want to be in DC.

I don't want to be near where she was assaulted, where she died.

I had brunch with her here six or seven months ago.

Everything is different now.

I know people live in her favorite neighborhood, Bloomingdale. But, I don't ever want to be here again.

The house is not far from T's place.

It's suddenly feeling very Irish. People are laughing. Glassy eyes. An overwhelming look of shock. A three day Irish wake is definitely called for but I cannot do this.

I needed to leave.

It was so cold. Sheets of ice on the sidewalks and roads.

I felt this strange slow tearing sensation. I was driving out of her tomb. Through locations that had taken her away. I wasn't sure if I would make it home alive.

My car started acting funny but I was out of the city now.

I was one highway exit from my house. I was almost home.

She was close to home too, when he walked up to her.

It's getting dark.

Lights come on.

My car doesn't want to run. I have to pull over.

I'm stuck.

Some dark force just tried to suck all of the life out of me and now I'm stuck.

I call AAA. I don't have AAA but it's the only thing I know to do. Turns out you can sign up from the side of the road.

They're sending someone out.

Alan has been working all day and has a show tonight and we need that money and I don't want to bother him. Besides, what's he going to do?

The tow truck is on the way.

I turn up the radio and scream songs out at the top of my lungs.

Here it is.

It's so cold and I'm wearing a dress and heels. What's wrong with me?

Why am I wearing this?

Because Tricia is dead.

SHE'S DEAD!!!

Right.

The tow driver lets me ride in his cab back to his shop which is just off of the far end of Main Street. Just over the train tracks. I ask if he can drive me home.

He says no, he's not supposed to.

It's so cold. I would walk a few miles, but it's so cold.

I explained that I was on the way home from my murdered friend's funeral and I'm just trying to keep living and I don't know why my car died except I think maybe everything is dying now.

He asks where I live and when he realizes it's less than five miles away he tells me he will drive me home under the condition I never tell a soul.

Okay?

I have to get out of the very tall cab of the truck in the parking lot where I live and walk to my front door. This seems like an impossible task. Everything is ice. Perhaps I'll slip and everything will be done.

He tells me to be careful.

I walk slowly and sometimes sideways. I make it to my front door and let myself in and hold Jasmine and tell her all about it.

Alan gets home after his show and I explain what happened and he wants to know why I didn't call him.

I don't want to mess up everyone's life.

It turns out the clutch in my car disintegrated. It just stopped existing.

If that had happened in the city, I would have become incredibly reactive. And then people would have called me a Karen and shot video footage of me and showed the world what a fucking screaming sobbing entitled mess I am.

Tricia was killed on December 25, an alleged "holy" day.

Her birthday is on February 25, I'm so glad she was born.

For some reason January 25 has become this kind of fulcrum point. I can't lose three months every year to trauma. Tricia would be so pissed off at me if I did that.

She's got no patience for me with this trauma, she wants me out there living and laughing.

In therapy I'm learning to predict what might be a trigger and then make adjustments for that before it might happen. It's a fuck-ton of work.

There are two drug dealers outside of my dining room window.

I told Darlene, my therapist, that I tried to do my homework but I was distracted by these drug dealers three feet away from me on the other side of my window. My husband had seen them trying to turn a five year old into a mule in the firelane.

Tricia's killer was smoking something for what looks to be days as he drove her in her car around the city under Christmas lights.

My therapist tells me drug dealers outside of my window are not acceptable.

We have spoken about Quantum Physics. She has explained to me that there are "pockets of chaos" in the Universe. It's a scientific fact. And through no fault of her own, Tricia stepped into a pocket of chaos.

Only she never says Tricia. She says "Trish". Every single time this happens, without fail, I hear "it's Tricia!" in the irritated tone that comes with an eye roll that belongs to Tricia alone.

When that happens, all I say is, "I think I might be going crazy.". Then my therapist says something I can not understand because all I can hear is Tricia saying, "That's not very nice."

Am I dead or crazy yet?

No.

Fascinating.

For Tricia's birthday, I am suddenly invited over to a mutual friend's house. Abigail apologized, "I don't know why I forgot to invite you. She was always talking about you."

Abigail insisted on going through all of T's things and helping her mother sort things out. She insisted on taking control of her ashes and for some reason, it seemed to be really healing for her to put them EVERYWHERE.

I found out about this gathering a little late.

We gathered for her birthday. Maybe ten of us. Someone decided we were the people closest to T.

But, that's a really strange call to make. She was close to a lot of different people from a lot of different walks of life.

I saw a rainbow when I stopped on the way for the obligatory bottle of wine. I took it to be a sign that Tricia wanted me there. She was always showing us rainbows.

We were in the backyard. They had worked together to come up with a service. They passed something around. It was in my hands.

It was her.

It was Tricia.

It was her ashes.

In my hand.

I asked.

"Is this her?"

"Yes."

"NO!"

Like always, I went along with what was happening. I rubbed her off of my hands and into the soil.

Abigail had given me a craft thing that T never finished and a plaque that said "create" and her fairy horns that she'd worn at the Renaissance festival. She bequeathed things to each of us.

It was kind.

She said, "These will be the last things Tricia ever gives you." I didn't like that.

She made up a donation thing so people could give money. I didn't understand what she was doing.

But, it was determined that we each had our own way to grieve. None of us were there to judge the other.

This is why T always chose her party guests so carefully.

Discernment.

I was not comfortable at all though I took comfort in seeing so many mutual friends.

I didn't want to do that again. I needed more therapy to deal with the fact that her bodily remains were in my hand. I never wanted that. I can still feel them. Was that ash bone or flesh? That's not what she wants me to focus on. That's not her anymore.

SHE'S GONE!

That's who she used to be and I have to come to terms with who she is now. Well, I'm attempting to come to terms with who she is now. I feel the weight in the ashes. The weight of her struggle. The way she fought him off, scratched his face, fractured his cheek bones. I don't want to feel this!

She doesn't want to be remembered like this!

[flourish: MT22]

2017. 29-March. Stepping Back.
Running a low grade fever
again
I keep pushing
because
She wants me
creating
Discernment
Artistry
Levity
And working to
Remove all people and things
from my life that do not feed
the beauty of my soul
Looking at this from many sides
therapy

How to take care of me
when
As Tricia once told me
I thought you wanted to run a theatre
I didn't realize you wanted to change
the whole damn world
Yeah
So more press coming out
tomorrow
And books are on the way to
sell
My therapist asked me a question
What would they think?
What would these women think
If someone told them in 1910
That
Their plays would get national coverage
In 2017?
Sit with that.
Fill
Up.
This next chapter will be
all about
Surrounding myself with those
who inspire
Because life is too short for
the other.
Time for tea.

Next up is Andrea's play. It's a two-hander and I really could use a two-hander right about now.

It's surreal. It's kind of a romp through color and sound and lust and connection. I love it.

I love costuming it. I love directing it.

It's the end of the rehearsal process and I realize I need a powerful image at the end. Something that will leave the audience with a brain impression in terms of image.

A boat!

I need A BOAT!

We can rig it to the ceiling and they can crank it up at the end. One character will drown on the stage below as the other lifts up through the air to escape.

Yes!

I NEED A BOAT!

I call Rob.

"I need a boat!"

"What size?"

We decide a small boat not being used at the lake during the cold months will do. I also told him this is an assemblage set. So, he brings a bunch of things he's got laying around and we use all of them.

In a matter of two days Rob's sent his crew with a boat on the back of a trailer. They ask where I want it and plop it right down. And they will come back to pick it up as well. This is so much easier than getting a Beetle through the front door.

We also need a tree to spontaneously bloom. Paul comes back and he rigs the boat and he builds these tubes that he pushes leaves through. I'm in the booth. Cramming these tubes on cue.

We still have to tech all of this in.

Katie Hileman
Curtis Jordan Photography

It's Thursday and I can't breathe.

I call the number on my insurance card and speak to a nurse. I tell her what's going on and she tells me I probably have gerd. She tells me to cut all acidic food out of my diet and she tells me what to buy over the counter. She tells me if it gets worse to call back.

It's Tuesday morning and we have tech rehearsal at 2 for the boat and lights and such. I can't breathe and my left hand has gone numb.

I call and Alan takes me in.

I tell the Doctor I've actually been feeling better and that it's probably gerd. I wanted to play it safe though because my left hand was tingling and felt like it might go numb.

He then launches into three stories, much like the detective did after I'd been mugged. Each story is successively more horrifying and they all end in death, just like the detectives. He's telling me that one woman came in saying that and then she left in a body bag.

I start sobbing.

He says, "Well, don't cry.".

He pushes into the center of my chest with three fingers and asks me if it hurts.

"YOU'RE POKING ME IN THE CHEST. YES! THAT HURTS."

He asks me if I have been doing any heavy lifting.

I tell him I've been moving a boat.

"A boat?"

"A boat."

"A boat?"

"I run a theatre. We occupy two completely different Universes. You'll never understand this. Move on."

I tell him I have a tech rehearsal I have to get to.

He tells me, no. He thinks I might be having a heart attack and he may need to rush me to the hospital for surgery. He just has to do some quick tests first.

I text Alan who is still in the lobby and convey this to him.

He tells me he doesn't think so. He tells me it's probably gerd.

They hook me up like Frankenstein's monster after they have me take all of my clothes off and put on a paper robe that leaves my ass hanging out.

I'm lying on the table connected to all of these wires. I don't know what they are doing. Running tests from another room I guess.

All of the lights go out.

Maybe I'm dead.

Maybe this is it.

It's all over.

I've already texted my team to tell them I may be having a heart attack. They may have to rush me to the hospital and cut my chest open. Would they be willing to run tech rehearsal without me?

At first they respond with things like, "of course."

But then it hits them and they all start panicking.

It's still dark.

I'm still lying here.

After an eternity the nurse comes in.

The lights automatically come on because apparently they are motion sensored.

News to me.

I'm still crying and asking her if they are going to take me to the hospital.

With a mix of irritation and slight boredom she drones, "You'll have to wait for the Doctor to talk to you."

I ask more questions but the nurse tells me that I'll have to wait for the Doctor.

I wait and wait and wait.

My ass is very cold.

I am alive.

He never comes back.

The nurse comes back YEARS later shocked to see that I'm still there with my ass hanging out.

She tells me, "It's GERD."

And gives me some prescription to be filled near the front of the building.

Oh, my God!

I text Alan. I text my team.

"NOT going to the hospital. Apparently, NOT having a heart attack."

WHY, if you thought someone was having a heart attack, would you TERRIFY them???

I wait in line to get my prescription and Alan meets me there. My ass is no longer hanging out.

When I get to the front of the line at the pharmacy I'm a standout because I only have one prescription. The pharmacist actually says, "is this all?"

YES!

YES, that is all and it's too much. I will take this for one month and then I will make every adjustment I can on my own.

Which means no longer eating all of the things I know to be food. I follow the dietary path of the sloth now. Amy buys me a picture book entitled, "Life in the Sloth Lane". Everything is going to need to slooooow down. Acid needs to be replaced with alkaline. I'm a chemistry experiment. I am alchemy.

The blueberry hibiscus tea at Sip is a win. No coffee, which I've been living on for years. No wine, which I've also been living on for years. No tomato sauce, no chocolate, years and years, blah, blah, blah.

The show is looking good.

I'M ALIVE!!

The cast of two shows up for their call before a performance. They open the back door and then quickly close it because there's a snake on the steps.

Now the last time I had a snake on the back steps, my Monster had come to see a Heartfriends show. She was chain smoking and pacing up and down the sidewalk. My performers were warming up through their songs. And Buddy the Maintenance man slaughtered the snake on the steps. There was blood everywhere. Then he hosed it down. And then we performed for children.

I'd told Carolyn about that. I told her I thought the devil had arrived. She disagreed. She told me that snakes represent transformation. The snake was coming to celebrate a shedding of skin into a new way of being.

Carolyn turned the murder of Tricia into a fable for me when I could no longer read the paper or watch the news. She told me that Tricia had three days and nights inside of the tomb and then she was free.

My therapist told me that when you see a pocket of chaos, get away from it.

Snake.

I shut the door quickly.

I started running.

Myrrh was already sitting at the front desk.

I ran past her and out the front door throwing up my hands and shouting, "snake!".

I ran over to Sip and looked at all of the customers on their laptops pondering who looked most nature-knowing.

I went up to one graying gentleman and interrupted his internetting asking, "do you know anything about snakes?"

"No."

NO!

I run back over and start picking lettuce out of the front window garden planted by the last cast and now growing. I run with it toward the back past Myrrh who is reading her book in her spot at the front counter.

Myrrh is asking me what's going on. The actors have already walked around the building and let themselves into the dressing room below the snake.

"There's a snake. I need to get it off of the steps,"

I run past her toward the back holding a handful of lettuce and hearing her say, "Well, don't FEED it. You should poke it with a stick."

"I AM NOT poking a serpent with a stick."

By now I'm at the back of the theatre. I quickly open the door and hurl lettuce down the steps.

The snake does not care.

I call Rob.

"What is it now?"

"Snake! There's a snake on the back steps. What should I do?"

"What color is it?"

"Black."

"What is the shape of its head?"

"I don't know, Rob. I'm not sketching it."

"It's probably just a black snake coming out to sun itself."

"How do I get it to leave?"

"Which way is it facing?"

"What?"

"Where's the head, is it closer to you or further away from you?"

"Further away."

"GOOD! That's good."

And now, I can hear Rob trying in earnest not to laugh at me. The same way Bill Bailey tried not to laugh at me when I kept trying to find the electrical box for "Hitchcock After Dark" but consistently opened the septic tank instead. So gross!

"Just grab a broom and poke its tail. It'll leave".

"Fah! I'll call ya back."

"Okay. Good luck." I have no doubt he laughed his ass off for a minute or two after he hung up.

I slowly opened the door. I poked the serpent with a stick. Nice and slow it slivered down the exact steps one of my actors fell down during "Claudie Hukill". It tucked under a mat at the bottom of the steps. A mat we've stepped on so many times. And then, it disappeared into the woods where I staged, "We Are Samurai". At least, that's what I told myself.

It's a good sign.

Change is coming. "Transformation is nigh". That's something T would say.

The show went well. Andrea flew in to see it. I'm not sure if she understood my staging but I absolutely loved it.

It was colorful and imaginative and daring and fully realized!

Katie Hileman
Mike Landsman Photography

Claudia's play was about the first known Eurocentric female mathematician. I pulled so many of my favorite actors in for that show.

To prepare for that show, Paul took us out on his sailboat in Annapolis. I told the team to pretend it was the Aegean Sea. I made snacks.

Claudia was back and it's always good to hang with her.

She likes to write in a lot of props. We had two dancing tigers and a mouse that needed to be chased by one of them.

I found these remote controlled mice. But, they weren't accurate. Poor Matt was wearing a tiger bodysuit and chasing a mouse all over the stage. It was hilarious. Once again, he was a sport.

I was on stage as Ericho, snake goddess of the underworld.

Snake Goddessing with Matthew Marcus and Ann Fraistat
Mike Landsman Photography

Amy was on stage and Ann played the title role. We had two of our Katies as well.

There was a magical moment as we were building the show. Amy was working on the set, Kris was adjusting the lights, Neil was playing around with sound, and I was building an altar on the stage. No words were spoken between us. Each of us was in our own zone. But we were connected and present with each other too. Together alone. Alone together. We were building one world together, each contributing something different. It was palpable.

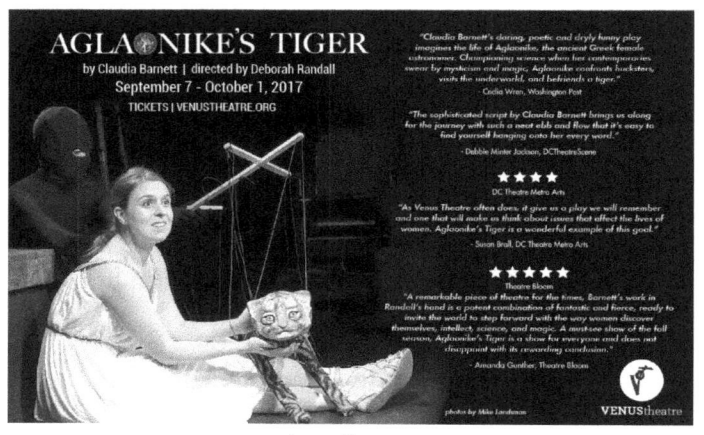

Ann Fraistat
Mike Landsman Photography

We have a little problem.

There's been this woman hanging out behind the building. I should have known from a few shows back. I'd asked Amy to cut wood back there instead of on the sidewalk in front of the storefront. Amy told me it was kind of creepy. There was this woman back there. And then, things would disappear. Like during, "We Are Samurai". After I'd set up the back garden, someone stole one of the cafe tables.

I knew we had a homelessness problem in Laurel.

Four different counties touch edges here. For the homeless this means they can jump from one county to the next whenever they are being chased out of one to set up camp in another. At the end of C Street is the Little Patuxent River. On the theatre side is Prince George's County, but on the other side is Howard County. So, we get these tent cities that pop up on one side or the other depending on the politics of the day. Down by the race track was a big tent city and a woman died there during the hurricane because there was no way to get a warning to any of them in time about the dangerous weather.

During "Garbage Kids" we'd researched this pretty heavily. Visiting the day center made it clear. There were lots of people there to shower, get a change of clothes and maybe grab some food to eat there and some to take with them.

In the winter, various churches worked together to provide shelter so people wouldn't freeze to death.

One lady wore her hair in a bob. She was always at the park near the river with a rolling cart and a lot of bags. It reminded me of the first show I directed, "Bag Lady". Only there was nothing intimidating about this woman. She looked like a corporate exec who couldn't find her office. She never said much and was polite if approached. She'd just sit on that same bench in that same spot with all of her belongings surrounding her and stare at the river..

Then there was a town favorite. Someone was always buying him lunch someplace on Main Street. One of our business neighbors caught him naked in the river, bathing. He liked to pee on the outside of the trash cans.

We also have a lot of halfway houses and drug recovery facilities. These are all great things. But, people fall off the wagon and things happen that don't always bode well for small businesses.

For a time, I hired a man to clean our gigantic windows. He charged us $20. He came with a bucket and a squeegee and he always did a good job. We would get to talking. He told me he was a recovering alcoholic. He said his daughter wanted to be an actress. When the plumbing exploded in the basement, he came with his boss to assess the situation.

He was so reliable.

And then he'd acquired a bicycle. He would make his rounds and clean the windows pedaling around Main Street with his bucket and squeegee in tow. Eventually he had an assistant.

One night I saw him coming down the alley with about four other men. Drunk out of his mind and trying to start fights. After that, I never saw him again. I mostly think about his daughter these days. What an unfair hand she's been given!

All we can do is our best.

So, this woman behind the building, I'm assuming she's homeless.

More cats are appearing now.

There are these cats that seem to be living behind the building and this woman is putting out food and water for them.

Matt hopped into the dressing room downstairs wearing his tiger suit. He's a little freaked out.

There have been opossums and raccoons, and we don't know what else is coming to eat from the cat dishes and he and one of the Katie's walk right past them barefoot.

It's scary.

I leave a note saying the bowls have to be moved, they are too close to my actors. I call Laurel Cats because I know they are a great rescue organization. They tell me to leave their phone number on a note and they will talk to her.

I see the man next door, the one who offered to slather lotion all over my body during a summer festival, talking to the Cat Lady. I see her body language and I can tell she's trying to "charm" him. He's loving the attention.

We're sold out.

It's time to go up and start the show.

The Cat Lady is out there.

I tell her that she has to move her bowls. She's drawing wildlife way too close to the paths of my actors.

Another business has some steel back there.

This Cat Lady loses her mind. She starts screaming at me saying, "There's always ONE bitch!!".

This feels so familiar.

Mama?

She was screaming and pointing in my face. I'm clear. I know exactly what she's doing. She's trying to provoke me so she can play victim later.

She's throwing the steel around. My actors are upstairs and checking through the back door. We're at go-time.

Holding.

Over and over she's screaming at me, "There's always ONE bitch!". She's telling me her cats live here and that if anything ever happens to them, she will kill me.

I'm staring right at her knowing that we need to get the show started.

Holding.

L is the Stage Manager for this show.

The Cat Lady was screaming at the cast to come down the steps too. She wanted to take us all on.

I'd backed up about two businesses by now from her screaming straight into my face but she was still stepping into me saying, "There's always ONE bitch."

I started saying, "I am THAT bitch, where do you live? What's your name?"

This was a cyclical dialogue that went around in circles at least three times. Her eyes were wild and dilated.

I had to walk around the building to get to the front for my entrance. I had my cell phone in the lobby and called the police from the front sidewalk. They asked if I would be there.

I told them I would be there but we were about to start the show and I would come around at intermission. As I stood at the front, I could hear her throwing steel all over the place and screaming about there always being one bitch in the back.

I thought about the fact that I have to walk around the building four times during the first act. This is another case of me staging myself to do something I would NEVER ask another actor to do.

We start the show.

At intermission I see the police around back. I point to her and say, there she is. She flips out again.

Looking back I realize that I had two snakes around my neck. They were puppets that I could move and I was dressed as the dark snake goddess of the underworld. So, someone prone to reactive behavior and possible delusions may have a reaction to my appearance. Especially when I'm telling them, "I am THAT bitch" and asking them over and over where they live.

The police pull me aside and tell me they know her. She does this. It's her thing.

She finds commercial properties and then brings her cats there to live.

I've never heard of such a thing.

I also saw a glimmer in L's hand and realized quickly it was the blade of a pocket knife and that's when I knew for sure that we were cut from the same cloth. Neither of us would have backed down. It was a good thing the police got involved. Now we can focus on the show.

Except, her cats are still there and she's not moving the food bowls.

Later L and I would have a quick exchange that consisted of me saying, "she must not know I grew up in Prince Georges". And L saying, "she must not know I grew up in North Jersey."

There was silence. And then there was laughter.

The landlord has died and his sons are in charge of the property now. They are lovely toward me. They tell me they will put up signs and that they do not want her on the property, or her cats.

The police gave me her name and address.

She's still stalking me.

Being stalked seems to come with my job description.

You're not supposed to be afraid of other women. It's not really stalking if it's women.

Not sure where that came from, but it's spinning in my head.

The Cat Lady is taking care of a family of raccoons in the dumpster in the parking lot next store now too. A FAMILY, there's about five of them in there. She's riding by in her car and looking to see if my car is there. She's hanging out around corners. She's using our trash can specifically to throw away her cat food cans. It's a bad smell and it festers with the heat of warm weather.

The good news is there is a Bed and Breakfast opening up in town. Claudia is staying there and they haven't even officially opened. The tour is adorable. They have prints up on the second floor of a girl and what we think is a tiger. Turns out it's another kind of cat, but still! The man of the home works for NASA. They have a moon room downstairs.

Kris and Amy have had to build a moon that goes through various stages for the show.

So much synchronicity.

The show does well and I introduce Claudia to Carol in Tennessee. Carol was my co-director of the original Bad Girls Festival and she's now teaching at a University in Tennessee. Carol also stages this play. Her students play the harp and she's got a sprawling proscenium. Her skill set has only expanded and I'm so happy for the meeting of these two.

All in all, a win.

And now we are going back to producing one of our playwrights from Australia. Alana Valentine has an incredible process. She immersed herself in worlds and interviews people for what seems like a never ending period of time. And then, she writes.

"Soft Revolution" was such a game changer. We're taking on her "Ravens" now. This is a completely different play. Well suited for our location. We follow a woman who is a sex worker and an addict.

It's powerful.

Visually stunning too.

This is a four hander, all women playing incredibly vulnerable characters.

I see the cat bowls at the bottom of the steps and I throw them into the dumpster.

The play is pure truth and power. We've got a choreographer on board and a dance pole center stage.

I find this very humorous because there is a Venus Theatre in Canada that is a strip club. Every so often someone will call me and tell me to send some girls over. I always say that I'll send some girls over alright. And they'll perform such text in your living room that your Johnson will just fall right off.

Now we have a stripper pole. One of the actors from the Suffrage collection is cast and she is our dialect coach. An Australian dialect is quite a challenge.

The power of these four women is undeniable.

Suzanne Edgar
Mike Landsman

The show veers into poetry and ends with a pole dancing recitation of Shakespeares, "The Phoenix and the Turtle".

Also Tara is back and the mask work is ridiculous.

A nod to the 1928 Magritte series called, "The Lovers" is a part of this too.

Visually stunning and elevated and also raunchy. We choreographed a pole dance to the Prince song, "P-Control". It made men blush and I love that. It's one thing when they see women objectified on their own terms. But when women decide to claim their sexual power, MEN. FREAK. OUT.

It was glorious.

After the show the lobby was packed. Wendy was there and Brendon brought their two children to meet up after the show. It was incredible to meet them.

Everyone was having a good time and then the Cat Lady slammed the door open and started screaming at me and walking toward me. Through a packed lobby of people. She was holding up two bowls and asking over and over, "Did You Do THIS?"

I said, no because I knew she was about to blow and this was my business. It occurred to me that she's always appearing when I have sold out houses. Somehow we coaxed her out of the room. But she stayed in her car and drove it up and down the street for a long time.

I decided I needed to sue her or to at least get a restraining order because she wanted to do damage to me or my business or both.

I found out that the dentist at the end of the row now owns the building. I let him know what was going on and told him I was going to sue her and he said he hadn't seen anything. I didn't ask him if he'd seen anything. But, that was his response.

Carolyn wired money to me and told me to treat myself to lunch after the hearing. Alan came before his lessons and sat with me in the Hyattsville Courtroom, very concerned. She was on the other side of the aisle. Tweaked out and bouncing. Wearing the same pink Victoria's secret relaxed wear as she always wore.

We were called to the front. She was mumbling under her breath that I was a liar and she was going to come after me. I mentioned this to the judge.

He asked her about the cats. He wanted to know if she had moved them. She said she had.

He asked her how far.

She said not far.

"Fifty feet?"

"No, not that far."

"Ten feet?"

"No, not really. Maybe five feet."

She told him that the man who owned the building gave her permission. But, the man she'd been flirting with did not own the building.

I explained that she had been stalking me.

She admitted that she always waited until a lot of people were around before she approached me.

This really freaked me out.

He asked which unit I rented and told me that she was placing the food at the unit next door so I had no say. I explained that my actors walked past within an inch and he said it didn't matter.

She knew every rule and how to break it. He asked her if she knew how serious the allegations were. She said she did and that's why she showed up because she didn't want to end up in jail.

I swear there was a silent "again" that she simply did not say out loud. She told him she'd worked at a jail.

He denied my request and she yipped for joy.

I felt like I'd just confronted the energy of my Mother. I didn't back down. And I know the social implications. I may be viewed as an entitled white woman who doesn't have compassion for the less fortunate.

Carolyn calls and talks to me while I order lunch at Busboys and Poets on her dime.

I tell her that this hostile woman won.

She tells me that I won. I won because I confronted her and now she knows I'll confront her again.

We also talked about the fact that I did keep my composure and this was a very triggering event.

I wanted a room of one's own so that I could lock the door and feel safe. But, this didn't feel safe. Not at all.

I was just about to put a call out for scripts when the new slumlord called. He told me he wanted to move me over one unit.

I told him, no.

I know every inch of my space. I've created and worked hard for it. I won't move.

He can just find another tenant.

A few days go by and I've been upset. Pretty upset. I've got Jasmine at the lake and it's an emotional place for me because it's where I talked on the phone to Tricia at least once a week the last year of her life.

As we're getting into the car the phone rings and it's him.

He tells me he and one of the other tenants changed their minds. I don't need to move, I can stay.

I reluctantly said, "thank you?"

It seems like no one really respects me or my business or the vision.

I thought I wasn't doing this anymore and here I am.

I put out a call for scripts and I'm laughing. I've been doing this at the end of every year for a while and the call has gone from two paragraphs to about five. Tricia would call me after it went up and ask me to tell her the story that was behind the new "rule". She would be laughing and telling me how she already tried to imagine what must have happened to cause me to write the latest paragraph.

After my share, she would tell me that it was a better story than the one she had imagined.

I miss her.

She's not coming back. Her murderer is going to be sentenced. I wish I could kill him. I feel her with me saying, "Stay away from him. Stay far far away from him." And then she tells me that if I go there I'm never coming back. I'll never be the same person again.

I'm asking her questions. I'm asking her about Jasmine because she's old now but she's not going to leave me. She knows I need her.

T keeps telling me, "20". My dog is going to live to be 20. The 2020 elections are coming. We need to get Trump out of office.

She's sending me messages like: "Get your house in order." "Man your station."

She's given me the same three words: levity, artistry, and discernment.

Nicole reaches out to me. She's now running the RiverShe Arts Collective. She's telling me that someone she knows backed out of a contract with DCAC. She has this space and do I want to present anything.

YES!

DCAC is where Tricia and I met. I want to tell her story. I want to try to tell her story. I'll write a ten minute piece and see how it goes.

Grief is a private thing. Like waves in the soul and rises and falls in its own time creating storm centers and unexpected moments of calm. Mourning is communal though. It needs to be experienced in groups. And trauma! Wow, trauma is something else entirely. Trauma is not about Tricia. Trauma is about the decayed humanity that caused that to happen to Tricia. Trauma is the inability to accept the level of evil you have witnessed.

Trauma is entirely manmade. The other two come from a need to separate the terrestrial from the spiritual in ourselves so that we can honor them.

[flourish: MT23]

TRIGGER WARNING!

2017. 14-September. Which Scarf?

We're back

To this

3-5 hour

Sleeping pattern

Up before the sun
Thoughts spinning
Images flying
Psychological collage
of nonsense
and love
and pain
everything now
PTSD
It's a diagnosis
Something to learn to live with
Backlog
Seeing
Experiencing
Violence
Silenced
That's PTSD
It comes with triggers
You know
Those things
Those things
That ignorant people
Make fun
of
Triggers
So avoidance
That's good
Stay away
Carry

venus

On
With
Life
But triggers
Are like the guys
I dated when I was young
You think they're gone
And BAM,
There they are again
Grinning at you
With flowers
Avoidance
Can't work
When there is
Media saturation
Unless
the residence
Is a deserted
Island
Bucket list
Yesterday
There was no way
To avoid
Truth
Violent truth
Murderous
Raping
Truth
So

Deborah L. Randall

I
Embraced
It
I know
What happened
I read
Every detail
Like a
novel
Her death
Occupies the mind
The masses
And
I
Try
Not to vomit
So
Let's
Review
This
Except
The thing
Is
I can't sleep
Will
Likely
Stop
Eating
For a time

Because
The first detail
I can't get past
The first
Detail
She was
Strangled
To
Death
With her own
Scarf
Which scarf?
Was it
One I made
For
Her?
Because
I knitted
A lot
of scarves
Thinking
Believing
Knowing
The love
I called
Them
Portable
Hugs
Stitch by stitch

Thinking of the
Wearer
Friend
Wanting
Wishing
Insisting
They
Never
Feel
Cold
Again
Was it
One
I made
Her?
Did my intention
To share
Love and warmth
Become
The weapon
That
Took
Her
Last
Breath?
Which scarf?
Is it one Clinton
Made for

Her?
Because
His
Were
Always
Better
Which scarf?
Was it a thrift store
Purchase?
Was it
Green?
I made her
A lot of
Green
Ones
WHICH FUCKING SCARF!?!?!?!?!?

It's a lot.

[flourish:MT24]

2017. 15-September. Choosing.
It wasn't a crossroads
It was a fork
One way to death
The other to life
Life seemed
More painful
But death

Was too predictable
So, I veered left
Into life
And today
Today is a marker
Seven months
Of intensive therapy
Two months
Of Pilates
Five months of
No alcohol
No caffeine
And one new understanding
I'm here
I'm awake
I'm alive
So…
WATCH OUT!

[flourish: MT25]

2017. 7-November. Remember.
You've been loved
Remember
When they ask you about that grin
In the face of so much darkness
Remember
It's bigger
Love is bigger than every other thing

venus

Remember
You've been loved.

2018 - Grief

"Living and Dying with Tricia McCauley" by Deborah Randall direction Deborah Randall costumes and props Deborah Randall|set Amy Rhodes|lights Kristin A. Thompson sound Deborah Randall|stage management Amy Rhodes, Krishaun Walker|front-of-house Amy Rhodes, Krishaun Walker|construction Deborah Randall, Krishaun Walker, and Amy Rhodes|graphic design Laura Matteoni Schraven| cast Deborah Randall|

"The Speed Twins" by Maureen Chadwick direction Deborah Randall costumes and props Deborah Randall|lights Kristin A. Thompson|set Amy Rhodes| sound Neil McFadden|sound assistant Rose Ligsay| stage management L| front-of-house Myrrh|construction Deborah Randall and Amy Rhodes|graphic design Laura Matteoni Schraven| cast Queenie played by Nancy Linden|Ollie played by Jane Petkofsky|Shirley played by Ann Fraistat|ensemble L, Myrrh Cauthen|

"This Little Light" by Jennifer Faletto direction Deborah Randall costumes and props Deborah Randall|set and lights Amy Rhodes|sound Neil McFadden|stage management L| wigs L| front-of-house Myrrh Cauthen|construction Deborah Randall and Amy Rhodes|graphic design Laura Matteoni Schraven| cast Modern Day Sadie played by Katie Hileman|Old West Sadie/Marie played by Deborah Randall|Shipwrecked Sadie/Victor played by Christina Day|Extra-Solar Sadie/Sharee played by KyoSin Kang|

"Running on Glass" by Cynthia Cooper direction Deborah Randall costumes and props Deborah Randall|set and lights Amy Rhodes|sound Neil McFadden|stage management Amy Rhodes and Krishaun Walker|front-of-house Myrrh Cauthen|construction Deborah Randall and Amy Rhodes|graphic design Laura Matteoni Schraven|ensemble Deborah Randall and Tina Canady|

Just knowing I'd be speaking my words about my relationship with Tricia in the DCAC space lit a fire under me. I'd be in the exact room that I stepped into after being mugged on the steps of the Women's

Empowerment Center when I had to open the show holding the audience up at gunpoint.

I'd be staring at the spot where Tricia stood, protecting me from myself, my fears, and possible intruders.

I'd be in the room.

There's something sacred about being in a space where many people create. I guess that's why the Ancient Greeks considered their stages altars of offerings. They call the altar to Dionysius thymele and it's located within the orchestra. Theatre, when it's alive, is always an offering.

I spoke the first pages. I wasn't sure if I'd want to run out of that room before I finished and I made plans to be able to do so. The buildings surrounding are nicer now but the rats seem of the same bloodline as the ones I'd shoot my plastic gun at as I prepared to play Mary in "Why We Have A Body" in the back alley.

I did it.

It worked.

It took Nicole asking me. The same woman who led the Wild Wise Woman Retreat in the mountains all of those years ago. The same woman who's triplets I held an outdoor summer camp for on the Chesapeake Bay.

She seems to pop up out of nowhere at the exact right moment and because of that, a new solo show is being born.

Next up, was a page-to-stage reading at the Kennedy Center.

Amy and her son were in NYC that morning but drove down to DC early so that Amy could read the stage directions. I was performing in a rehearsal room above the Opera House. There was a grand piano in the room and a wall of mirrors.

I played Pat Benetar through my bluetooth speaker and set up candles and a memorial area for T.

So many of her friends came.

By the end, I was completely sobbing. The room was completely sobbing.

I had to leave and hide in the backstage bathroom to really cry it out. This is weird because as a producer I like to talk to my audience after a show.

Once I made my way back into the room there were still so many people. Familiar faces I hadn't seen for so long and new faces too and so many hugs.

As we were leaving I saw Gregg Henry at the bottom of one of the red carpet ramps. No words. We just gave each other a kiss. Then he asked how it went. I nodded but couldn't say much.

Once again, being in that place sent a message to my soul that I was on the right path and that I would find home. It was the same message from all of those years before, just keep going.

No transitions, just process.

Amy's son looked at me when we were outside at the Kennedy Center. He gave me feedback. It was exactly what I needed to hear. It seems like just yesterday he was eight and Amy was teaching him to use a power drill in the theatre.

He always liked to play sick so he could stay home from school and hang out with us working at the theatre all day when he was young.

Gabe Rhodes leaps with glee at the Kennedy Center

He's all grown up. He's completely articulate. A wonderful dancer, he leapt outside at the Kennedy Center. We were in the zone. It was what I felt deep down but couldn't quite access, his leap. This was working.

I could keep going. I set a date to open the season with this one woman show tribute.

I needed to because I didn't want the monster to have the last word.

It was just in November of last year that her Monster was sentenced to 30 years in prison.

I didn't think I believed in Capital punishment after a decade of Molly Maguire research but in this case I do. I wish he was dead. We'd all sleep better.

On that day, I knew I couldn't be there so I was able to schedule an ankle tattoo. I asked that they not have the news playing on the TV screen.

I think this wreath of cleavers around my ankle is giving me power. Even though T didn't like tattoos. The last time I saw her her nose was pierced, so. Tit for tat.

[flourish: MT26]

17 November-2018. BECOMING.

One year

As the years go by

One now

Since

Justice

Justice?

Justice!

Couldn't find it...

One year since

The sentencing

venus

30 years for a life

His words

Printed in

The Washington Post

Her voice

Silenced

I was told

That I have one foot

In each world

And the trick

Is balance

That's the trick

One in

Each

World

My right foot

Had me outside

In the Courthouse

Raging

If I had bullets

They would all

Go into him

Justice!

My left foot

Sunk into the

Mud

Cold

And her voice

Came into

My head
Clear
Stay
Far
Far
Away
From
Him
It went against
Every instinct
My sense of justice
Was being challenged
It's always
A test
When faced with
A monster
Will you become
Them?
Will you grow into
You?
That's always
The test
My whole life
Looking back
I wanted to
Push the
Monster
Down the
Steps

After she

Chased me

Down the hall

So, I made

Sure that door

Was shut

Just in case

And let her

Terrorize

Me

Why?

Because of

What I was

CHOOSING

to become.

I learned to run

And to duck

And to cover

And to absorb the blows

Now

My friend

HIM

She was very clear

Stay

Far

Far

Away

I had to

shut that door

Deborah L. Randall

Because of
What I was
CHOOSING
to become.
Screens everywhere
The date upon us
She was clear
If you go
You won't ever
Really come back
You won't be you
again
Stay far far
Away from him
So, I scheduled
An appointment
To get a tattoo
On my left ankle
The soft one
The introspective one
A wreath of love
and laughter
Cleavers
the happiest plant
She'd ever met
Just laughing
All the time
Hoping
Praying

I could honor
HER
This way
With laughter
With joy
With love
With light
An addition
To becoming
ME.

I found a red couch. We turned the space into a thrust. It's a pretty small thrust but we made it happen. There was a fish named Pisces downstage center.

Telling the story of Tricia Lisa Helfert Photography

People came from all over the country to see it. I don't know who they were but I know they were there. I live streamed for the first time. Being a purist I have never believed in putting theatre onto two dimensional mediums. But, some people really wanted to see it. So, they tuned in around the country and from other continents.

Tricia had dual citizenship and had thought about moving to Great Britain.

Of course some of her ashes were mailed to a friend out there. They were scattered in Avalon. On that night there was a fierce storm. The sky turned purple. A professional photographer happened to be shooting Avalon the same night Tricia's ashes were being scattered there. I have this image hanging on my studio wall. It's purple and there are lightning bolts. Looking at it makes me feel so much better. It is full of rage and power and that's how I feel about what happened to her too.

We have to extend! We're selling out over and over.

I was able to use one of her last voicemails to me to close the show. Just an empty stage with her voice and the last thing she says is, "Love you".

Tonight I was setting up and it was raining outside. It started raining sideways. I checked all of the instruments. My backstage was upstairs for this show, thank the heavens. I didn't want to have to deal with the feral cat lady again. Especially not by myself.

There was a flash of light and a big boom!

Sometimes transformers blow. It happened just after we closed, "Devil Dog Six". I ordered take out and it was delivered and the whole team ate and chatted by candlelight. It was perfect.

This transformer was on a telephone pole behind the space. Our building was the only one without electricity. PEPCO must know me by now.

It felt personal.

People started showing up. Amy was there. We were asking people if they could come back on another night when the electricity was back up. Most of them said yes.

About eight of them only had that night available to watch the show.

The last show Tricia saw was, "Garbage Kids". She sat on the far side of the house and our constant friend of the theatre, Elizabeth sat on the close side. We closed that show to those two people.

Getting people in to see new work, especially work that empowers women, has been a depressing uphill (up-mountain?) slog. There's no way we're turning the audience away.

I still have a plan. I'm still on a schedule.

Amy and I confer about how we are going to run the show without electricity. We have a whole slideshow tribute to her and the sound is run from a record player live on the stage. We realize that everyone has a cell phone now. So, we invite them to turn on their flashlights. Amy tells them that she will signal them to watch the video and at that time she will play the music that goes along with it on her phone.

Pisces is still alive. I think. And the sponge finally sunk and seems to be keeping things clean and possibly oxygenated. It floated on top of the water for so long.

It was so dark. The show was a completely different show. I had no time to rehydrate and let tech hold focus for a moment. We placed strategic flashlights around the set for me.

I felt the void.

I could feel the nothing.

It was so different in the darkness.

I found so many new things in the show.

At the end, I couldn't really leave the stage because it was so dark, I was going to trip backstage. So, I waited for a moment on the stage and the audience sat on and off of the sides of the red couch. They just stayed there.

I sat on the floor of the stage watching the shadows of them.

The couch had become significant because it was representing the couch that Tricia sat on in her group house while I developed, "Til It Hurts". She'd watch me go through the two act solo show and then give me her notes. She'd show up when she could when I was performing it. In a feminist bookstore on the second floor in DuPont Circle she sat on the floor stage right. She was wearing burgundy clothing with matching burgundy lipstick.

She was always there to anchor me and I was always playing for her laughter.

Always.

Am.

Still am.

She was in the room with me in a different way. In the way that it was late and stormy and everyone was tired and no one wanted to leave.

We started talking. And we talked into the night. Until I had to excuse myself and my full bladder and scramble my way backstage.

A lot of her interns and farming friends came. Some people in the audience flew in from the West Coast. I could hear them sobbing during my performance. I could hear them moving around and holding each other. I just kept going.

After that performance, one friend gave me two bags of Tricia's Holy Basil that she'd harvested. She said T taught her to put them in paper shopping bags to wick out the moisture and let them dry. That makes for delicious tea. I felt high when I drank it. Beyond relaxed.

Another friend came up to me after. She said that they'd checked Tricia's laptop to see what music she was listening to right before she left her home on Christmas Day. The preshow Pat Benetar album is the last thing she listened to.

It healed me to connect with people telling me I'd found the words and spoken them, when they were still searching for what to say.

K and Amy covered tech for me on this. They worked together seamlessly. I'm so grateful. K lives across the street in C Street Flats. She just walked in one day and volunteered. I knew I'd love working with K when someone walked into our theatre and started speaking to me. She interrupted them and said, "rank and purpose?".

I've longed for that. Boundaries and structure.

Discernment.

It was entertaining to see that it came from a soldier stationed at Ft. Meade. K has great stories and loves food. She tells us about "funeral chicken" which, she says, can only be found in the south at funeral repasses and this one gas station situated in a remote and unexpected location.

I trust K completely. Amy is a constant trusting partner. Without those two I would not have been able to do a run of this intense piece, never mind an extended run.

Add to that Kris Thompson's brilliant lighting and there was no way I was going to fail on this project.

Trust and Respect.

A mutual friend also gave me a painting he created that he had given to Tricia and she'd had hanging in her apartment. We hung it above the red couch.

My friend Sami offered up her calligraphy skills. She wrote the names of women we'd lost on beautiful river rocks. At first I placed them on the stage for dress rehearsals only. But, it felt so right having them there, they stayed for the entire run. Windy Winters was included in this horrifying collection. After the show closed Molly Ruppert put the rocks on display with her art gallery opening. Eventually, they were all released into the river.

I feel very different now.

Floaty.

I'm so excited to have Ann back on stage. I cast her a lot and there have been times in the rehearsal room where I just looked at her and she'd say, "okay, got it!". Then she'd make the adjustment I couldn't quite find the words to express.

It's an incredible experience in the process to operate on that level.

Ann Fraistat
Curtis Jordan Photography

This playwright is flying in from London with her partner, Chad. They've both written for the BBC and she's also run her own production company. This feels like a really big deal.

Amy and I have found a powerful color pallet for this one.

I think we can nail this. The play takes place in lesbian purgatory.

We're taking a lot of risks with wigs and costumes too. L is back as our stage manager and sometimes she's at the theatre until 2 or 3 in the morning taking care of the wigs. I don't like that at all. I appreciate her and I'm just hoping everything goes smoothly with the production.

I'm so excited to have Chad come into town with her partner!

I have some work to do at the theatre and then we're meeting at Olive on Main. About five blocks up. Across from Oliver's Tavern where T went into a state of zen over an Outfield cover tune.

I figure I can walk up and then walk them back down to the theatre so they can see Main Street. I've always been so in love with Main Street. I used to miss light cues at Petrucci's Dinner Theatre because the sunset at the top of Main absolutely blew my mind.

That was a long time ago. The trees have grown along the street now and they block the sunset.

I feel good. I'm showered. I'm wearing a dress. I've done my hair and I'm wearing make-up. I feel good.

As I'm walking up Main Street, a man in a van starts shouting at me from the other side of the street.

He's driving eastbound, I'm walking westbound. It's near the spot where I shouted down a gigantic St. Bernard who was hauling ass to cross the street and eat Mr. Gable. I remember this "Mom" voice coming up out of me. I'd never heard it before. I'd put Mr. Gable between my ankles to create a gigantic two headed creature.

I was saying, "NO! GO HOME! TURN AROUND!" The charging St. Bernard became terribly confused. It stopped in the middle of Main Street.

Frozen there it looked at me with pure puzzlement.

I broke this frozen tension by bellowing, "GO HOME!!" in a persephonus voice that had apparently just been born of me.

This now though was a rare moment that I was walking alone sans k-nine.

Always a mistake. I forget though. My dogs have given me such confidence over the decades.

This man is shouting from his van, "I like you. I like the way you look. Mamacita!" and then he makes yippee hooty sounds.

There is a woman. Her car is parked on the curb and she's taking product out of the back seat into her shop, Grace's Boutique. I believe this is Grace. We've never met but I've heard great things about her.

I go straight up to her and start talking.

"Hi. I know we've never met but there's a man in a van who is watching me. Can you pretend to have a conversation with me until he goes away?"

"Of course. You just stand here and talk to me as long as you need to until you feel safe. Anytime. I'm always here."

Now the man in the van has made a u-turn on Main Street and pulled his van over to the curb about a half block down on the same side of the street as me and he's behind me so I can't see him.

"I think he just parked, so this may take a few minutes."

"No rush. You keep yourself safe."

It occurs to me how kind she is and also, how any woman knows this scenario and will gather to protect complete strangers.

It's kind of a universal rule for women.

"I have a meeting a half a block up across the street. Two women have just arrived from London. I was so excited to meet them and to show them my theatre. But, now I'm not sure how well I'll be able to put a face on my company."

"You just keep yourself safe right now."

After more of this exchange the man drives up directly beside us and tries to make eye contact with me with all of his might. His truck is at a slow crawl and there is a backup forming behind him.

What's with people and stalking?

Another universal rule women intuitively know about being stalked is we don't give away our destination until we can determine the all-clear.

In this case, that means making sure his van has disappeared and that he's far enough away that he can't see what we're doing from his rear view or side view mirrors.

Now that he's far enough up 5th Street for me to move I break away mid sentence saying only, "he's gone. Thank you so much!"

I'm ten minutes late in meeting Chad and her partner. Luckily, they've already ordered drinks and are pretty relaxed.

Back when I worked at Gymboree my manager Liz would tell us to "articulate your subtext". It was her belief that people can sense things, so it's better to simply tell them what's going on than to try to cover it over and have them draw up their own narratives. This is always much worse than the truth.

Then again, I don't want to overshare. I just want to start on a clean foot.

Professional.

But here's the thing that any woman can tell you about this particular stalking scenario. Sometimes they loop back around.

Back in college, I showered and blew my hair dry TWICE before my stalker stopped walking circles around the theatre.

This van man might come straight into the restaurant. The Cat Lady had no problem doing this in my own space.

What would I do then? What would Ann Landers recommend?

I say hello to them both.

I apologize for being late. I simply tell them there was a man in a van stalking me up Main Street so I had to pause until he moved on.

Both of their eyes widen and rest into a very familiar place and we never speak of it again.

They are simply delightful.

There's a lot of gin drinking during the show.

We have an after party and the gin is flowing. I'm not drinking. I'm on top of this gerd living the sloth life.

Chad takes my guitar and flips it upside down as we're hanging out in the lobby. She starts playing it left-handed. She's playing and singing Joanie Mitchell songs and all of the songs of women from that era. We're all singing along. Myrrh never had gin before. She's now on the piano in the lobby and Chad's got her arm around her and it's one hell of a time!

I'll never forget it.

A gorgeous experience. In Chad's purgatory the women have to take a survey and tick off boxes regarding whether they'd come back again as lesbians or gay men.

Laura has created three strips of wallpaper that contain the most amazing women referenced in the show on them.

It's a gorgeous set, I'm proud of the costuming.

There is a film aspect in the show. At one point, all of the bottles behind the bar have to spontaneously explode.

There's no good way to do this in alley staging. Even with sugar glass.

During rehearsals I keep saying, "Myrrh will do that part". I've created the staging device where Myrrh and L represent the Powers that Be.

They are literally controlling our world as front of house, stage manager, and board operators, so why not admit it. L wears black angel wings and all black tech clothing. They develop a fem character to do all of the set changes and people think that's who they are and everyone wants to flirt with them.

I've got Myrrh in all black as well. Holding down front of house and helping L on scene changes. I've got her wearing a modern day miners headlamp on her forehead.

I tell her over halfway through rehearsals that I've staged her and ask if that's okay. She is excited about it.

I love these people.

So Myrrh begins laughing maniacally in the lobby and enters the stage with a nerf gun. In this awesome lighting design by Kris and sound design by Neil, lights are flashing and the sound is violent and ominous as Myrrh obliterates Amy's set with a nerf gun and then goes back to her desk in the lobby.

Fortunately, I was able to purchase plastic bottles for the bar so they just bounced.

Kris and Amy have worked together to mount the front end of a car over the bar and the lights come on for this section.

The first time we run this in rehearsal, the actors lose their minds. They are laughing so hard we have to call a break.

It works. I love my Powers That Be. I love turning stage directions into unexpected realities.

It was an awesome experience.

Myrrh

Jennifer's play has two very different acts. I love that. The idea is that names have meaning. Every character in her play has the same name but they live in a different place and time. That's one act. The other act takes place in a department store and we need mannequins.

L has named each mannequin and treats them delicately.

I'm staging with the trap door again and it's a blast.

We have a lot of fun with Jennifers script.

THIS LITTLE LIGHT
by Jennifer Faletto | directed by Deborah Randall
March 8 - 25, 2018

★★★★★
DC Theatre Scene

This Little Light, like so many Venus Theatre productions, is a gem that radiates the very joy it dares us to find in ourselves, and each other, when we fear we've lost it most.

Kelly McCorkendale, DC Theatre Scene

Watching this play is like listening to some of the Beatles' music, where the tempos and beats suddenly change but the song still flows so melodically. The playwright, director, and actors create a beautiful quilt with their little pieces of existence.

Susan Brall, DC Metro Theatre Arts

Deborah Randall's production ... is acted with the right philosophical breeze; Faletto's ... actable combination of winsome and lonesome makes "This Little Light" one of the determined Venus's best finds.

- Nelson Pressley, Washington Post

Photo by Mike Landsman
VENUS THEATRE

Jumping on stage with Kyosin Kang and Christina Day
Mike Landsman Photography

I found a pocket of down time to zip up to NYC and see what Cindy Cooper has done with her "How She Played the Game" script. It's now a two-hander called, "Running on Glass".

It's more ethnically diverse, which is great. Two television actors give it a solid read which I appreciate. A lot of times when I see plays I'm thinking about producing in NYC it's hard to get past the sheen of the actor wanting to be noticed for paid work. Sometimes it's actually easier for me to read the script than to get a sense of it from a reading like that.

But, this is a lovely evening. I decided to bring this work back to Venus.

I hired an actor trained at NYU to play the other character and I put myself in to revisit Trudy, and Babe, and Gretel.

We keep the room in thrust and Amy builds a ledge to frame the space. At the end it becomes filled with memorabilia from the characters. I wanted to build a museum of sorts on stage.

They are still so unknown and their stories are so valuable. I'm able to obtain signed baseballs and real photographs.

An English teacher selling weed products tells me she'll make it class credit for her students to come out.

This seems perfect. I remember this from the 80's. This is how it was always meant to be.

Only, the students don't really know how to be an audience. It's difficult for them to turn off their phones.

At one performance one young man keeps falling asleep in the front row and I keep waking him up with vocal volume and prop bangs. It's hilarious the way he startles.

I don't take kindly to disrespect in my house.

Cindy comes down to see it and we go out to a diner after. That's our thing. In NYC or around where I produce, Cyn and I will find ourselves a good diner and chat a while.

We end the year with this and I'm not sure about next year.

Although, stepping back into the character of Trudy has been invigorating and powerful for me.

Embodying Trudy again after many years Curtis Jordan Photography

Tricia is telling me 20. 20. 20. 20.

Levity. Discernment. Artistry.

Everything is different but I'm still in a swirl.

[flourish: MT27]

25. February 2019. Three Times.
Three
46
7
8
9
That's time
Without you here
As you would say
Revolutions around the sun
Cycles
Star shifts

venus

Planting seasons

gone

Still here

Without you

Or

In the resonant

Waves

of

You

The nonlinear

laugh lines

in Lights waves

In sound

In wave crashes

Leaves rustling

Everywhere

You

Nowhere

Too

We tried so hard to find you

T

We tried so hard

And we failed

And we are haunted

That we could

Not

Reach

You

When you needed us

Deborah L. Randall

To
We are haunted
By three
Three birthday's
You
Flicking a stick
Leaning on the sink
In the depths
Of all of your friends
It's hard to comprehend
The end
It takes me right back
To the spin
The cycle
The spiral
The contractions
And the release
of
Life
Three
Released
Three turns
Ago
And here were are
Wishing
We could hug you
Watch you
Trying on some
Pair of pants

venus

Someone else threw
Away
Because
You'd attained
Zero
Carbon footprint
You composted
And upcycled
And made use
Of throwaway things
And scoffed at a pedicure
Saying you didn't like
Other people
Cleaning your feet
As if
As if that was your
Job alone
And you were taking
Full responsibility
And when I
Spoke a cutting
Phrase
Said something that
would have leveled
someone else
You let loose
A laughter
A full gut
Cackle

And then you engaged
And that laughter
Exchange
Became its own
Eternity
On this day
Of three
GOD!
I am rageful
Missing you
I have so much to say.
So many questions
Still
Like
If I can manage
To live to 92
Twice the time here
As you
Maybe
Maybe
Maybe
I'll have lived
For you too
Thank you
For healing me
So deeply
For believing in me
So unconditionally
For trusting

So completely
In a world
That never
Deserved you.
If you were here
Now
If you were here
I'm not sure
I don't know
But, I think
We'd be laughing
Our asses off
And I'd be telling you
About hot flashes
How it feels like
You are transforming
Into an amphibious state
How places sweat
That were always dry
Before
Like the front of the neck
And you would tell me
About some herb
That would combat
My discomfort
You would roll
Your eyes at aging
And you would say,
Water.

Deborah L. Randall

That's all you can do
Is drink water
and then I would
Pull out a bottle
Of tequila
And challenge your
theory
And we would drink
And laugh
And dance our way
Through
Me and you
Like always
I'm not the one
Writing this script
And, I'm fucking furious
About that
I feel you with your little twig
Leaning back against
somebody's kitchen
Sink
Laughing with
your friends
Layers thick
Swishing your stick
Waiting for the next adventure
Carry on, T.
We love you.
We miss you.

venus

We feel you in
The ripples of
Love resonating on
And we promise
To honor our time here
Because that option
Was stolen from you.
It's the least
We can do
This is our justice
Living well
Drinking water
Laughing ridiculously
Standing in truth
Unapologetically
Fierce
For you, T.
For you.
Simple choices
Little tiny
Happy moments
The eternity of
You
Happy 49th Birthday,
My friend, Tricia McCauley.
I love you.

2019 - The Final Season on C Street in Laurel, MD

"Jane App" by Deborah Randall| concept and direction Deborah Randall| costumes and props Deborah Randall|set and lights Amy Rhodes|sound Neil McFadden|stage management Amy Rhodes and Krishaun Walker|front-of-house Amy Rhodes and Krishaun Walker|construction Deborah Randall and Amy Rhodes|graphic design Laura Matteoni Schraven|ensemble Deborah Randall and Tina Kumpel|

"#solestories" by Renee Calarco|direction Deborah Randall| costumes and props Deborah Randall|set and lights Amy Rhodes|sound Neil McFadden|stage management Amy Rhodes and Krishaun Walker|front-of-house Amy Rhodes and Krishaun Walker|construction Deborah Randall and Amy Rhodes|graphic design Laura Matteoni Schraven|ensemble Jasmine Brooks, Tina Kumpel, Jane Petkofsky, Graham Pilato, and Claire Gallagher|

"The Finger" by Doruntina Basha direction Deborah Randall costumes and props Deborah Randall|set Amy Rhodes| lights Kristin A. Thompson|sound Neil McFadden|stage management Deborah Randall|front-of-house Amy Rhodes and Deborah Randall| construction Deborah Randall and Amy Rhodes|graphic design Laura Matteoni Schraven| cast Shkurta played by Catherine Gilbert|Zoja played by Amy Rhodes|

"The Powers That Be" a Rock Opera by Deborah Randall and Alan Scott direction Deborah Randall musical direction Alan Scott costumes and props Deborah Randall|set and lights Amy Rhodes|sound Neil McFadden|stage management Deborah Randall and Amy Rhodes| fx harness rig Paul Kelm|construction Deborah Randall and Amy Rhodes|graphic design Laura Matteoni Schraven| cast Amina played by Jasmine Brooks|Benten played by Amy Rhodes|Inansi played by Myrrh Cauthen|Eire played by Cam Shegogue|Inari played by Rikki Lacewell|Anu played by Deborah Randall|

Something feels strange. For the first time, I really don't want to read submissions. It's been years in the making. An audience member told one of the actors after one of the shows that he had seen things he'd never seen before and that he had felt things he had never felt before.

Being a student of X, I took this as a great compliment. We are meant to reveal new things and take people to new places emotionally as artists.

It was the last bit that made my jaw drop.

The last thing he said was that he never wanted to see or experience those things again.

This flies directly in the face of everything I've been building for thirty years.

Sure, we had the guy who would sit in the front row with the never ending lunch box sized bag of chips that would just jam it into his face and crunch over and over never looking at the stage for a full act. We had the gallon jug of water lady who would gulp gulp gulp right in the lights. We had people who would leave their soda cans on the set.

I took things as a signal that ticket prices were too low. If they had to pay a little more, maybe they wouldn't treat it like the old cafeteria they used to neglect on an all-you-can-eat mission.

But this was different.

Some people don't want to feel anymore.

They don't want to feel at all.

This terrifies me.

So, I'm not sure what I'm doing here.

Life is about connection. THEATRE is about connection.

I'm seeing Lily Tomlin at her switchboard and hearing clicks of plugs being undone and connections being erased on the operating board of connection.

Exchanged for some kind of wireless self-obsession.

I gave a talk for entrepreneurs at UMBC after I was awarded alumna of the year for visual and performing arts in 2012.

The one question a student asked me that I absolutely could not answer was, where do you get your passion?

I don't know.

It's just always been there. I've given this question a lot of thought over the years.

Where do you get your passion?

Passion.

Passion comes from WANTING.

It's directly connected in theatre to actors needing an objective. What do you want? What is your goal?

When an actor understands their objective they can then amp up the stakes.

This may be an oversimplification. Plays are not cookie cutters.

In my pondering, this is what I've been thinking. With stakes comes tension.

The tension generated from different characters wanting/needing different things is the driving energy of the play.

Surreal work may yield a different process, but this is, as I say, an oversimplification.

Plays either have tension (passion) or the void of tension (passion).

What am I supposed to do now? Why am I fighting so hard for something that is not wanted, appreciated, or viewed as needed?

It's super strange because the mayor declared November Venus Theatre Appreciation Month in the town of Laurel until the year 2020. Bud was there at City Hall with me. It was so good to see him again.

Bud watched the Mayor honor me and Venus at City Hall

That seemed like a futuristic date I would never see.

20. 2020.

Everything is feeling so different.

I've decided to offer workshops for free. LoveShop Workshops. I want to guide women through their bodies using chakra points and get them to share their stories and get them to play. I need to take a temperature on things.

Every workshop blows my mind.

One woman from town is stopping me in my tracks. She's a survivor of child sexual molestation.

She's on a walker now. She's a senior citizen.

She's spent the bulk of her adult life with a very abusive man. Decades.

I can see all of this in her body.

As she shares her story, much like the stories shared all of those years ago at the House of Ruth, I am filled with a childlike joy brought on by her courage and sense of play but also a very adult sadness understanding the reality she's had to survive.

I remember the waiting room at RAINN after I had to call a suicide hotline and was then instructed to go there. When my father hugged me at a funeral, which was the only time I ever saw him. Times meant to honor someone else, so I was never going to make that about me. I would simply take in the pain. When he hugged me for the first time since 1984 there was a loud knowing in my soul. It said, "He Loves You! He Loves You Too Much!!!!"

The first sentence brought pure joy to the five year old version of me who missed her Daddy. But, the second sentence made me feel like everything I ever believed about him was a complete deceptive lie.

I put a good face on the rest of the day and he disappeared again. The next day I had to call for help because I felt like I wasn't supposed to exist. I knew he'd done things to me but I didn't know what. I had to go into recovery so that I could move forward with my life. This is what brought me to the RAINN offices.

I never got used to the scene inside those offices. Everything was half-scale. Chairs and tables and little toy chests are half the size of what they were supposed to be. As if, growth stopped for some horrendous reason. Walls covered with childrens books showed promise of an innocence stolen. There were different little girls in the lobby every time I went. There were white noise machines outside of every single therapist's door going down the hallway to let us all know our story was safe there.

I thought it was just me. I thought it was just my era. I could see with my own eyes now that this was actively still happening to more children than I could imagine. It makes me nauseous still, just the thought of it.

There's only one reason any of us were there, we'd been sexually violated by a man that was supposed to be protecting us when we were children.

I learned a lot through that recovery. The definition of incest as told to me is, "abuse of power".

I'm a grown woman now, just coming to terms with all of this. Many of these girls were still in the single digits. Maybe two Jimmy lifetimes to speak of. MAYBE!

Years would go by and I'd see my father again at a funeral. The more frail he appeared the more free I felt. I stopped changing my hairstyle and color because I no longer had to worry about him recognizing me from behind.

Everything came to a head at my Aunt Virginia's funeral. The two years prior I was called and told she was asking for me. So, of course I showed up. But I made it clear to the rest of my family that I could not be in the same room with my father. I don't ever want to have to call a hotline again. It's my job to identify my triggers and take action to keep myself safe. In one conversation she thanked me for her birthday card. I told her I hadn't given her one, I'd only baked her a cake. She disagreed and pointed to a card on the table that my Father had given her and apparently signed my name to it.

These little denials and violations ripple out and can kill a person.

I was happy to be visiting her and to be reconnecting with my cousin Joe. He's the one who got me into music before I went to kindergarten. We stood on the top of a hill where her coffin was perched at a cemetery that could probably use some regulation accountability. Walking up there was like parkour. There was bad astroturf rolled out over planks and plywood covering open graves. Most of the people in attendance were older. My Father was in a wheelchair due to his Parkinsons, and his wife was on a walker due to her evil.

Joe was not wearing a coat. He was shivering and cold. My father sat to the left of him in his wheelchair. I stepped in behind Joe's right shoulder because I wanted to give him my scarf. He was shivering and he'd already jumped up once and grabbed Ginger's coffin.

I did not realize I was in the striking range of my Father. It's always been the unspoken rule that funerals are about the dead we are honoring and nothing else. Before the service was over he looked back at me and into my eyes and in front of everyone, he blurted, "WHO ARE YOU?"

Thanks to my toolbelt now turned tool warehouse I said with confidence and no hesitation, "I AM YOUR DAUGHTER!"

And then he reached across my cousin and grabbed me and pulled me into him from the front during my Aunts burial. He was clutching me into him and saying things I could not understand until I heard, "You know I love you, I always love you." By the time I pulled away from his shockingly strong grip, I saw his wife halfway down the parkour hill of corpses fumbling with gigantic tennis shoes and a walker that was shaking. Two men, I think both from my fathers Masonic Temple or whatever, ran and flanked her to keep her from falling over and get her in the vehicle.

My other cousin stood beside the coffin facing us and when she could she said, "So, anyway, we're going to gather at Mom's house if any of you would like to come."

I wasn't going to go but I went. I brought Joe his Rum Cake cupcakes because he was asking for them. And my Father, as per usual, never showed up.

Years later he would call me sobbing and text me, "I'm sorry you had an asshole for a farther." That's how he spelled it. In a text. Yeah, I'm sorry about that too and thanks for the closure.

Now I was looking at a geriatric woman who had little stuffed animals and baubles dangling from her walker taking my workshop. She wore mismatched colorful clothing. She carried a very small sketch book and had several others that she'd already filled in her hanging bag. Whenever she felt uncomfortable, she would sketch the scene.

She's just remarried a man she trusts.

She shares so many things with us. Each woman does. They share their stories and I am hit hard with the realization of the sacred quality of this work. Woman's-work.

Maybe men aren't meant to understand it. Though many really seem to and some are surely victims themselves. There are also a fair number of women who come to Venus shows alone. They have asked their husbands to stay home. They tell me this is what they are doing for themselves.

I've been discounting how few places there are for women to go and to just BE. To witness. To experience without having to be a performative female..

It seems ironic. I'm asking them to stop performing on my stage.

The thing about having a script is a collective group of actors agrees to explore a specific language in a specific world.

I've done a fair amount of devised work as well.

My heart lives with scripts.

I find them to be sensual and sacred even when they are ridiculous.

One of my students in the workshop is young. She's been in the basement bedroom of her parents' place spending a lot of time in bed.

I understand depression.

She lights up in this workshop. She is incredibly talented.

She's game for anything.

So, I decided to begin the year with an experiment. Something we've entitled, "Jane App ". I was wondering what it would be like if there was a virtual button on a smartphone that allowed access to the reproductive history of women.

PRESS RELEASE

Dear Member of the Press:

Thank you so much for covering #JaneApp.

It's been an interesting process. An iteration. I wanted to use the technology that sits in our hands every day as a vehicle to deliver live theatre. So, I thought an episodic piece would work best. I spent some time researching the Jane movement. I was able to meet with two of the founders, Heather Booth and Eleanor Oliver. I wanted to take their stories and incorporate them into my vision.

Recently, I realized that this project in some ways is a nod to Mary Shelley. This is my Frankenstein. My way of putting the pieces of a person together to create some kind of utopian ideal of how we could be. If we could wish away tragic death. If we could embrace that spark of life.

It was a few weeks into the process that I added a rewrite which understood the same actor to be playing all of the Janes. That this was the woman who's hand Reggie had held. That this was the only person she could really see. This is my way of celebrating surviving trauma. It's my way of celebrating the power of the mind to create what it can no longer see and in that imagining, heal itself. THAT'S how powerful we are!

I wanted to show different films at the end out of frustration born of my 19 years of producing works for women. In the male canon, very little context needs to be explained because we all live in that world. But for women, we can end up spending much of the time explaining a history before we even begin to explore character and conflict. So, exposition quickly becomes a lesson of something unknown. This can exhaust the energy of a work before it really sees the light of day. So, in showing these films, I share a history which I believe should be known as a part of the American experience. But, it's not.

There are more films coming out. One called, "Roe." "She's Beautiful When She's Angry" is the first film we'll show. Heather Booth recommended it. And, in talking with Mary Dore, the creator, I came to understand that she is still in debt paying for her project. So, another frustration is the financial inequities which go to keep the work erased. It's just so frustrating. "Reversing Roe" is another film I intend to show on the second Friday. This is another critical history.

So, I hope this will be a real experience that in some ways raises more questions than it answers. My sound designer says the project puts a lot of elements in a blender that don't seem like they should go together but somehow do. He said it was part listening to a book on tape collective as a community, part theatre, part performance, and a unique poetic experience.

I can only call it an iteration.
Born of my experience and ability. I hope that you will enjoy it!
All Best!!

I read a lot of books and did a lot of research. I would begin with one scene and each week I would add a scene. Until we told the story of women's reproductive health in America.

During this process, I reconnected with Paula Kamen. She wrote a play called, "Jane: Abortion and the Underground" which Venus read at George Washington University around 2006. She tells the incredible story of the Jane Movement in Chicago in the 70's.

I also reconnected with Heather Booth. Heather is one of the founders of the Jane Movement, not to mention a political organizer and soldier for the rights of women.

I reconnected with another founder of the movement named Eleanor that worked with Heather in founding Jane. In fact, Heather was the main organizer and Eleanor volunteered her phone to receive all of the calls coming through.

They would put notices up on campus that read, "Need Help? Call Jane.". Elanor's phone number was listed there.

At one point, the Jane's were blindfolding women and taking them to two or three locations before they'd let them know where they were. They were largely privileged white women who would volunteer their apartments for procedures. And they learned how to do the procedures themselves after they'd hired men who overcharged or were inappropriate. One man stepped forward and taught them.

They did get caught. They'd hidden all of the index cards with all of the patients on them. On the ride to the police station they were eating them.

They annoyed the officers because they were left alone in a room together and took over a desk there.

Roe was passed when they were in holding cells which is why many of them did not spend a century in jail EACH.

Somehow, I was able to reconnect Eleanor with Heather.

We met at Eleanor's apartment in DC, not far from where I would have met up with Andrea Dworkin.

I recorded our conversation.

Soon after, a film came out about the Janes which was long overdue.

Heather and Elanor came to our final performance. I'd written about a clinic bombing.

After the live performance and before we showed the film featuring Heather and all of her work, she approached me. Her assistant was with her this time.

They were very clear that I had a room filled with people and they needed to know how I was going to organize them?

I had to explain that I allow my audiences to draw their own conclusions. But, that's not what they meant.

How are you going to move forward with this momentum to change the world? That's what they meant.

Heather offers to speak.

ON THE VENUS STAGE!

Sure.

She speaks to our packed house for about 40 minutes. She and Eleanor leave after that and the rest of us stay and watch a film about the incredible career of Heather Booth.

It was entirely surreal.

In the audience that night was Renee Calarco. Renee had been posting her Sole Stories on Facebook. I called her and told her I didn't feel like taking regular submissions. I asked her about the Sole Stories project. She said it wasn't a play but she'd been toying with the idea.

So, I told her we should take a journey. Explore iterations.

She agreed.

I was back to having a script in my hands and it felt like coming home again.

"Sole Stories" was a delight. Renee was so generous with her talents. It definitely felt like Tricia energy. Like all of DC Theatre was gathering to support one of their own. Stories were shared in the lobby. Lots of stories were shared about the Bug. The show was simply delightful.

I could not believe it when I received a submission from a publisher representing a playwright from Kosovo. KOSOVO!

It was amazing.

I had to do it. It was another two-hander and everyone knows how I feel about those.

Amy Belschner Rhodes and Catherine Gilbert
Curtis Jordan Photography

Amy came back onstage with a new, young talent named Cat.

This play was stylized. That was clear. How to convey that stylization on a small American stage in the suburbs was a big challenge.

There were moments of fast paced whimsical characters, punctuated by a woman who had lost her son and her husband and because of that, her house.

Another situation where two very different generations of women had to figure out how to work together.

The absence of men is a real issue in cultures whose women do not have rights to property. This play addressed that.

Where do they go?

This was my question about the women of the Molly Maguires. It feels like I've come full circle with the question and now I need to figure out what the response has been over these more than two decades of exploration.

The weight of it.

We decided to build a dining table and chairs that had sunken into the floor with the weight of time and oppression.

The final show of 2019 is something Alan and I collaborated on together. A rock opera.

Curtis Jordan Photography

We went away for a week and stayed in this house on the river in the middle of nowhere. Suddenly Alan pointed out dolphins in the water. I thought he must have been seeing things. But there they were. A pod, swimming along.

It was a beautiful moment. We'd secured a VRBO that takes pets. Sadly, one month before her 20th birthday we had to say goodbye to Jasmine. She was not going to leave me. She saw me through the darkest days and back to the shores of the living. So, we had to decide to let her go.

I owe my life to that dog.

Losing her catapulted me into another place.

I'd had full conversations with her. I promised her that I would treat myself as well as I had treated my dogs. I promised her I would get my house in order and that I would not get another dog until I was in a different place emotionally and spiritually.

She was gone.

She was free.

We went away and I wrote and wrote.

I listened to so much music and I wrote. I based characters on female goddess archetypes again.

Alan and I retreated and wrote a rock opera

This process is something I experience intimately. There can't be a lot of clamoring about. It's essential to get still and to listen. That place of observation allows for the opportunity of new creation. Connected creation.

I wish I could figure out how to share this experience openly but it always seems to happen in darkness.

We name the show, "The Powers That Be" which is a nod to the amazing work of Myrrh and L in "Speed Twins". It's a riff on the Public Enemy song. The show also has a couple of satirical riffs with songs from, "Fiddler on the Roof". An inside joke with myself. The first time I'd ever performed one of my own monologues was that audition for Fiddler.

I rewrote "Tradition" and turned it into a song called, "Permission". My mentor taught me that whenever there was a slight against me I could redirect the energy out of feeling wounded and consider it permission to say whatever I wanted to say artistically. The song is a way to celebrate that guidance.

This direction has saved me so many times. It's allowed me to laugh when I would have otherwise crumbled. It's a familiar thing for me to do.

Taking the permission to express exactly what I needed to say is what this project was all about.

There are so many school shootings, I included a candle lighting ceremony just for the massacres up to this point in THIS YEAR. The world feels like it's wobbling out of its spin because people have decided to stop feeling. I need to call that out.

I set the play in the "Light of the World" church in Mexico. It's near the Wal-Mart shooting in Texas. The central figure bursts into the church holding the dress her toddler was wearing in the shopping cart when she was shot and killed.

The church has been passed on through three generations of men. Pedophiles.

Each of the other characters is an archetypal goddess.

Once we got back from the retreat, Alan and I sat at our dining room table and wrote over 20 songs in two days.

We were in the zone. I read my poetry to him. He plucked away at his guitar.

The page-to-stage festival put us on the "Evan Hanson" stage for the first ever reading of this. It was weird being in an equity space. We weren't allowed to touch the music stands. Not even to move one over three inches.

Kathleen Warnock asked if I wanted to bring something to her, "Drunken Careening Writers" in NYC.

YES!

That's when I wrote the Prologue.

Amy and I bussed up to NYC and had a grand time. We arrived at the reading early and crashed an ERA party/speaking event before it was our time to go downstairs. The room was filled with powerhouse feminists.

It's shocking to really take in the power of denial. It's amazing to think about Alice Paul. About standing in her house and now standing here with ALL of these women. Incredibly gifted women are still fighting for equality all of these decades later.

It's infuriating.

Downstairs, Kathleen filled the room with writers from all over the country. One man was a writer on, "A, My Name Is Still Alice.". Violet took me to see, "A, My Name Is Still Alice" at the Georgetown Foundry in the 80's. That show changed my perception of what women can do on stage. I can't believe I'm talking to him.

He told me how they had to dumb down a lot of the monologues in order to get the show produced off-broadway. Such a crime.

I met so many people that night. BRILLIANT people. Cindy Cooper was there with her friend Dorian. Just an INCREDIBLE evening.

In the prologue, I explored the double-bind. I wanted to give this show opening a visual by suspending myself from the ceiling tied up and having to release the ties that double-bind me while being spun around, speaking one monologue after the other.

Back at the theater, Amy was running the show from the stage in character. Myrrh was also on stage and throwing one slur after another at Trump. It was so fun to write words for Myrrh to say that I knew I could never get away with speaking.

The show ends with a song called, "Jeffrey Epstein Is Dead".

That monster you thought
Lived inside your head
That terror that ripped you
Up out of bed

That self-diagnosed
Existential dread
It was never your delusion
Jeffrey Epstein is dead

The world is brighter now
That one monster is dead
And all his dirty secrets
No longer live inside your head

Justice to the raping ones
Who served the Saviors bread
It was never your delusion
Jeffrey Epstein is dead

We dance on their graves
And we open our shades
One monster dead
Many more to behead

We are lighter now, women
Lighter and free
Jeffrey Epstein is dead (repeat)

It was my voice. It was my vindication.

Through this project, I honestly gave myself (and, I hope my audience) permission to celebrate and dance on the graves of the men who assaulted us.

There were two women who turned around and left the show as soon as the doors were open and they saw me hanging from the ceiling.

People had to walk past me hanging from the ceiling to take a seat.

I wanted them to see how normalized so much insanity has become. I wanted them to FEEL the absurdity of that.

Some did NOT want to see, and others took it in. I could tell who had been molested and sexually assaulted solely on their reaction and understanding of the show. Isn't this a grace? To find a way to give us an outlet. Isn't this an incredible grace?

One critic who tried to dissuade any other critic from covering me decades ago paid to come and see it and asked if the script was available.

Another artist said my writing reminded her of Ntozake Shange. She told me the piece should be running in tandem with an exhibit going on at the Smithsonian at the same time.

Amy Belschner Rhodes is in charge of me not passing out as I hang in a harness from the ceiling undoing all of those double-binds

I feel.

I feel.

I feel like I finally said what I needed to say. One of my actors from different productions told me it was too much.

Yes.

It's all too much.

[flourish: MT 28]

Living and Dying
I died with her
My belief in the goodness of man
Died with her
My need to explain the situation
Died with her
My final remnants of innocence
Died with her

She lives with me
Her laughter at the ridiculous
Lives with me
Her love of plants
Lives with me
Her reverence for the Pisces soul
Lives with me

Wanting to know more
Lives with me
Her passion for beauty
Lives with me
Her need to discuss until the sun comes up
Lives with me
Her blessings on their heads
Live with me

See?

Some of me died with her
But more of her lives with me

So

I am better for having known her
My heart is not harder
My mind is wiser
And I don't know why
She swam back to me for
23 years
I only know that she did
We were friends
We are friends
Because she's curled up
In my heart now
now
Like a kitten on a couch.

20

2020

"Man your stations." "Get your house in order."

Tricia was telling me what was coming but I couldn't see it. I don't think many could see what was coming.

I was still in producer mode. Still having no inclination to read new submissions.

Amy and I celebrated Tricias birthday on February 25th by going to the ocean and spelling out, "T Was Here" with flowers and shells in the sand. There were rumors about Covid so we were almost joking about it.

Our lease was up at the space in another year.

I went into fight mode because that's my preset.

We decided we could revamp the space. I applied for grants and got a lot of them. We came up with a new aesthetic. Elizabeth and I riffed about so many projects. She would draft them and then the city would fall flat. I figured this was a way she and I could make something good happen but it ended up being me wasting her time. This is all because while I understood artistry, and levity, I still needed to learn how to practice discernment. I see that now.

I found an HVAC system that made the air 95% pure. It was a $28,000 system. I applied for a $25,000 grant and got it. There was a great rep working with us who was willing to donate his labor to help make up the difference.

We were going to put a bathroom at the front in the lobby.

We had to clear out anything that seemed to collect dust. I didn't think the audience would want to sit in a space that felt unclean in any way. I wanted to do a lot with color and have everything sanitized regularly.

I snapped this picture in the last moments on C Street of the heartbeats of my artistic team.
Kristen Thompson (so many lighting designs)
Neil McFadden (so many sound designs) Amy Belschner Rhodes (so many set and light designs. So many construction hours, so many roles, and countless adventures)
THANK YOU!!

The businesses on either side of us left.

Amy and I filled three dumpsters, made two 15' truck-filled donations to community forklift, and COUNTLESS thrift store drop-offs. It's amazing how much we've collected.

Rob is no longer working for the city. I'm explaining to my contact at the city that Joe is leaving SIP across the street. She says that the pandemic is hard on businesses. I tell her it's not the pandemic. I tell her that he has customers lined up the block waiting to get in. It's not the pandemic.

I explain to her that we have brought amenities to C Street and we are being mistreated. It seems like, I tell her, now that the developers are here, you don't have to work so hard to promote the businesses that made the area appealing.

I mention that I hope we become an arts district soon. She tells me that's not happening anymore. Too much work.

It makes no sense for us to stay here.

I call a friend I respect very much as I sob. I explain that Tricia sat in these seats. I tell them that her handwriting is still on the back wall. I feel like I'm leaving her behind. She tells me that Tricia is with me and not in that place.

After Amy and I clear out the basement, we notice a pool of water form and disappear. We think this is connected to the toilet being flushed next door. Turns out, we've still been standing in raw sewage.

I let the landlord know we will not be renewing our contract. We will be leaving. I return a $25,000 check to the city in November, Venus Theatre Appreciation Month.

By 2021, we are out of the space.

We keep a 10x10 storage space for the first year.

In 2022, we downgrade even more and I reorganize the crawl space in my home to store lights and pipe and drape and other essentials.

Deborah L. Randall

[flourish: MT29]

I could hardly breathe
The walls were closing in on me
And mine

Sometimes the only thing
Left to do is

Let

go

Epilogue

Theatre, for me, is a verb. Theatre (v.) Imagining a world together, live.

The ways and processes that allow us to imagine together in one living breathing space are as varied as the people working on them. Nothing happens in the theatre until a group collectively DECIDES it will happen. This is the only way I can explain landing some of my strongest work with half the rehearsal time, with a domestic abuser on the prowl, or in a room that has been compared to a shoebox.

We make the decision together and we respect whatever roles we've agreed upon. We understand that everyone really has the same job. Each person on the project is there to set the others up for success. What does success mean? Well, the team would have to decide that too, right?

For me, success has meant exploring worlds created in colorful minds. Worlds that include compelling female characters. For me, success means taking a risk and growing from the fruits of that journey.

I appreciate the canon of existing work, but I'm more interested in the peers of Sappho, Aphra Bahn, and Lady Gregory. I'm more interested in the stories of women whose actual names I will never know.

This is probably because for most of my life they've been silenced. I am a woman. I am a WHOLE person and I need to see that reflected back to me in my culture. It's no surprise that one of the antonyms for canon is disbelief.

The impact of disbelief and erasure I have received hit such a fevered pitch, I almost couldn't take it anymore. About ten years ago my friend (and incredible choreographer) Maria asked me to write my story down. She used the word "memoir". She told me other people would benefit from hearing my story of triumph. My story of triumph? My immediate thought was, "I'm too young to have a memoir!". But then, I looked at the year on the calendar.

Through the decade of exploring my story in writing certain energies were called up. This usually happens when I produce plays too so it was not much of a surprise. At one point my Aunt called after eight years of estrangement. She didn't say hello or ask me how I was doing. She observed that I wasn't a cute five year old anymore and raised her voice and told me not to make a film about the family. I never intended on making a film. I haven't heard from her since.

This is pure fear. I've been staring at this fear forever and I'm tired of being afraid. Sick of it.

In the words of Anne Lamott, "If people wanted you to write warmly about them, they should've behaved better".

My family, my history, is simply my origin story. It doesn't define who I am, it's merely a launchpad into this life. The direction has been largely up to me. The past is incapable of understanding what I've accomplished. It's the PAST and nothing is growing there. In situations with difficult people who tried to hold any power over me, Tricia would alway say, "Blessings on their heads".

I can still hear her saying this and I can see her wiping her hands twice. Done and done.

I have always known and continue to believe that my purpose is to explore the stories of women.

The future will be so different, I hope. There will not be this patriarchal push down. The female dichotomy will no longer be about being outwardly pretty enough to be seen but inwardly demure enough to be heard (just a little bit).

It amazes me how many stories we'll never know. During my Molly Maguire exploration, I met a direct descendant at an Olive Garden in Tysons Corner, VA. We had the same first name and the same birth day and month. I told her about her Great Great Grandmother over endless breadsticks.

In my industry, the powers-that-be don't seem to view me or my work as successful. That's because they are transactional. In order to sell the most tickets, they make the safest choices. I can't tell you how many times I was asked to cite where what I wanted to do had already been successful someplace else. They've pushed away the innovators.

I don't call that winning.

Without risk, new works will never see the light of day. The flavor-of-the-month minority play reading that keeps established organizations qualifying for money intended for true minority org's with no staff is nothing less than criminal to my mind. They're literally killing any real growth.

The collaborative tribe we've built together at Venus Theatre understands our own definition of success. This tribe includes the audience, front-of-house, playwrights, actors, and every single person who DECIDED on whatever given night that a specific world would appear. It also includes consistent angel donors who completely changed my life and the life of Venus. Donors who simply asked me to "keep going!". Incredible people DO exist in the world. I will never be able to thank them enough.

This adventure has been worth every sacrifice.

Once I realized we had to leave our space of 15 years I was in the old familiar. It felt like beginning a process. Back to the table.

Covid hit at the same time.

I began to realize what things like dinner at home were. At home? Wow. I began to experience pajamas - whenever! I began to look up recipes and think about what I wanted to cook. I could rest. When storms blew through I didn't bolt up out of a cold sleep screaming about the Venus sign potentially turning into a kite-like-guillotine hurling down C Street. I used my practical theatre skills acquired over so many years to fix things in my own house. I claimed my studio and started playing music again.

I went into the cave. I dreamed again there.

I was longer hunted by the people who were supposed to protect me. Once you've experienced the worst, the light circles back and the giggles eventually return too. I have a loving husband, Alan Scott, and two rescue dogs, Ziggy Stardust and Joonbug, to fill my life.

As I worked on this memoir, it felt like something was missing. I told my story draft after draft. I began to realize my passion and excitement came from one source, the living playwright. When I discovered the living playwright my whole world shifted because I knew I wasn't alone. Because I knew dreamers dream and the brave ones get it down and then share it with as many people as possible. This is something as a child I never knew was possible.

Everytime we made it so at Venus, I could feel my soul soaring. I could feel a new social synapse formed and firing.

Connection.

Over the Covid-years I shared a lot of ideas with my team. We decided that along with this memoir, we should release an anthology of monologues for women. This was different but familiar. I put out my usual call. I could immediately feel Tricia poking fun at me. I began to feel the energy of the frolic again.

This time, I could choose more than four plays to produce in one year. This time I could jump genres. This time, I could decide how to organize the chapters and what to name them.

"Frozen Women/Flowing Thoughts" was born of this. It's an anthology that contains the woman-empowering works of 76 different playwrights from all over the globe. There's a directory in the back that will allow the reader to access full bodies of works from each of the playwrights.

Theatre isn't made of bricks and mortar. Theatre is made of people.

My big hope now, is that everyone will pick up the anthology and contact playwrights or their agents for rights and start producing in every nook and cranny imaginable.

Since our last production in November 2019 at Venus, I've yet to go back into a theatre to watch another play. It's been five years now and I'm starting to think I should reevaluate things again.

There are certain areas of the city I still cannot visit. If I force myself I may need days, weeks, or months of recovery time. Crimes against humanity pack a lifelong punch for some of us. All I can do is wake up each day and decide to live, decide to find a way to play. Decide that if I am gifted this next Jimmy Lifetime, I damn sure better decide how to explore every precious morsel-moment.

Working up "Living and Dying With Tricia McCauley" taught me about waiting out the darkness. It was really challenging to work that piece. When the darkness hit it could freeze me up. But I knew if I found a way to sit as comfortably as possible in the darkness, the light would come back around again. The trick was not to panic and just breathe.

Whatever we decide collectively, that's the world we're going to occupy.

Isn't that something else?

About The Author

Deborah L. Randall is the founder of Venus Theatre Company, the longest-running regional women's theatre in the nation. Deb is a producer, director, actor, playwright, and poet. She offers empowerment workshops for women and is proud to speak on her experiences. Deb's been called a "script-whisperer" by her team. Encouraged by her creative team and others she has decided to tell her story in this hybrid memoir/history/poetry experience.